Activities for the Spark

Curriculum for Early Childhood

by Beverly S. Lewman and Susan A. Fowler

Redleaf Press

© 2001 The Board of Trustees of the University of Illinois
Cover and interior design by Percolator
All rights reserved.

Published by: Redleaf Press
a division of Resources for Child Caring
450 N. Syndicate, Suite 5
St. Paul, MN 55104

Distributed by: Gryphon House
Mailing Address:
P.O. Box 207
Beltsville, MD 20704-0207

The contents of this curriculum and training manual were developed at the Department of Special Education in the College of Education at the University of Illinois under grant DE-H024D70012 from the U.S. Department of Education. However, those contents do not necessarily represent the policy of the Department of Education, and you should not assume endorsement by the federal government.

Copying of *Activities for the Spark Curriculum for Early Childhood* or any portion thereof is prohibited except for reproduction of forms or other materials intended for copying and distribution as handouts in order to facilitate practical use of the material.

ISBN: 1-929610-08-4

The following have granted permission to reprint covers:

The Lady with the Alligator Purse. Used by permission of Little, Brown and Company.

The Little Mouse, the Red Ripe Strawberry, and the Big Hungry Bear. Used by permission of Child's Play.

Mama, Do You Love Me? by Barbara M. Joosse, illustrated by Barbara Lavallee © 1991. Published by Chronicle Books, San Francisco. Used with permission.

Book cover from *The Napping House* by Audrey Wood, copyright © 1984 by Don Wood, reproduced by permission of Harcourt, Inc.

Reprinted with permission of the publisher, Children's Book Press, San Francisco, CA: *Nine-in-One Grr! Grr!,* text copyright © 1989 by Cathy Spagnoli, and illustrations copyright ©1989 by Nancy Hom.

Polar Bear, Polar Bear, What Do You Hear? by Bill Martin, Jr., illustrated by Eric Carle. Illustrations copyright, © 1991 by Eric Carle. Reprinted by permission of Henry Holt & Co., LLC.

The Snowy Day by Ezra Jack Keats, copyright © 1962 by Ezra Jack Keats, renewed © 1990 by Martin Pope, Executor. Used by permission of Viking Penguin, an imprint of Penguin Putnam Books for Young Readers, a division of Penguin Putnam Inc.

Cover from *Tree of Cranes* by Allen Say. Jacket art copyright © 1991 by Allen Say. Reprinted by permission of Houghton Mifflin Company. All rights reserved.

The Very Quiet Cricket by Eric Carle, copyright © 1990 by Eric Carle. Used by permission of Philomel Books, an imprint of Penguin Putnam Books for Young Readers, a division of Penguin Putnam Inc.

Contents

*The number in parentheses indicates the level of sophistication of the story based on the story line, detail of illustrations, text, vocabulary, and themes. Stories are rated 1, 2, or 3, with 1 being the simplest and 3 being more sophisticated.

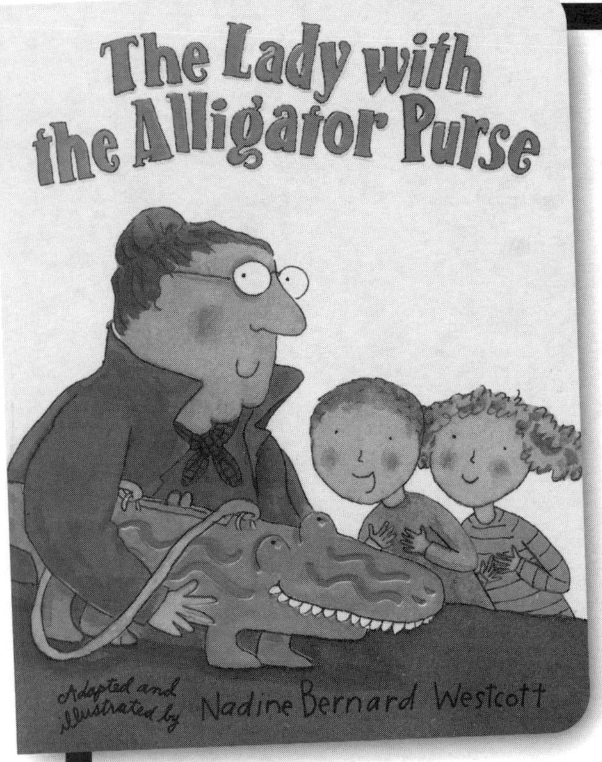

The Lady with the Alligator Purse

by Nadine Bernard Westcott

New York: Little, Brown, 1988

Story Synopsis: This joyous story is the familiar rhyme, "Miss Lucy Had a Baby," with a modern twist. Instead of naming a childhood disease as the cause of the child's illness, the Lady with the Alligator Purse says, "Nonsense!" She does not prescribe medication; instead, she prescribes pizza. This unit is a classroom favorite with entering three-year-olds and older children alike; children often chant along with the story as they become familiar with it.

Classroom Use: All children seem to enjoy this story and the related activities. It is a simple story that may be used effectively early in the school year. It fits well with other stories related to family and health. The themes and concepts for this unit are *in/out, eating, telephone talk,* and *helping sick people.*

Considerations: The illustrations are cartoonlike and have more detail than is suggested for best practice with young children. The book is also small and may be used most appropriately with small groups of children. The last illustration portrays the Lady with the Alligator Purse sliding down the banister. If you use this book, you may want to discuss the fact that it is dangerous to descend stairways in this fashion.

Special Materials: Most materials suggested for this unit are typically found in preschool classrooms. One make-believe activity suggests props for doctor and nurse play such as Band-Aids, craft sticks, cotton balls, and gauze.

ACTIVITY MATRIX

The Lady with the Alligator Purse

Day	Concept	Music Activity	Art Activity	Make-Believe Activity
Day 1	In/Out (Cognitive, Language, Motor)	Move in and out of a circle on the floor. Make shakers by putting objects into containers.	Put materials in egg cartons and take things out of egg cartons.	Play with babies, putting them into and taking them out of pretend bathtubs.
Day 2	Eating (Social)	Sing food songs.	Make food sculptures or pizza.	Pretend to feed babies.
Day 3	Telephone Talk (Social)	Make paper cup telephones, hum into them. Hum into kazoos.	Talk about artwork on pretend telephones.	Pretend to use telephones while taking care of babies.
Day 4	Helping Sick People (Social)	Make a tape recording of songs that would help a sick person feel better.	Make get-well cards with crayons, glitter, scraps.	Pretend to be doctors and nurses.
Day 5	Baby Care			

Theme of the Day:
In/Out

Day 1 Group Time: Introducing the Book

What to Do:

This story is the familiar one that has been chanted or sung for many years. If you know the melody that traditionally is used for this rhyme, sing the story and encourage the children to join you as they become familiar with the rhyme.

Introduce the activity. Tell the children that you will sing (or read) them a very silly song story today, one that would never really happen.

Sing the song or read the story. Sit with the children around the circle on the floor. Sing (or read) the story slowly, giving the children opportunities to ask questions.

Discuss the story. Ask the children what happened in the story. What did the baby eat? Why was his mother worried? Did they ever try to eat soap or drink any of the water in the bathtub? What did it taste like? Ask why the baby didn't eat the bathtub. What did the Lady with the Alligator Purse say was the matter with the baby?

Introduce the theme of the day: In/Out. Ask the children to stand around the circle as you go through the story again. Tell them that you are pretending that the circle is Tiny Tim's room. For the verse when the doctor, nurse, and lady "came in," encourage the children to step in the circle as you stress the word *in.* For the verse when these characters "went out," encourage them to step out of the circle. Tell the children they will think about *in* and *out* in the centers today.

MATERIALS

- Book, *The Lady with the Alligator Purse*
- Chalk or masking tape to make a circle on the floor for the children to stand around (make the circle before the activity)
- Empty can
- Several beans or small rocks
- Egg carton from the art center
- Playdough
- Glitter
- Baby doll
- Container, large enough for doll to sit in

Introduce the arts activities.

Music and Movement Center

What the children will do: Move in and out of a circle taped on the floor and make shakers to use. Show the children how to drop beans (or rocks) into an empty can. Shake it so they can hear the sound. Say that today in the music and movement center they will move in and out of a circle as the song tells them to do, and they will also make their own shakers.

continues . . .

Art Center

What the children will do: Put materials in egg cartons. Give each child a small piece of playdough. Then show them the egg carton and put a piece of playdough in each section. Pass the egg carton around, asking the children to put their pieces of playdough in the egg carton too. Sprinkle some glitter on the playdough in the egg carton and tell the children they can put different things in egg cartons in the art center.

Make-Believe Center

What the children will do: Put babies in and take them out of baths. Put the doll in the container as you explain that you are putting the baby in a bathtub the way Miss Lucy did in the song. Pretend to wash the doll and tell the children they may put babies in pretend bathtubs in the make-believe center.

Have each child choose an arts activity.

Notes:

Theme of the Day: In/Out

Day 1: Music and Movement Center

What to Do:

Relate the activity to the story. Remind the children that the doctor, the nurse, and the Lady with the Alligator Purse all came into Miss Lucy's house and then went out of Miss Lucy's house. Say that they will play a game to music and will go in and out of a circle like the people in the story went in and out of the house.

Play "In and out the Circle" game. Tell the children to listen as you sing, "Step in and out the Circle" to the tune of "Go in and out the Window." Have them try to do what the words say without a demonstration from you. Compliment them for listening carefully. Then repeat the song and join in the actions.

Step in and out the circle.
Step in and out the circle.
Step in and out the circle,
As we did before!

Walk all around the circle . . .
Now jump in the circle . . .
Now sit in the circle . . .

MATERIALS

- A circle 6 or 7 feet in diameter marked on the floor with chalk or masking tape
- Cassette player
- Recorded music with a strong rhythmic beat that is appropriate for children to move to
- Plastic containers with lids, one per child and adult
- Dry beans or other items to put in containers to make shakers
- Adhesive tape

Ask the children for additional ideas. How else could they move around or in and out the circle? Use the children's suggestions.

Move to recorded music. Leave the circle on the floor and play the recorded music. Invite the children to move any way they choose. Join in and model moving in and out of the circle. Stress the words *in* and *out* as you talk about ways you and the children are moving. "Sean and Latrell are in the circle. Now they're out of the circle." "I put just my foot in the circle." Prompt the children to also talk about what they are doing. "Antwon, are you in the circle or out of the circle?" As the children move in and out of the circle, encourage them to move in ways that address individual learning goals. "Louis, stand on one foot in the circle." "Casey, jump up with both feet in and out of the circle, like I am!"

Put objects into shakers. Turn off the music and assemble the children with you on the floor. Show the children how to make shakers to use as they move to the music. Show how to drop beans into a plastic container and put on the lid. Then shake the shaker rhythmically. As the children make their own shakers, discuss how they are putting beans in and perhaps taking some out. After a child makes a shaker, encourage him to listen carefully to the sound it makes. Then tell the child to put in or take out some beans and shake the shaker again. Does it sound the same? (Before the children use the shakers to move to music, they may need to tape the lids securely in place.)

Move with the shakers. Play the music and show how you can move in and out of the circle while shaking a shaker. Older children might enjoy forming a line behind a leader to weave in and out of the circle.

Theme of the Day: In/Out

Day 1: Art Center

What to Do:

Relate the activity to the story. Remind the children that the doctor, the nurse, and Lady with the Alligator Purse all went in Miss Lucy's house and then they went out of the house. Tell them that they will put things in containers and take things out of containers.

Let the children play freely with the materials. Join in and show how you can put a variety of items in an egg carton and take them out as you talk about what you are doing. "I put yarn in the egg carton." "I'm taking out the pine cones." Prompt the children to talk about what they are doing as well. "What did you put in here?" "What did you do with the crayons?"

Use a paper punch. Show how to use a paper punch to make circles to put in an egg carton. You might hold the paper over the egg carton as you punch the circles, and talk about how they are falling into the egg carton.

Encourage cutting. Show how you can use scissors to cut small pieces of paper, yarn, string, or fabric to put in an egg carton. Prompt the children to talk about what they are doing.

Encourage counting. Ask the children to count things as they put them in the egg carton cups, helping them count as needed. Ask the children to take things out of the egg cartons, emphasizing the word *out* as well as quantity words and numbers: "Take out all the beads." "Take out some cotton balls." "Take four circles out of the egg carton."

Brainstorm other objects to put in the egg cartons. Encourage the children to name other things to put in their egg cartons. Their suggestions might be realistic, such as small things in the room, or silly, such as "elephants," "the moon," or "birthday cakes." Let them find some of the more realistic objects suggested and put them in the egg cartons. If a suggested object is too large but is available in the room, such as "a book," let the children try the idea and find out for themselves that it won't fit.

Glue the objects in place. After the children have worked with the materials for a while, offer them glue to squeeze into the egg carton cups to hold the materials in place.

MATERIALS

- Egg cartons
- Playdough
- Glitter
- Small materials, such as beads, Styrofoam chips, cotton balls, pine cones, rubber bands, stamps, crayons, and chalk stubs
- Yarn, string, or small pieces of fabric
- Paper
- Paper punch
- Scissors
- Glue

Theme of the Day: In/Out

Day 1: Make-Believe Center

What to Do:

MATERIALS

- Baby dolls
- Small- to medium-sized boxes, or bowls and plastic tubs
- Bars of soap
- Water toys
- Washcloths, towels, or scraps of fabric
- Pitchers of water (optional)

Relate the activity to the story. Remind the children that first the doctor, the nurse, and Lady with the Alligator Purse went into Miss Lucy's house and then they went out. Say that they will put babies in the bathtub and take them out the way Miss Lucy put her baby in the bathtub and took him out.

Discuss the activity. Put a doll in a container (and pour in water if it is available) as you talk about how you are putting the baby (and water) in the tub as Miss Lucy did in the story. Put in the washcloths and water toys, emphasizing the word *in* and encouraging the children to describe what you are doing.

Discuss bathing babies. Remind the children that Miss Lucy let her baby drink the bath water and eat the soap and comment that this is not the best thing for a baby to do in the bathtub. Ask the children to describe things to do with a baby in a bathtub; they might suggest wash the baby, play with toys, splash water.

Encourage the children to pretend to bathe babies. Let the children put dolls in the other containers and pretend to give them baths. Join in and show how to wash a baby, shampooing its hair, playing with a water toy, taking the baby out of the water and drying it, as you emphasize the words *in* and *out.* As the children bathe the dolls, talk with them about what they are doing and ask questions to extend their play: "How will you wash the baby's hair?" "What could your baby do with the boat?" "How could you use the towel?" "Your baby is crying? What's wrong? How could you make the baby feel happy?"

Theme of the Day:
Eating

Day 2 Group Time: Introducing the Theme of the Day

What to Do:

Review the previous day's activities. Show the children the shakers and artwork they made the previous day. Discuss how they put things in and took things out of the shakers and egg cartons. Then talk about how they put babies in and took them out of baths.

Sing or read the story.

List things that cannot be eaten. Show the pictures of the baby when he is drinking the bath water and eating the soap. Remark that people don't really eat those things. Point to some things around the room and ask the children if they ever eat those things. Ask them to name other things that people do not eat, encouraging everyone to name at least one thing.

MATERIALS

- Shakers and artwork from previous day
- Book, *The Lady with the Alligator Purse*
- Baby doll
- One pretzel per child
- Pieces of fruit and a small paper plate

Introduce the theme of the day: Eating. Give each child a pretzel to eat, and talk about how good they are. Show the children the doll and pretend to feed it a pretzel, commenting that the doll likes to eat pretzels too. Ask the children to name other things they like to eat. Tell them they will think about *eating* in the centers today.

Introduce the arts activities.

Music and Movement Center
What the children will do: Sing "food" songs. Sing a portion of a song about food (for example, the "Apples and Bananas" song). Tell the children they may sing songs and pretend to eat food in the music and movement center.

Art Center
What the children will do: Make food sculptures. Show the children the fruit and the paper plate. Show how you can arrange two of the pieces of fruit together on the paper plate. Tell the children they may make a real snack in the art center.

Make-Believe Center
What the children will do: Pretend to feed babies. Show the baby doll and have it cry as you tell the children that the baby is hungry. Pretend to feed the baby another pretzel and tell the children they may pretend to feed babies in the make-believe center.

Have each child choose an arts activity.

Theme of the Day: Eating

Day 2: Music and Movement Center

What to Do:

Relate the activity to the story. Remind the children that the baby ate the soap and that later everyone ate pizza. Remind the children that soap is not the right thing for them to eat. Say that they will sing songs about food today.

Sing about foods named by the children. Sing the song that was sung when the activity was introduced, and encourage the children to sing with you. Ask the children to name the foods they like to eat. After they mention several foods, repeat the song, substituting the foods that the children named for the ones you sang about previously. Repeat this procedure until each child has mentioned a food.

Sing a song to tune of "Mary Had a Little Lamb." Give each child a spoon and show how to make a stirring motion with a spoon. Tell them to pretend they are cooking soup to eat. As the children stir, sing the following to the tune of "Mary Had a Little Lamb." Sing the song again, encouraging the children to sing along with you.

We are making soup today,
Soup today, soup today.
We are making soup today.
We are making soup!

Discuss kinds of soup. After you finish the song, ask the children to tell what kind of soup they made. To prompt them you might say, "I made tomato soup. What kind of soup did you make?" If most children name the same kind of soup, ask them to think of other kinds.

Sing about other foods. Put the plastic replicas of food (or pictures of food) where they are easily accessible. Prompt the children to each choose one. Help the children name each piece of food. Sing the melody of the song "If You're Happy and You Know It" adapting the words to "If you have a banana, hold it high . . ." (This portion of the activity should be adapted for the level of the group. Three-year-old children should use plastic replicas of either fruits or vegetables. Older children will be able to categorize—that is, "If you have fruit, hold it high.")

MATERIALS

- **Large pot or other large container**
- **One spoon per child**
- **Plastic replicas of food or food pictures**

Theme of the Day: Eating

Day 2: Art Center

What to Do:

Relate the activity to the story. Remind the children that first the baby in the story ate the soap and that soap isn't the right thing to eat. Then say that everyone ate pizza. Say that they will make food sculptures out of food they like to eat. (To make this activity relate more directly to the story, you can provide the ingredients to make individual pizzas instead of food sculptures.)

Make food sculptures. Ask the children to put on their gloves. Then ask them to choose the foods they like to eat. Give the children plates to work on and ask them to make the foods look nice on the plate. Show how to make a sculpture with the food. For example, stick pretzels into a piece of banana, then put a dab of peanut butter on the end of each pretzel and stick a raisin on it. If the children want to use bananas, tell them to cut pieces with a plastic knife rather than using a whole banana.

Pour food coloring into bowls. Ask the children to pour the food coloring into the bowls. Emphasize the names of the colors. Dilute the food coloring by helping the children add water to each bowl of food coloring.

MATERIALS

- Bananas (or canned fruit such as peach halves, pear halves, or pineapple rings)
- Other foods for making snack, such as stick pretzels, peanut butter, graham crackers, raisins
- Plastic knives
- Food coloring and one small bowl per color
- Water, to dilute food coloring
- Small clean paintbrushes
- Small plates
- Protective gloves, one set per child (latex, if you know that the children are not allergic to it)

Encourage children to paint their food sculptures. Have the children put on protective gloves so they will not stain or lick their fingers. Let the children use paintbrushes to paint their sculptures with food coloring. As they work, encourage them to talk about their beautiful sculptures and how good they will taste.

Identify each child's work. When each child finishes a food sculpture, print his name on the plate, so that he can eat his own food sculpture during snack.

Theme of the Day: Eating

Day 2: Make-Believe Center

What to Do:

Relate the activity to the story. Remind the children that everyone in the story ate pizza. Suggest that little babies don't eat pizza. They just drink milk. Say that Miss Lucy's baby was not a tiny baby. Say that they will pretend to feed babies today.

Use playdough to represent food. Tell the children that playdough is not something they should eat, just as bath water and soap are two things that aren't the right things to eat. Pretend to prepare the food by cutting it with a plastic knife, mixing it in a bowl, "cooking" it on a play stove, and pretending to pour a drink into a baby bottle or cup.

Pretend to take care of babies. Let the children play freely with the props. Join in and model different activities related to preparing food and feeding a young child:

- Cradle a baby doll in your arms and feed it a bottle.
- Prepare doll for eating in a high chair or at a table by pretending to wash its face and hands, putting it in a high chair or chair, putting a bib on it.
- Pretend to feed doll with a spoon or serve doll food to eat on a plate.
- Wash doll after eating.

Discuss play. As the children use the materials, make comments and ask questions to prompt language and help them extend their play. "Your baby wants a drink. What should you do?" "What could you cook on this stove?" "Please show me how to feed this baby."

MATERIALS

- **Baby dolls**
- **Play dishes and cookware, including plastic knives**
- **Playdough**
- **Other available materials for pretending to feed babies, such as bibs, baby bottles, toy high chairs, toy stove**

Theme of the Day:
Telephone Talk

Day 3 Group Time: Introducing the Theme of the Day

What to Do:

The music and movement center and the art center activities for today are limited to six children each because of the individual attention the adult must provide. If only two adults are in the room, either the music and movement center or the art center should be used, with the second center being the make-believe center.

MATERIALS

- Book, *The Lady with the Alligator Purse,* (with page marked where Miss Lucy calls for help)
- Toy telephone
- Homemade cup-and-string telephone
- Paint, brush, and paper
- Baby doll

Sing a song and review the previous day's activities.

Sing the food song from the previous day with the children. Ask them to tell about the snacks they made and what they did with the dolls on the previous day.

Sing or read the story. Sing or read the story and encourage the children to sing or chant with you.

Introduce the theme of the day: Telephone talk. Show the children the page where Miss Lucy calls for help. Ask the children what Miss Lucy did to get help. Emphasize that she used the telephone. Ask them if they know how to use the telephone to call for help. If the children know how to dial 911, encourage them to do so, using the toy telephone.

Make a telephone's ringing sound and answer the toy phone. Briefly pretend to talk to someone: "Yes, the children sang a song. Yes, it's funny. I have to go now. Good-bye!" Discuss experiences the children have had talking on the telephone. Then tell them they can pretend to talk on telephones in the centers.

Introduce the arts activities.

Music and Movement Center

What the children will do: Make paper-cup telephones to use. Show the children a paper-cup telephone. Have another adult hold one cup against his ear as you pull the string taut and say something into the other cup, as if you were on the phone. Tell the children they can make their own phones to use in the music and movement center.

Art Center

What the children will do: Talk on pretend telephones about their artwork. Make some marks on the paper with the paintbrush, and then make the sound of a telephone and hold your hand to your ear as

continues . . .

you pretend to answer it. Pretend to talk to someone on the phone, telling the person about your artwork. After you hang up the pretend phone, tell the children that they will paint in the art center and then call and tell someone about their paintings.

Make-Believe Center

What the children will do: Pretend to use telephones while taking care of babies. Hold a baby doll in your arms and make a telephone ringing sound. Answer the toy phone and have a brief conversation: "Hello. Hi, Rachel! My baby is sleeping now. I can come to your house when he wakes up. Good-bye!" Tell the children they can play with toy phones in the make-believe center.

Have each child choose an arts activity.

Notes:

Theme of the Day: Telephone Talk

Day 3: Music and Movement Center

What to Do:

This activity should be limited to six children per adult helper.

Relate the activity to the story. Remind the children that when Miss Lucy needed help, she called the doctor, the nurse, and the Lady with the Alligator Purse on the telephone. Say that they will get to make toy telephones today.

Make paper-cup telephones. Help the children assemble a toy telephone. Adapt the amount of direct assistance to the skill level of each child, although most children will require quite a bit of help.

1. Cut a piece of string about 3 feet long.
2. Poke one end of the string through the hole in one cup from the outside to the inside.
3. Tie a knot in the end of the string inside the cup.
4. Repeat the procedure with the other end of the string in the other cup.

MATERIALS

- **Paper cups with a hole poked in the bottom center of each**
- **String (3-foot pieces of string should be precut for three-year-olds)**
- **Scissors**
- **Kazoos**

Practice using telephones. Help the children pair up. Tell each child to hold one of the cups, so that the pairs of children are connected by the strings. Help them pull the strings taut, but not too tight or they will come out of the cups. Have one child in each pair hold his cup to his mouth. Have the other child hold her cup to her ear, giving physical guidance as needed.

Hum into the telephones. Tell the child who has the cup to his mouth to hum. It will be easier for the child who is listening to detect the vibrations of humming than talking. Talk with the other child about what she hears. Have the children switch the positions of their cups and repeat the procedure.

Continue the humming sound with kazoos. Distribute the kazoos. Have the speaking child hum into the phone with his kazoo. Encourage the children to take turns playing the kazoo into the phone and listening to the sound.

Encourage the children to talk on the pretend phones. Once the children are familiar with the procedure of one child listening and the other making sounds, encourage them to pretend they are talking on a telephone. To prompt them, suggest things for one child to say, and the other to answer.

Theme of the Day: Telephone Talk

Day 3: Art Center

What to Do:

This activity should be limited to six children per adult helper.

Relate the activity to the story. Remind the children that Miss Lucy used the telephone to tell people her baby was sick. Say that they will pretend to use telephones to tell people about their artwork.

Discuss the activity. Show them an art print and discuss it. Ask such questions as what animal they see, what colors they see, if they see straight lines or curved lines. Have them name items in the picture. Tell them that they will make their own painting, using any colors they want to use, and that you will pretend to call each one of them on the telephone to talk about what they are doing.

MATERIALS

- Art prints with bold, sweeping, colorful lines, appropriate for use with young children
- Several colors of paint
- Several colors of paper
- Paintbrushes in different sizes
- Paint sponges

Encourage the children to choose materials and paint. Encourage the children to choose colors of paper, sizes of brushes or sponges, and colors of paint they wish to use. Let the children paint as they wish.

Pretend to call each child on the telephone. As they work, pretend to telephone one child at a time. Encourage the child to hold his hand to his ear and engage in the telephone conversation. Ask the child questions about his artwork, emphasizing techniques the child has used and the marks and shapes he has produced. "Hello, Joey, tell me about the painting you made." "Did you use a big brush or a little brush?" "What colors did you use?" "What did you do with the sponge?" "Did you make long lines or short lines?" "How did you make dots?"

Telephone again, asking about another child's painting. Telephone the children again and ask them to tell things about each other's paintings. "Did Shante make big circles or little circles? What else do you see on her painting?" "Who used the color green?" "How many paintings did Adam make?"

Theme of the Day: Telephone Talk

Day 3: Make-Believe Center

What to Do:

Relate the activity to the story. Remind the children that Miss Lucy was taking care of her baby when it got sick. Say that she used the telephone to call people for help. Say that they will take care of babies and talk on the telephone.

Call children on a pretend telephone. Encourage the children to use the props to set up doll play as they wish. As the children play, make a telephone ringing sound. Name a child to answer another toy phone. "Dionne, the phone is for you!" When the child answers the phone, begin a conversation that relates to doll care. "How is your baby? Is she still sick?" "What are you and your baby doing?" "Where are you going today with your baby?" Telephone each child at least once and encourage them to call each other on the phones. If needed, suggest things that they can say to each other.

Join in the play. Choose a doll and join in the make-believe play directly. As you play, suggest different reasons to use the toy telephones. "Your baby looks sick. Call the doctor!" "I'm going to order a pizza for supper tonight. What's the number?" "My baby wants to talk to his grandpa on the telephone."

MATERIALS

- **Dolls**
- **Props for child care with dolls, such as blankets, baby bottles, beds, rattles, and other toys**
- **Two or more toy telephones**

Theme of the Day:
Helping Sick People

Day 4 Group Time: Introducing the Theme of the Day

What to Do:

Review the previous day's activities. Show the children the paper-cup telephones. Ask two volunteers to demonstrate how they used them. Show the paintings from the previous day and pretend to telephone the children. Ask them what they did in the art center. Discuss how they talked about their babies on the toy phones in the make-believe center.

Sing the "Miss Lucy" song or read the story. Use the book to sing or read the story, encouraging the children to join you.

Discuss *doctor/nurse;* introduce theme of the day: Helping sick people. Show the children a picture of the doctor and nurse in the story, and discuss how they could help Miss Lucy's baby if it was sick. Show the children the doll and pretend that it is crying. Soothe the doll and comment that it might be sick. Tell the children they can pretend to help sick people in the centers today.

MATERIALS

- Paper-cup telephones and artwork from previous day
- Book, *The Lady with the Alligator Purse*
- Cassette player
- Blank tape
- Piece of paper folded in half
- Glitter and glue
- Doll
- Craft sticks

Introduce the arts activities.

Music and Movement Center

What the children will do: Make a tape recording of music that would help a sick person feel better. Sing the first two lines of "Twinkle, Twinkle Little Star." ("Twinkle, twinkle little star. How I wonder what you are.") Then ask the children to sing it with you to record on the tape recorder. After you record the two lines of the song, play it for the children to hear. Comment that music like that would make a sick person feel better. Tell them they can record songs they like in the music and movement center to play for pretend sick people.

Art Center

What the children will do: Make "get well" cards. Show the children the piece of paper folded in half. Spread some glue on the front of it and sprinkle glitter on the glue. Tell the children that they can decorate cards in the art center, and give the cards to sick dolls in the make-believe center.

Make-Believe Center

What the children will do: Pretend to be doctors and nurses. Use a craft stick as a thermometer to take the doll's temperature. Tell the children that the doll is sick and you want to take it to the doctor. Tell them they can pretend to be doctors and nurses in the make-believe center today.

Have each child choose an arts activity.

Theme of the Day:
Helping Sick People

Day 4: Music and Movement Center

What to Do:

Relate the activity to the story. Remind the children that Miss Lucy was worried because her baby was sick. Talk with the children about being sick. Ask what makes them feel better when they are sick. Say that listening to happy music can make people feel better and that they will make a tape to make people feel better. (If a child in the class is home sick, the tape could be made specifically for the child and sent to the child's home.)

MATERIALS

- Cassette player and blank tape
- Blankets or large pieces of fabric
- Pencil and paper
- Musical instruments

Record a song. Ask the children to sing a song (any song they know well) for you to record.

Encourage the children to pretend to be sick and listen to the tape. Ask them to each choose a blanket and lie down on the floor, pretending to be sick. Play the recorded song for the children to listen to. Discuss whether this song would make a sick person feel better. Accept all responses.

Brainstorm songs. Ask the children to name other songs they like so that they can tape those songs. You may need to prompt them by making a suggestion. Write down all their suggestions and read the list back to them, asking for additional suggestions.

Record the songs. Help the children choose the songs to sing for their tape. After all the songs have been recorded, play the tape for the children.

You might also let the children play instruments for the tape if there is time. Play the tape for the children to hear as they again pretend to be sick. If it is practical, suggest that they take their recording to the make-believe center to play for the sick babies.

Theme of the Day:
Helping Sick People

Day 4: Art Center

What to Do:

Relate the activity to the story. Remind the children that Miss Lucy's baby was sick. Say that it makes sick people feel better to know that other people are thinking about them. Say that they will make cards to make sick people feel better.

Encourage the children to fold the paper. Give each child a piece of paper and show how to fold the paper in half to make a card. Give assistance as needed, but encourage the children to try to fold it without help. Do not expect perfectly folded cards.

Encourage the children to decorate their cards. Put out all the materials and encourage the children to decorate the cards as they wish. Work with the children, making and decorating a card. As you work, talk about how the cards would make sick people feel better. Ask them to think of people they know who might like the cards.

Write messages. Encourage each child to think of a message for you to write in her card. The children might pretend to write additional messages. Ask the children to show their cards to each other and either pretend to read the messages or have you read what they told you to write.

MATERIALS

- **Pieces of paper, 8 by 12 inches each**
- **Crayons and markers**
- **Other art supplies such as glue, glitter, and scrap materials**

Theme of the Day:
Helping Sick People

Day 4: Make-Believe Center

What to Do:

Relate the activity to the story. Remind the children that they will pretend to be doctors and nurses and make sick people feel better because the baby in the story was sick. Show them the props, encouraging them to name each one.

Let the children play freely with the materials for doctor/nurse make-believe. Join in and show some ways to care for the dolls:

- Take the doll's temperature with a craft stick or pretend thermometer.
- Put the doll in bed and cover it up.
- Give the doll medicine and drinks.
- Listen to the doll's heartbeat and take its blood pressure.
- Give the doll an injection.
- Pretend to wipe a wound with cotton.
- Put a Band-Aid on a wound or wrap it with gauze.

Encourage the children to discuss what they are doing. As the children use the materials, ask questions and make comments to prompt language and help them extend their play when needed. "How could you listen to the baby's heart?" "This is a pretend thermometer. What does a nurse do with this?" "This baby is sick. What's wrong with it?" "What does the doctor do when you're sick?"

MATERIALS

- Dolls
- Props for doctor/nurse play, such as Band-Aids, craft sticks, cotton balls, gauze strips, items from play doctor kits
- Beds for dolls or boxes to serve as beds
- Doll blankets or scraps of fabric

Theme of the Day:
Baby Care

Day 5 Group Activity

What to Do:

Relate the activity to the story. Remind the children that Miss Lucy was taking care of her baby when the baby got sick. Ask what happened to make the baby sick. How did the baby get well? Tell them that they will pretend to take care of babies today.

Introduce baby-care play. Ask the children to name some of the things they did with babies in the make-believe center on previous days. Their comments might include that they gave them baths, fed them, and took care of them when they were sick.

MATERIALS

- Props for baby care used in the make-believe center on previous days
- Chairs
- Dress-up clothes

Ask them to name other things they could do with babies. If needed, make some suggestions yourself: take them for a walk, take them for a drive in a car, take them to a playground, take them swimming.

Ask the children to think of props they could add to the make-believe center for each of their ideas: "What could you use for a car? a stroller?" "How could you make a slide for a playground?" "What could you use for a swimming pool?" Help them set up the props they think of, giving suggestions to expand their ideas. These might include:

- A car: four chairs, two in front and two in back. Put a box on one chair for a car seat.
- A stroller: a box or small wagon.
- A slide: a box with a long block or piece of cardboard resting on one end.
- A wading pool: a box or bowl. For a wading pool with real water, use a water table.

Give the children time to play. See suggestions below.

Review the activity. Sit with the children to review the activity. Ask the children what they did. How did they take care of their babies?

Suggestions for Implementing Baby Care Play:

Encourage the children to continue the themes they enjoyed on previous days in make-believe, helping them think of ways to add to these themes. For example, for doctor/nurse play, they might add dress-up costumes or set up a hospital.

continues . . .

Join in and model new ways to care for the babies based on the props added. For example, you might push the stroller to the "park" and then have the doll slide down a slide, or you might put Styrofoam chips in a box to serve as water in a wading pool.

Make comments and ask questions that will prompt children to interact with each other and extend their play when needed. "Ask Janey where she and her baby are going." "Your baby needs a bath! Kevin is giving his baby a bath." "Let's take our babies to the park. Who else could come with us?"

Encourage the children to soothe the dolls by singing a lullaby.

Older children might enjoy acting out the story. Children would take turns acting out the five characters while the other children sing or chant the story.

Notes:

SKILLS & GOALS MATRIX

The Lady with the Alligator Purse

	Skills or Behaviors	Goals and Objectives
Cognitive	• Name things that are in or out of a container	• Increase concept and vocabulary development • Increase understanding of opposites
	• Identify and label colors	• Increase color concept and vocabulary development • Increase visual awareness and discrimination
	• Identify and categorize foods	• Increase classification skills • Increase general vocabulary and concept development
	• Use one object in play to represent another object (paper cups for telephones)	• Increase symbolic functioning • Increase general reasoning and problem-solving abilities
Language	• Identify own written name	• Increase visual awareness and discrimination • Increase understanding of symbols • Increase understanding of concepts about words
	• Step in and out when requested to do so	• Increase receptive and expressive vocabulary • Increase capacity to follow simple directions
	• Chant rhyming syllables	• Increase auditory awareness • Increase phonological awareness
	• Use appropriate language for telephone conversations	• Increase functional use of language • Increase receptive and expressive vocabulary
	• Hum a song and use humming with kazoos	• Increase awareness of pitch and tone • Increase breath control and capacity

SKILLS & GOALS MATRIX (CONT.)

	Skills or Behaviors	Goals and Objectives
Social	• Take care of babies (dolls) by bathing and feeding them	• Increase awareness of routine self-care skills • Increase ability to follow rules in group activity
Social	• Discuss how people feel when they are ill	• Increase understanding of point of view and feelings of others • Increase ability to speak in a group setting
Social	• Practice adult caretaking roles	• Increase understanding and practice of empathic behavior • Increase appropriate social behaviors in supervised setting
Fine-Motor	• Shake shakers to make noise	• Increase hand strength • Increase bilateral control
Fine-Motor	• Put small objects into containers	• Increase finger dexterity • Increase visual-motor coordination • Increase control of release
Fine-Motor	• Use paper punch to make holes in papers	• Increase bilateral coordination • Increase hand strength and dexterity
Fine-Motor	• Use variety of household materials to make a collage	• Increase tactile awareness • Refine pincer grasp • Increase visual-motor coordination
Gross-Motor	• Pretend to stir while holding a large bowl	• Increase gross-motor planning and coordination • Increase dynamic balance • Increase arm and leg strength
Gross-Motor	• Follow a leader in a line while moving in and out	• Increase motor planning and control • Increase ability to imitate movements
Gross-Motor	• Follow directions to move in various ways	• Increase movement repertoire • Increase gross-motor planning • Increase ability to move based on auditory input • Increase awareness of body in space
Gross-Motor	• Shake objects	• Increase motor planning and control • Coordinate fine- and gross-motor movements

STORY OF THE WEEK / EL CUENTO DE ESTA SEMANA

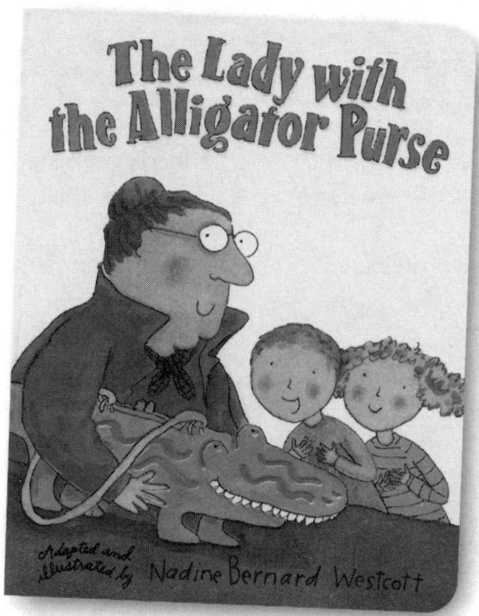

The Lady with the Alligator Purse

by Nadine Bernard Westcott

The Spark story for this week is *The Lady with the Alligator Purse*. It is based on an old children's rhyme that begins, "Miss Lucy had a baby, she called him Tiny Tim." In this version of the story, Miss Lucy puts her baby in the bathtub. He drinks all the water and eats all the soap. Miss Lucy calls the doctor, nurse, and the Lady with the Alligator Purse. Ask your child what the doctor, the nurse, and the Lady with the Alligator Purse said about the baby. What did they say was the matter with him? ("Mumps," said the doctor; "measles," said the nurse; "nonsense," said the Lady with the Alligator Purse.) Ask your child what the Lady with the Alligator Purse said Tiny Tim needed (pizza). The themes to go with this story are *in/out, eating, telephone talk,* and *helping sick people.*

El cuento de Spark de esta semana se llama *The Lady with the Alligator Purse* (a dama con la cartera de cocodrilo). A este cuento lo conoce mucha gente. Durante muchos años, los niños han estado cantando sus canciones: "La señorita Lucy tuvo un bebé al cual lo llamó el pequeño Tim". La Señorita Lucy puso a su bebé en la bañera y él se tomó toda el agua y se comió todo el jabón. La Srta. Lucy, entonces, llamó al doctor, a la enfermera y a la dama con la cartera de cocodrilo. Pregúntele a su niño o niña qué dijeron el doctor, la enfermera y la dama con la cartera de cocodrilo sobre qué tenía el bebé ("sarampión" dijo el doctor, "paperas" dijo la enfermera, "tonterías" dijo la dama con la cartera de cocodrilo). También pregúntele a su niño o niña qué dijo la dama con la cartera de cocodrilo que necesitaba el pequeño Tim (pizza). Las ideas temáticas que van con este cuento son: *adentro/afuera, comer, hablar por teléfono* y *ayudar a la gente enferma.*

© 2001 The Board of Trustees of the University of Illinois. May be reproduced for use by teachers.

The Little Mouse, the Red Ripe Strawberry, and the Big Hungry Bear

by Don and Audrey Wood

Singapore: M. Twinn, 1984

Story Synopsis: This is the story of a little mouse who picks a red, ripe strawberry, and after hiding it, guarding it, and disguising it to protect it from the Big Hungry Bear, finally shares it in order to avoid having the Big Hungry Bear take it away.

Classroom Use: This is a very simple, beautifully illustrated story that is highly enjoyed by children in preschool programs. Teachers report that at the first of the week, children think it is the bear that shares the strawberry with the mouse, but by the end of the week they aren't so sure. This unit reinforces sharing and provides an excellent opportunity for children to grasp the concept of *half.* It may be used any time of the year. The themes and concepts stressed in this unit are *senses, colors, half,* and *share.*

Considerations: If you have children in your room who need to increase their ability to share, this is an exceptionally good unit to use. The primary point made in the story is that the mouse shared the red, ripe strawberry at the end of the story.

Special Materials: Nothing is suggested for use in this unit that is not already available in most preschool programs or in your home.

ACTIVITY MATRIX

The Little Mouse, the Red Ripe Strawberry, and the Big Hungry Bear

Day	Concept	Music Activity	Art Activity	Make-Believe Activity
Day 1	Senses: Hear, See, Smell (Science)	(Hear) Compare sounds and movements of the bear and the mouse.	(See) Look through the book together. List what they see. Provide a variety of materials to enable them to make whatever they choose.	(Smell) Children pretend to be the Big Hungry Bear and try to find an object by using their sense of smell.
Day 2	Colors (Cognitive, Kindergarten Readiness)	Play recorded music as children march around color shapes. When the music stops, sit on the nearest shape. Sing color song.	Mix paint in resealable plastic bags. Discuss resulting colors and paint freely with the paint.	Use play food of different colors. Pretend to be mouse and bear preparing dinner.
Day 3	Half (Math)	Divide the children into 2 equal groups. Count children, stressing half. Children play instruments loudly with bear music and quietly with mouse music.	Make art prints with halves of vegetables dipped in thick paint.	Children cut paper fruit in half, then share their fruit with a stuffed animal friend.
Day 4	Share (Social)	Pass an instrument around circle, singing the Share Song to the tune of "Mary Had a Little Lamb."	Children make Styrofoam structure to use as a hiding place for the strawberry. Limited supplies to share.	Share food supplies to make individual snacks.
Day 5	Strawberries (Nutrition activity)			

Theme of the Day:
Senses—See, Hear, Smell

Day 1 Group Time: Introducing the Book

What to Do:

Read the story. Read the story slowly, providing opportunities for the children to discuss what is happening. Encourage them to stamp their feet and join you as you say "boom, boom, boom," and sniff with you as you read the words, "sniff, sniff, sniff."

Discuss the story. Ask the children what happened to the strawberry. Lead a discussion that includes such questions as whether or not they like strawberries, if they have ever picked strawberries, if they have ever seen a real bear. Did they know that bears like to eat berries? Have they ever seen a real mouse? Where?

MATERIALS

- Book, *The Big Hungry Bear*
- Drum
- Red tissue paper
- Banana or other item with a strong odor

Introduce the concept of the day: Senses—see, hear, and smell. Discuss the picture where the person who is talking to the mouse says, "Oh, I see." What does the person see? How does the person know that the mouse is going to pick the strawberry? What body part did the person use in order to see?

Remind the children that the mouse hadn't known that the big hungry bear loved strawberries until her friend told her. Show the picture in the book where the mouse hears about the bear. How does the mouse feel? Remind them that the bear tromped through the forest looking for berries. Strike the drum loudly three times.

Say that this is the way the bear may have sounded while tromping through the forest. Ask the children what body part they used to hear the drum. Say that they heard the drum with their ears.

Ask them how the bear finds ripe strawberries. Encourage the children to join you as you model sniffing as the bear sniffed, "sniff, sniff, sniff." What body part did they use to sniff? The bear uses his nose to smell the strawberries.

Say that they are going to use their eyes, ears, and noses today to see things, hear things, and smell things in the centers.

Introduce the arts activities.

Music and Movement Center

What the children will do: Make sounds and move like the bear and the mouse. Have a child demonstrate how a bear might tromp through the forest. As the child demonstrates, sing the first verse of the song

continues . . .

below to the tune of "Twinkle, Twinkle, Little Star." Have another child demonstrate how a mouse might sneak through the forest. Sing the second verse to the song as the child moves. Ask which animal made the loudest sound. Which one could they hear? Say they will move like the bear and the mouse in the music and movement center today.

The big hungry bear tromps through the forest green
Sniffing for a berry that he can't see
Tromp, tromp, tromp go his big bear feet
Tromp, tromp, tromp go his big bear feet
The big hungry bear tromps through the forest green
Sniffing for a berry that he can't see!

The hungry mouse sneaks through the forest green
Hiding the berry so the bear can't see
Sneak, sneak, sneak go her little mouse feet
Sneak, sneak, sneak go her little mouse feet
The hungry mouse sneaks through the forest green
Hiding the berry so the bear can't see!

Art Center
What the children will do: Use different materials to make strawberries. Show the children the picture on the front of the book. Ask them what they see on the book that is red. Take a piece of the red tissue paper. Crumple it up into a round ball. Say that you made a strawberry! In the art center they will use paper, markers, playdough, or tissue paper to make anything they want to make that they see in the book.

Make-Believe Center
What the children will do: Pretend to be the Big Hungry Bear, trying to find the strawberry by sniffing. Say that the bear could find the strawberry because he could smell it. Say that they will find things by smelling them too. Show the children the banana (or whatever you have that has a pleasant, strong odor). Have your assistant hide her eyes. Hide the banana under a piece of cloth while the children watch. Ask your assistant to see if she can find it by smelling. Say that they will all use their noses to try to find something in the make-believe center.

Have the children choose an arts activity.

Notes:

Theme of the Day:
Senses—See, Hear, Smell

Day 1: Music and Movement Center

What to Do:

The emphasis for this activity is *hear.*

Relate the activity to the story. Remind the children that the mouse hadn't heard that the bear loved strawberries until her friend told her. Ask if they think the mouse could hear the bear tromp through the forest.

MATERIALS

- Drum
- Triangle and striker

Have children stamp their feet to make sounds like the bear. Stamp your feet as the children remain seated. (If there are children who cannot move their feet, encourage them to strike their hands on the floor.) Play a steady, booming sound on the drum as they stamp their feet to the beat. Ask if the bear is loud. Could the mouse hear the bear coming? Does the bear care if the mouse can hear him?

Stand and move to the drum beat. Ask the children to stand and pretend to be the bear tromping through the forest on their big bear feet.

Think of other ways a bear might move. Ask the children to sit. Ask who can think of another way a big bear might move. Have the child demonstrate an idea, then have the other children move as the child did. Continue as long as the children suggest ways to move like a bear.

Move like the mouse. Ask the children to sit. Ask them if they think the little mouse would be loud as she moved through the forest. Would the mouse want to make a sound that the big hungry bear could hear? Have the children stand and sneak through the forest the way a little mouse might sneak. Play the triangle as they move like mice. Encourage them to move any way they want to move while they pretend to be little mice sneaking through the forest.

Sing a song. Encourage the children to move any way they want to move as you sing the following song to the tune of "Twinkle, Twinkle, Little Star." They should move like big bears, then like little mice. Encourage the children to sing with you as they begin to learn the song.

The big hungry bear tromps through the forest green
Sniffing for a berry that he can't see
Tromp, tromp, tromp go his big bear feet
Tromp, tromp, tromp go his big bear feet
The big hungry bear tromps through the forest green
Sniffing for a berry that he can't see!

The hungry mouse sneaks through the forest green
Hiding the berry so the bear can't see
Sneak, sneak, sneak go her little mouse feet
Sneak, sneak, sneak go her little mouse feet
The hungry mouse sneaks through the forest green
Hiding the berry so the bear can't see!

Theme of the Day:
Senses—See, Hear, Smell

Day 1: Art Center

What to Do:

The emphasis for this activity is *see.*

Relate activity to the story. Remind the children that the mouse's friend saw the big ripe strawberry that the mouse was getting ready to pick. Say that they will see what else is in the book.

Look through the book together. Write down the children's suggestions. Look through the book. Ask the children to tell you what they see in the pictures. Use the paper and marker to list all the things they mention that are in the book. When they have stopped making suggestions, show them the list of all the things they used their eyes to see in the book. (If the group includes a child with a visual disability, provide an item from the story to feel, such as a real strawberry or a leaf. Then ask the child to describe it to the group.)

MATERIALS

- Book, *The Big Hungry Bear*
- Large piece of paper and marker (for list)
- Playdough of various colors including red, green, and brown
- Tissue paper of various colors
- Butcher paper
- Markers

Show them the materials. Remind the children of the way the tissue paper was used to make a strawberry. Say that you made the strawberry because that is what you saw in the book. Show them all the materials that they can use to make whatever they wish to make that they see in the book. (Encourage older children to plan by telling you which object on the list they are going to make. Write the child's name beside each item on the list.)

Encourage the children to make what they saw. Work with the children as you, too, make an object from the book. Encourage the children to use the materials as they wish and to look at the book as they work. Don't expect representational reproductions of any object. Encourage experimentation.

Theme of the Day:
Senses—See, Hear, Smell

Day 1: Make-Believe Center

What to Do:

The emphasis for this activity is *smell.* Hide one of the objects before the activity begins. Hide it in the immediate area where the activity will take place.

MATERIALS

- **Object with a strong odor (two of the same object)**

Relate the activity to the story. Remind the children that the bear could smell strawberries from a long way away. Tell them that once he smelled a strawberry, he kept sniffing as he looked for it. Say that bears have a very strong sense of smell. Ask the children if they have ever smelled anything and then tried to find it.

Have the children smell the object. Pass the object around and encourage each child to smell it. Discuss the odor. Do they like the way it smells? Have they smelled it before? Do they think they could find one by smelling for it?

Try to find the object by smelling for it. Encourage the children to pretend to be the bear, sniffing around to find the object. Whoever finds it can pretend to be the mouse and hide it for the other children to find. (For older children, add other objects at this point.)

Theme of the Day:
Colors

Day 2 Group Time: Introducing the Theme of the Day

What to Do:

MATERIALS

- Artwork from previous day
- Book, *The Big Hungry Bear*
- Shape (preferably red, and large enough to place on floor)
- Globs of fingerpaint (two different colors)
- Resealable plastic bag
- Two craft sticks
- One piece of white construction paper
- Plastic food and play dishes

Review the previous day's activities. Remind the children that on the previous day they heard, saw, and smelled things in the centers. Ask for a volunteer to show you how to tromp like the bear and another volunteer to show you how to sneak like the mouse. Show some of the artwork from the previous day, asking the artists to tell about their work. Ask how they found the banana (or other smelly object) in the make-believe center. What did they do like the bear? Sing the song from the previous day and encourage the children to sing with you.

Read the story. Read the story, again encouraging the children to be involved in the story by stamping their feet and saying, "boom, boom, boom" and by sniffing when you read "sniff, sniff, sniff."

Introduce the theme of the day: Colors. Show the children the front of the book. Encourage them to name the colors they see. Then sing the following words to the tune of "Skip to My Lou." You can encourage the children to stand if they are wearing the featured color. If you have a child in the group who is unable to stand, encourage the children to raise their hands in response instead of standing.

Red, red, who's wearing red?
Red, red, who's wearing red?
Red, red, who's wearing red?
Stand up if you're wearing red!

After singing about several different colors, (the children wearing the color should sit after each verse), sing something that will bring all the children to their feet. For example, sing "Head, head who has a head?" Be sure to include specific colors that individual children may need to learn. Say that they will be working with colors in the centers today.

Introduce the arts activities.

Music and Movement Center

What the children will do: March around shapes like the mouse guarding the strawberry. Show the children the large shape and say that you are pretending it is the strawberry. Show the illustration in the book that shows the mouse marching with the key. Ask for a volunteer to pretend to be the mouse marching

continues . . .

around the strawberry to guard it. Say that in the music and movement center they will pretend to be the mouse and march to music.

Art Center

What the children will do: Mix paint in resealable plastic bags, then paint with the color they create. Show the children the resealable plastic bag. Show them how to take a craft stick and place globs of paint inside the bag. Close the bag. Squeeze the bag to mix the paint. Involve the children by passing the bag around and give several children the opportunity to squeeze the bag. After the paint is mixed, show them how to open the bag and squeeze the paint out onto the paper. Say that today in the art center they will mix paint and paint with the color they make.

Make-Believe Center

What the children will do: Pretend to be the mouse and the bear as they prepare dinner. Show the children the play food you have gathered. Ask them what color each food is. Ask a child to place some of the food on the plate. Tell the children that in the make-believe center they will pretend to be the mouse and the bear fixing food to eat together.

Have each child choose an arts activity.

Notes:

Day 2: Music and Movement Center

What to Do:

Consider the individual goals of the children in your classroom as you choose colors and shapes for this activity. You might want to put chalk marks on the floor to guide children in placing their shapes with enough room to march around them.

MATERIALS

- Floor shapes (red, green, blue, yellow)
- Cassette player
- Recorded marching music

Relate the activity to the story. Ask the children if they remember how the mouse guarded the strawberry. What was he holding when he was guarding it? Why would he hold a key? Encourage them to realize that the chain around the strawberry has a lock and that the key would unlock the lock. Ask them what else they see on the floor around the strawberry (thumbtacks). Remind them that they are going to pretend to be the mouse guarding the strawberry, but they will guard shapes instead of strawberries.

Identify and place shapes. Show each shape. Ask the children to identify the color and shape of each one. Encourage each child to choose a shape and to place the shape on the floor.

Explain the game. Say that you are going to start the music and that they should march around the shapes like the mouse until the music stops. When the music stops, they should sit on the closest shape. The first time through, lead the line. Weave around all the shapes; demonstrate marching like the mouse guarding the strawberry.

Continue the activity, encouraging a child to be the line leader. Repeat as long as the children are interested in the activity.

Close the activity by singing the following words to the tune of "Skip to My Lou."

Red, red, who's wearing red?
Red, red, who's wearing red?
Red, red, who's wearing red?
Stand up if you're wearing red!

(repeat, changing colors)

Theme of the Day: Colors

Day 2: Art Center

What to Do:

Relate the activity to the story. Remind the children that there were many different colors in the book. Show them the picture inside the house where the mouse is guarding the strawberry. Have them name the colors in the picture. Show the children the different colors of fingerpaint.

Place paint in a bag and squeeze to mix the colors. Place all the materials in the center of the table where the children have free access to them. As you join the children, show how to choose two colors, placing a glob of each in the plastic bag. Show how you can mix the paint in the bag. Encourage the children to choose two colors, mix them, then choose a piece of paper to paint on. Ask them to name the color they mixed.

Experiment with the paint. Encourage the children to paint, first with the color they mixed, then with other colors if they wish to do so.

MATERIALS

- **Book, *The Big Hungry Bear,* with page marked where mouse guards strawberry**
- **Open containers of red, yellow, and blue fingerpaint**
- **Small plastic bags (enough for each child and adult to have one)**
- **Craft sticks (one for each color of paint)**
- **Paper (different colors to provide child choice)**

Theme of the Day: Colors

Day 2: Make-Believe Center

What to Do:

Relate the activity to the story. Ask the children what the mouse did with the strawberry. Suggest that since the bear and the mouse both like to eat strawberries, maybe it would be a good idea for the mouse to invite the bear over for dinner.

Have the children prepare for the dinner. Encourage the children to set the table, place food on the plates, and get everything all ready for company. As the children work, discuss colors of food, sizes and shapes of plates, colors of plates, and so on.

Have individual children pretend to be the bear and the mouse. Suggest that one child pretend to be the mouse and another one pretend to be the bear. Help them play the roles by asking such questions as, "How would the bear walk? How would he talk? How would the mouse walk? How would she talk?" The other children can be friends who came to dinner. Encourage the children to change roles.

MATERIALS

- Housekeeping center
- Play food
- Plates
- Forks, spoons, knives

Theme of the Day:
Half

Day 3 Group Time: Introducing the Theme of the Day

What to Do:

Review the previous day's activities. Ask the children to tell you what they did the previous day in the music and movement center. Help them remember that they marched around shapes and pretended to be the mouse guarding his strawberry. Show some of the artwork, asking children to identify their work and name the colors they used. Ask what they fixed for dinner in the make-believe center. Sing the "Color Song" and encourage the children to stand as you sing about the colors they are wearing.

Read and discuss the story. Encourage the children to participate by sniffing, saying boom, and tromping their feet at the appropriate place in the story.

Introduce the theme of the day: Half. Read the section of the story again, that says "cut the strawberry in two and share half with me." Show the children a graham cracker square (or a strawberry if you have one). Stress that you only have one piece (or one strawberry). Then break or cut it in half and give half of it to your assistant. Say that you can share when you break it in half because then you have two pieces of the same size. Say that they are going to talk about *half* of things today in the centers.

MATERIALS

- Artwork from the previous day
- Graham cracker (or strawberry and knife)
- Book, *The Big Hungry Bear*
- Cassette player
- Recordings of high, light music and slower, louder music
- Potato, cut in half
- Container with thick paint
- Piece of paper
- Strawberry made of construction paper, with a dark line drawn down the middle
- Scissors
- Blocks
- Stuffed animal

Introduce the arts activities.

Music and Movement Center

What the children will do: Divide into groups, then play instruments to music. Play a little of the high, light music. Ask which animal might move to this music. Then play a little of the other music. Ask if they think the bear would move like this. Tell them that they will divide into mice and bears and choose instruments to play in the music and movement center today.

Art Center

What the children will do: Make fruit or vegetable prints. Show the potato that you have cut in half. Show them how the two halves fit together. Then dip half the potato in the paint and press it on the paper. Say that they will make prints from halves of vegetables in the art center today.

continues . . .

Make-Believe Center

What the children will do: Cut paper fruit in half, then share with a friend. Show the children the paper strawberry. Model cutting it in half on the dark line. Explain that you are cutting it in half. Use the blocks to make a chair for your stuffed animal friend, then pretend to feed half of the fruit to your friend. Say that they will cut a piece of paper fruit and feed it to a stuffed animal friend in the make-believe center today.

Have each child choose an arts activity.

Notes:

Theme of the Day: Half

Day 3: Music and Movement Center

What to Do:

This activity works best when there are an even number of children.

Relate the activity to the story. Remind the children that the mouse divided the strawberry in half, then gave half of it away and ate the other half.

Divide the group of children in half. Tell the children to stand up. Have them help you count them, then say you need ____ to be bears and ____ to be mice. Ask the bears to sit on one side of you and the mice to sit on the other side. Say that the group is divided in half.

Choose instruments to play. Place the instruments where the children can reach them easily, then encourage them to choose an instrument to play. Ask them if the bears should play loud instruments or quiet ones. Ask if mice should play loud instruments or quiet ones.

Play sections of the music and encourage the children to play their instruments. Encourage them to play loudly with the "bear" music and quietly with the "mouse" music.

Play music again, for the children to move. Have the children change roles, with the mice becoming bears and the bears becoming mice. Let the children choose whether they want to move to the music or play an instrument. Some children may be able to do both.

Sing the Big Hungry Bear song to the tune of "Twinkle, Twinkle, Little Star."

The big hungry bear tromps through the forest green
Sniffing for a berry that he can't see
Tromp, tromp, tromp go his big bear feet
Tromp, tromp, tromp go his big bear feet
The big hungry bear tromps through the forest green
Sniffing for a berry that he can't see!

The hungry mouse sneaks through the forest green
Hiding the berry so the bear can't see
Sneak, sneak, sneak go her little mouse feet
Sneak, sneak, sneak go her little mouse feet
The hungry mouse sneaks through the forest green
Hiding the berry so the bear can't see!

MATERIALS

- Music instruments, enough for each child to have one
- Cassette player
- Recordings of high, light music and slow, loud music

Theme of the Day: Half

Day 3: Art Center

What to Do:

Relate the activity to the story. Remind the children that the mouse cut the strawberry in half and shared it with his friend. Say that their food has already been cut in half and they are going to paint with half a piece of food.

Match and name food halves. Show the pieces of food to the children. Encourage them to fit the matching pieces together. Say that when something is cut in half, both pieces are the same size. They are the same, not different. Encourage the children to name each item.

MATERIALS

- Pieces of fruit or vegetables, cut in half
- Thick paint, red, yellow, and blue
- Paper (several different colors to provide choice)

Let the children experiment freely with the materials. Place the paint, paper, and food pieces where they are easily accessible, and join in the activity. Encourage the children to compare the prints made by different pieces of food. Which food makes the biggest print? If you use both halves, does the print look the same or different? If you print over a print you already made with a different color, what happens? Does the print change color or stay the same?

Theme of the Day: Half

Day 3: Make-Believe Center

What to Do:

If the group includes children who cannot cut, cut some of the paper fruit in half before the activity begins.

Relate the activity to the story. Remind the children that the mouse cut the strawberry in half and shared it with his friend. Say that they will cut a piece of paper fruit in half, then share it with a pretend friend.

Cut the paper fruit in half. Place the fruit and scissors in the center of the table where they are easily available and encourage each child to take a fruit shape and a pair of scissors. Ask each child to label his fruit and its color. Give help as needed as they cut their fruit in half.

Encourage children to choose a stuffed animal friend. Ask the children who the mouse's friend was in the story. Say that they can pretend that the stuffed animal is the friend with whom they share their fruit. Encourage them to use any of the housekeeping materials, blocks, or whatever they wish to create an environment in which they may share their strawberry with their friend. (For example, they may wish to make a block chair for their friend, or create a box table to place dishes on.)

MATERIALS

- Pieces of paper fruit with a heavy black line drawn down the center (strawberries, bananas, oranges, apples, etc.)
- Scissors (enough for each child to have a pair)
- Stuffed animals, enough for each child to have one
- Blocks, empty boxes, dishes

Theme of the Day:
Share

Day 4 Group Time: Introducing the Theme of the Day

What to Do:

Review the activities of previous day. Ask the children what they did on the previous day. Ask who played instruments like bears and who played instruments like mice. Show several of the art prints, encouraging the children to tell what they used to make them. Then show the two halves of the paper strawberry. Ask a child who she shared fruit with.

Read the story. Read and discuss the story. Encourage the children to participate by sniffing and stamping their feet when appropriate.

Introduce the theme of the day: Share. Show the picture in the book where the text says, "Share half with me." Ask what *share* means. What is the mouse in the picture doing? Is he keeping the whole strawberry for himself? Show them the cookie. Say that it's your cookie. Should you eat the whole cookie in front of them, or should you share your cookie? Encourage a discussion, then break pieces off your cookie and give a piece to each child. Stress that you are sharing with Jamela, sharing with Jason, sharing with Tyler, and so on.

MATERIALS

- Art prints from previous day
- Two halves of paper strawberry
- Book, *The Big Hungry Bear*
- One large cookie
- One musical instrument
- Several pieces of Styrofoam, tape, one pair of scissors
- Several small plates with one type of fruit on each
- Two small paper plates
- Two spoons

Introduce the Sharing Rhyme.

If you don't want to give what you have to a bear,
Just look for a friend and share, share, share.
Sharing with a friend lets them know that you care,
So look for a friend and share, share, share.

Introduce the arts activities.

Music and Movement Center

What the children will do: Share musical instruments with friends. Give a musical instrument to your assistant. Sing the Sharing Song as you pass the instrument back and forth between the two of you.

Sharing Song

(to the tune of "Mary Had a Little Lamb")
Share, share, share your toy,
Share your toy, share your toy,
Share, share, share your toy,
Share your toy today.

continues . . .

At the end of the song, play the instrument. Say that in the music and movement center, the children will share a musical instrument.

Art Center

What the children will do: Make structures to hide the strawberry in. Work with your assistant to role-play the activity. Each of you should have several small pieces of Styrofoam, but share one pair of scissors and one roll of tape. Role-play how to ask politely for the needed supplies and how to say thank you. Tell the children that they will make Styrofoam structures in the art center today, but they will need to share the materials with each other.

Make-Believe Center

What the children will do: Share supplies to make a fruit salad snack. Take one of the small plates of fruit and give the other one to your assistant. Explain to the children that you want to make a snack out of several kinds of fruit but you just have one kind and you like the other kind too. What can you do? Lead the discussion until someone suggests that you can share with your assistant. Take one of the empty plates and give one to your assistant. Share the fruit with each other, then say that this is what they will be doing in the make-believe center today.

Have the children choose an arts activity.

Notes:

Theme of the Day: Share

Day 4: Music and Movement Center

What to Do:

MATERIALS

- Musical instruments

Use an instrument that is a classroom favorite.

Relate the activity to the story. Have the children sit in a circle on the floor. Remind them that the little mouse shared his strawberry with a friend and that they are going to play a musical game where they share their musical instruments with each other.

Discuss sharing an instrument. Give the instrument to a child and encourage him to play it. Ask if anyone else likes to play that instrument. If no one speaks up, insist that it is your favorite instrument. Ask if it would be fair for the child to get to play the instrument all the time without your having a turn. Encourage a discussion. Say that today everyone will have a turn to play the instrument.

Sing the Sharing Song, then explain the game. Have the child put the instrument down while you sing the Sharing Song to the tune of "Mary Had a Little Lamb."

Share, share, share your toys,
Share your toys, share your toys,
Share, share, share your toys,
Share your toys today.

Encourage the children to sing the song with you, then start the game. Encourage the child with the instrument to pass the instrument to the next person as you sing. The children will pass the instrument around the circle. At the end of the song, have the child who has the instrument play it. Then say it's time to share the instrument again and repeat the process of singing the song and passing the instrument around until the song ends. Stress that everyone is sharing the instrument.

Theme of the Day: Share

Day 4: Art Center

What to Do:

Relate activity to the story. Tell the children that at first the mouse tried to hide the strawberry, and then later on decided to share the strawberry with a friend. Say that today they will make something to hide the strawberry in, but that they will have to share their materials with their friends.

Encourage children to gather materials and start building. Show the children the supply of materials and encourage them to gather what they think they will need. If children are older, encourage them to make one group structure, sharing materials and working together. Younger children may be happier making their own creation. Since most of the supplies are limited, encourage them to share with each other, asking if they may please use something, then thanking the friend who shared with them.

MATERIALS

- Pieces of Styrofoam, such as packing material
- Empty toilet paper tubes
- Empty boxes of varying sizes
- Masking tape (one dispenser)
- Toothpicks or golf tees if available (limited number)
- Markers (limited number)
- Crayons (limited number)
- Craft sticks (limited number)

Theme of the Day: Share

Day 4: Make-Believe Center

What to Do:

If fruit is not available, substitute other food such as cereal, pretzels, and raisins to make trail mix.

Relate the activity to the story. Remind the children that the mouse shared his strawberry with his friend and that they are going to be sharing food with their friends today.

Distribute the food. Give each child a small bowl of one kind of food. Say that they will be making their snack so they will want to have several different kinds of food on their plates. Ask what they could do, how can they get some of the food that someone else has?

Make supplies readily available. Place spoons and small plates in the center of the table where the children can easily reach them. Tell everyone to get a plate and a spoon. Encourage each child to tell what is in the bowl he has.

Encourage sharing. Model the desired behavior by asking a child for some of her food and putting a spoonful of your food on a child's plate when requested. Continue until each individual has a variety of food.

Eat the snack. Let the children eat the snack or place the child's name on it and cover it until later.

MATERIALS

- Bowls of fruit, precut into small pieces (each bowl should contain only one kind of fruit)
- Small empty plates
- Spoons

Theme of the Day:
Strawberries

Day 5 Group Activity

What to Do:

Relate the activity to the story and discuss strawberries. Show the children one of the pictures in the book where the mouse is next to the strawberry. Say that the strawberry in the book looks very big. Why do they think it looks so big? Help them to understand that the strawberry looks big because the mouse is so little. Show the children the strawberries. Put a strawberry on the floor next to a child. Does the strawberry look big or little? Discuss whether strawberries are a fruit or a vegetable.

MATERIALS

- Book, *The Big Hungry Bear*
- Strawberries (fresh or frozen whole berries)
- Other ingredients as indicated

Discuss picking strawberries. Ask the children how the mouse in the story picked the strawberry. If necessary, show them the picture of the mouse on the ladder. Say this is pretend, that mice don't really climb ladders to pick strawberries. Ask if they have ever picked strawberries. Did they have to climb a ladder to pick the berry?

Brainstorm ways to eat strawberries. Ask the children how they eat strawberries at their house. Do they eat strawberries on ice cream? Encourage them to suggest ways to eat strawberries as you list their ideas on the paper. Read the ideas back to them to encourage other ideas. The suggestions might include:

- Strawberry sundaes
- Strawberry milkshakes
- Strawberry shortcake
- Strawberry pie
- Strawberry jam
- Strawberries on cereal
- Strawberries and cream

Describe what they will make. Tell the children that all those ideas sound good and that they are all going to work together to make a strawberry dessert today.

Suggestions for Implementing the Activity:

Encourage the children to help wash the berries, stem the berries (if necessary), measure ingredients, mix ingredients, and set the table to eat the treat after it is finished. Throughout the activity, discuss different

continues . . .

fruits and where they can be found. Ask what other types of fruit the children have helped gather, and discuss their favorite fruit. Any strawberry treat may be prepared. Children can help measure and make such foods as:

- Strawberry milkshakes
- Instant vanilla pudding with strawberries
- Strawberry toppings for ice cream (strawberries and sugar blended together in a blender)
- Strawberry shortcake (an easy way is to make the shortcake with prepared cakes or biscuits)

The recipe for one simple baked dessert follows:

Wash, stem, and slice one quart of strawberries.
Sugar as desired.
Set sugared strawberries aside.
Sift together 1 cup flour, 1 cup sugar, 2 teaspoons baking powder, ½ teaspoon salt.
Add 1 cup milk to the dry ingredients.
Stir together with a wire whisk.
Melt ½ stick of margarine in a 9-inch square pan.
Pour the batter on top of margarine. Do not stir.
Spoon strawberries on top of batter.
Bake 45 minutes at 350 degrees.

Notes:

SKILLS & GOALS MATRIX

The Little Mouse, the Red Ripe Stawberry, and the Big Hungry Bear

	Skills or Behaviors	Goals and Objectives
Cognitive	• Recognize and name colors and/or shapes	• Increase ability to sort by color and/or size • Improve visual discrimination
	• Compare quiet and noisy sounds	• Increase understanding of opposites • Improve auditory discrimination
	• Identify halves of objects	• Increase understanding of whole-part relationships
	• Identify body parts	• Increase visual memory skills • Increase general vocabulary and concept development
	• Label objects in a book and make a list	• Increase awareness of written language • Increase ability to associate pictures with written labels
Language	• Learn, and sing, a song	• Increase receptive and expressive vocabulary • Increase phonological awareness
	• Identify quiet and noisy sounds	• Improve auditory awareness and discrimination
	• Recognize and label events of the story when asked	• Increase preliteracy skills: understand story structure, become familiar with written language
	• Use "please" and "thank you"	• Increase functional use of language • Increase use of socially appropriate language

SKILLS & GOALS MATRIX (CONT.)

	Skills or Behaviors	Goals and Objectives
Social	• Sing a song with others	• Increase participation as member of a group
	• Act out a part in a story	• Increase understanding of point of view and feelings of others • Increase ability to speak in a group
	• Participate in an art project as part of a group	• Increase appropriate verbal interactions with peers • Increase appropriate social behaviors
	• Share objects with peers	• Increase ability to play cooperatively with a peer • Increase pro-social behavior with peers
Fine-Motor	• Use halves of vegetables for stamps	• Refine pincer grasp • Increase visual-motor coordination
	• Squeeze paints in a bag	• Increase bilateral coordination • Increase hand strength
	• Play musical instruments	• Increase wrist rotation • Increase bimanual coordination
	• Smear fingerpaints	• Increase visual-motor coordination • Increase use of shoulder, arm, wrist, and hand in coordinated movement
Gross-Motor	• Move quietly like a mouse	• Increase motor planning • Increase dynamic balance • Increase awareness of body in space
	• Move rhythmically to music	• Increase gross-motor planning and control • Increase auditory-motor coordination
	• Walk in and out of shapes on the floor	• Refine mobility control • Increase awareness of body in space
	• Stamp feet	• Increase gross-motor control • Increase body awareness • Increase leg strength

STORY OF THE WEEK / EL CUENTO DE ESTA SEMANA

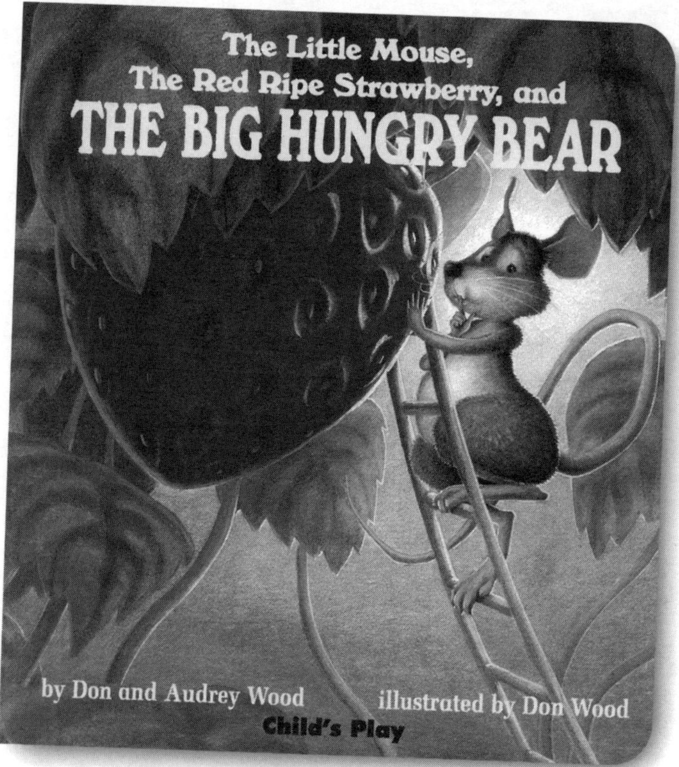

The Little Mouse, the Red Ripe Strawberry, and the Big Hungry Bear

by Don and Audrey Wood

Edición en español: ***El ratoncito, la fresa roja y madura y el gran oso hambriento***

The Spark story this week is *The Little Mouse, the Red Ripe Strawberry, and the Big Hungry Bear.* You may be able to find this book at the library. The story is about a little mouse that picks a red, ripe strawberry. His friend tells him that big hungry bears love strawberries and can sniff them out no matter where they are. Ask your child what the mouse did (cut the strawberry in half and shared it with his friend). The themes to go with this story are *senses (smell, hear, see), colors, half,* and *share.*

El cuento de Spark de esta semana se llama *El ratoncito, la fresa roja y madura y el gran oso hambriento.* Usted puede conseguirlo en cualquier biblioteca. El cuento es sobre un ratoncito que encuentra una fresa roja y madura. Su amigo le cuenta lo mucho que le gustan las fresas a los osos grandotes y hambrientos. Ellos las pueden oler desde donde sea que estén. Pregúntele a su niño o niña qué hizo el ratoncito (cortó la fresa por la mitad y la compartió con su amigo). Las ideas temáticas que van con este cuento son: *las sensaciones: oler, oír y ver; los colores, la mitad* y *compartir.*

© 2001 The Board of Trustees of the University of Illinois. May be reproduced for use by teachers.

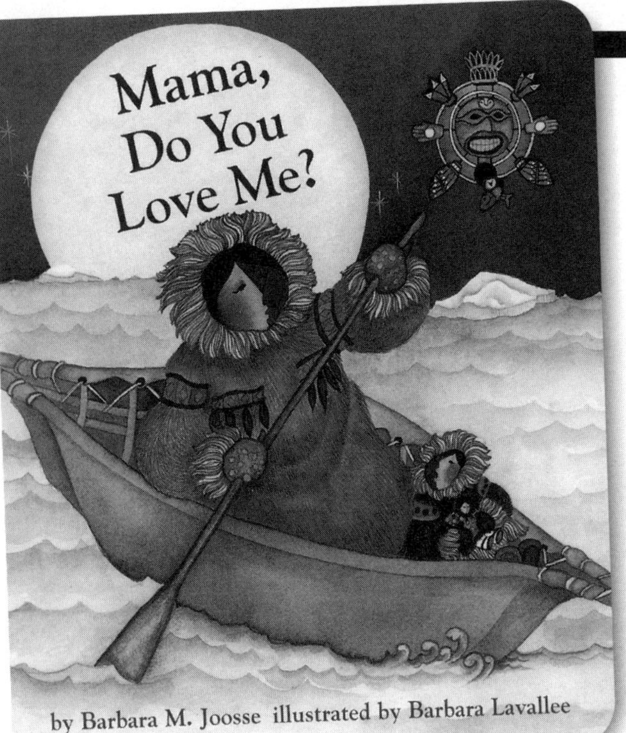

Mama,
Do You
Love Me?
by Barbara M. Joosse illustrated by Barbara Lavallee

Mama, Do You Love Me?

by Barbara M. Joosse

San Francisco: Chronicle Books, 1991.

Story Synopsis: *Mama, Do You Love Me?* is a tale of unconditional love. Throughout the story, the child tests the mother's love, but the mother states that even though she might be sad or angry or upset or worried, she still loves the child. Teachers report that the cultural words inserted in the text are highly enjoyed by the children in their classes. For example, the word *mukluk* is a marvelous word to say, much more fun than *boots.* Although the story introduces a very different culture, it tells a universal tale about a mother's love for her child.

Classroom Use: Many teachers use this book during February, associating it with Valentine's Day. It also may be linked to other stories about cold weather and families. The themes and concepts for this unit are *people who love one another, large and small, cold,* and *feelings.*

Considerations: The setting is the Arctic and the clothing worn by the story characters is traditional Inuit dress. When you use this unit, you may want to tell the children that the story shows the way the Inuit people lived many, many years ago. If possible, show present-day pictures of people who live in the Arctic for comparison. Since the story includes unfamiliar words, it is wise to prepare before you introduce the story to the children. The author includes information at the back of the book about many of the terms in the book.

Special Materials: In addition to the materials typically found in preschool classrooms, this unit suggests poles with magnets and paper fish equipped with paper clips for a fishing activity.

ACTIVITY MATRIX

Mama, Do You Love Me?

Day	Concept	Music Activity	Art Activity	Make-Believe Activity
Day 1	People Who Love One Another (Social)	Showing affection and sharing instruments. Move to happy music.	Use art materials to make something for someone they love.	Pretend to take care of babies.
Day 2	Large/Small (Cognitive, Language)	Compare size and sound of instruments. Move in large and small steps.	Use large and small tubes to print circles, paint.	Play in sand table with wet sand and large and small sand toys.
Day 3	Cold (Cognitive, Language, Science)	Play a game to a cold weather rap and move to cold weather music.	Paint with ice cubes and paint powder.	Dress up for winter and pretend to do winter activities.
Day 4	Feelings (Social)	Music and art combined. Express feelings through moving or painting in response to different kinds of music.	See music.	Practice expressing feelings while playing with toys.
Day 5	Life in the Arctic			

Theme of the Day:
People Who Love One Another

Day 1 Group Time: Introducing the Book

What to Do:

Introduce the story. Tell the children that the story they will hear is about a little girl and her mother and how much the mother loves her little girl.

Read the story. Read the story and then talk about how the mother loved the child. Stress the idea that Mama's love was unconditional: she loved her "Dear One" no matter what might happen. Show the picture where the little girl breaks the eggs. Does the mother look angry? Read the part again that says, "Then I would be sorry. But still, I would love you."

MATERIALS

- Book, *Mama, Do You Love Me?* (with page marked where child breaks egg)
- Small box and wrapping paper
- Doll

Teach the song. Introduce the song by saying that you know a song that the mother in the story might have sung. Sing the following words to the tune of "Skip to My Lou":

I love you, yes I do
I love you, yes I do.
I love you, yes I do
I love you and you!

Repeat, encouraging the children to join the singing as they become familiar with the song. Model touching someone gently as you sing the song to model one interaction between people who care about each other.

Introduce the theme of the day: People who love one another. Say that all of the activities today will help them think about people they love. Have the children name people they love, such as parents, aunts, uncles, grandparents, cousins, teachers, neighbors, and friends. Say that they are like the little girl in the story. They have people who love them.

Introduce the arts activities.

Music and Movement Center
What the children will do: Show affection for each other and share instruments. Tell the children that when people love one another they usually feel happy. Sing the following words to "If You're Happy and You Know It":

continues . . .

If you're happy and you know it, touch a friend.
If you're happy and you know it, touch a friend.
If you're happy and you know it, then your face will surely show it.
If you're happy and you know it, touch a friend.

Say that in the music and movement center they will move to happy music, play instruments, and sing.

Art Center

What the children will do: Use art materials to make something for people they love. Tell the children that when people love one another they sometimes show their love by giving a gift to the person they love. Show the children the small box and quickly wrap the wrapping paper around it like a gift. Tell them they will be making and wrapping gifts for someone they love.

Make-Believe Center

What the children will do: Use dolls and housekeeping props to pretend to take care of babies. Cradle a doll in your arms and give it a hug. Tell the children you are hugging the doll like the mother in the book hugged her little girl. Say that they may take care of babies in the make-believe center.

Have each child choose an arts activity.

Notes:

Theme of the Day:
People Who Love One Another

Day 1: Music and Movement Center

What to Do:

MATERIALS

- Recorded music that sounds happy
- Cassette tape player
- Musical instruments: rhythm sticks, sand blocks, resonator bells, cymbals, cluster bells, triangle, tambourine, maracas

Relate the activity to the story. Remind the children that the little girl's mama loved her very much, even when she broke things. Say that when people love one another, they may get angry or upset with each other, but they still love each other. Remind them that when they are with someone they love they are usually happy. Now they will move to happy music and make happy sounds.

Move to music. Say that you will play some happy music and they can move to the music any way they want to move. Play the recorded music and join the children as they move. Encourage creative movement. Say such things as, "This happy music makes me feel like smiling!" or "This happy music makes me feel like hugging someone." Play through the tape, complimenting children for making unique and appropriate movements.

Encourage the children to choose instruments. Ask the children to sit in a circle on the floor with you. Be sure they are within easy touching distance of each other. Place the instruments in the middle of the circle and encourage each child to choose an instrument to play.

Play instruments to a song and model touching the child next to you. Encourage the children to join you in singing the "I Love You" song and playing their instrument to the music. (Don't expect three-year-old children to play and sing at the same time.) As you finish singing, hug or touch the child next to you in the circle, saying, "Most people like to touch people they like." Encourage each child to touch the person next to her.

Show how to share with others. Tell the children that friends also like to share things with each other, so each child will pass his instrument to the person he just touched. Show how you can pass your instrument to the child you touched.

Repeat the activity. Sing the song again, using the new instruments to accompany the song. Repeat the sequence, always passing the instruments around the circle in the same direction so that children have new instruments to play each time. This will provide an opportunity to practice sharing instruments and to practice singing.

Theme of the Day:
People Who Love One Another

Day 1: Art Center

What to Do:

Relate the activity to the story. Remind the children that the little girl's mama loved her all the time. Say that when people love one another they often like to give things to them. They will make gifts for people they love. Encourage the children to recall times they gave or received presents.

Make gifts for loved ones. Invite the children to make things for people they love. Let the children use the art materials as they wish to make their gifts. They might draw pictures, glue scrap materials together, cut pieces of paper and glue them on paper. Encourage the children to use scissors if they can; encourage them to tear paper if they cannot use scissors. Some children may be able to cut snips to "fringe" the edge of their work.

MATERIALS

- **Colored paper**
- **Crayons or markers**
- **Scrap materials, such as yarn, pieces of foil, Styrofoam chips, straws**
- **Scissors**
- **Glue**
- **Small boxes**
- **Wrapping paper**
- **Tape**

Wrap the gifts. Suggest that the children put their creations in boxes and wrap them like gifts. Let them wrap the boxes as much on their own as they can—perfection is not necessary. The children can either tape the wrapping paper in place on the boxes or wrap the paper around the boxes loosely for an adult to tape in place. Encourage independence, but offer help when needed to avoid frustration—wrapping boxes is a difficult task.

Label the gifts. Ask each child to name someone at home they would like to give their gift to. Print that person's name on the wrapped gift, or help the child print the name. Let them take the gifts home.

Theme of the Day:
People Who Love One Another

Day 1: Make-Believe Center

What to Do:

Relate the activity to the story. Show the children the page at the beginning of the book that shows the mother and child kissing each other. Say that when people love each other they often like to touch each other. Say that they will pretend that they are the parents and that the dolls are the children that they love.

Pretend to show affection for the dolls. As the children play in the housekeeping area, join in and model showing affection toward the dolls in different ways:

- hugging them
- kissing them
- singing to them
- smiling at them

Pretend to care for the dolls. If needed, show some different ways of caring for the dolls:

- feeding them
- dressing and changing them
- giving a bath
- rocking them to sleep
- looking at books with them

MATERIALS

- Book, *Mama, Do You Love Me?* (with page marked of mother and child kissing each other)
- Dolls or stuffed animals
- Housekeeping props

Theme of the Day:
Large/Small

Day 2 Group Time: Introducing the Theme of the Day

What to Do:

If children have not learned the concepts *large* and *small,* use the words *big* and *little.*

Review the previous day's activities. Remind the children that on the previous day they talked about loving someone. Sing the song "I Love You," and reach out to touch a child. Discuss the gifts they made and wrapped for someone they love. Encourage the children to share the different ways they took care of dolls in the make-believe center.

MATERIALS

- **Book, *Mama, Do You Love Me?***
- **Adult and baby plastic whales (or other animals)**
- **One large drum and one small drum**
- **Paper-towel tube, toilet-paper tube, and drinking straw**

Read the story. As you read the story, have the children look at the pictures. In the first two pictures and the last two pictures, ask the children: "Who is small?" "Who is large?" Discuss how Mama is large and Dear One is small.

Introduce the theme of the day: Large/Small. Use a pair of adult and baby plastic whales (or other animals). Move the adult whale around as you say, "This large whale is swimming in the water, like the whale in the book." Then swim the baby near the adult whale and say, "Here comes a small whale. The large whale and the small whale are swimming in the water. Which one is the large whale? Which one is the small whale?" Tell the children that they will be thinking about *large* and *small* things in the centers today.

Introduce the arts activities.

Music and Movement Center
What the children will do: Compare the sizes and sounds of instruments. Show the children the large drum and label it as large. Then play a slow beat on the drum as you take large steps in a circle around the children, chanting, "large steps, large steps, large steps, large." Then switch to the small drum and take small steps as you chant, "Small steps, small steps, small steps, small." Tell the children they may walk to the drums in the music center, taking large steps like Mama would and small steps like Dear One. They will also sing and play instruments.

Art Center
What the children will do: Use large and small tubes to print circles and use them in other ways for art creations. Show the children the tubes and straws, emphasizing that they are large and small. Tell them they may use these in the art center.

continues . . .

Make-Believe Center

What the children will do: Play in the sand table with wet sand and large and small sand toys. (If you don't have access to toy whales or other toy aquatic creatures, you will need to adapt the activity.) Show the children a large whale and a small whale and name them as large and small. Remind them that the whale in the book was swimming in water. Say that in the make-believe center they may dig large and small holes in sand for the whales and fill the holes with water, so that the whales can swim around like the whale in the book.

Have each child choose an arts activity.

Notes:

Theme of the Day:
Large/Small

Day 2: Music and Movement Center

What to Do:

Relate the activity to the story. Remind the children that the mama in the story was very large and the little girl was very small. Encourage them to discuss their own families. Who is large in their family? Who is small? Is anyone smaller than they are? Say that they will move like the mama and the little girl in the story.

Encourage large and small steps. Ask a child to show how to take large steps. Have everyone join the movement and take large steps like Mama. Have everyone freeze in place. Ask a child to show how to take small steps like Dear One. Have everyone take small steps.

Move to the sound of the drum. Beat rhythms on the large and small drums, alternating slow, ponderous beats on the large drum, as you chant, "large steps, large steps, large steps, large," and short, light beats on the small drum as you chant, "small steps, small steps, small steps, small." Ask the children to move back to the circle and sit down.

MATERIALS

- Two recordings of music, one slow and loud and the other faster and lighter
- Large drum and small drum
- Variety of musical instruments, such as large and small resonator bells, drums, triangle, jingle bells, tambourine, and sand blocks, in a box or large sack
- Blank tape
- Cassette player

Compare the sizes of instruments. Put the box or sack of instruments in the center of the circle and let each child reach in to take one. Help the children decide whether each instrument is large or small, by holding them next to the similar ones to make comparisons.

Seat children according to the sizes of their instruments. Invite all the children who have large instruments to sit together and all the children who have small instruments to sit together.

Tape the sounds of the instruments. Ask all the children who have large instruments to say, "Large!" for you to record. Then tell them to play together as you record the sounds of their instruments. Have them put their instruments down and tell the children who have small instruments to say, "Small!" for you to record. Then encourage them to play together as you record the sound of their instruments. (Encourage children who are waiting for their turn to act as an audience and clap when the other group finishes recording their sounds.)

Play the tape back. As the children listen to the tape of their instruments, talk about the sounds the instruments made, discussing any differences the children might be able to hear.

Play tapes that suggest large and small movements. Encourage the children to move to music that will enable them to experiment with large and small movements. Play the music and move to the music with the children. Say such things as "I can take large steps, can you?" or "This music makes me think of a small fairy moving. I wonder if I can look like a small fairy?" Some children may prefer to play instruments to the music.

Theme of the Day:
Large/Small

Day 2: Art Center

What to Do:

Relate the activity to the story. Show the children the last two pictures in the book and discuss the difference in size between the mother and the child. Ask what kind of a painting they think the child in the story might have made. Would it be large or small? What kind of a painting would the mama make? Say that they can make large or small paintings.

Let the children experiment with the materials freely. Join in and show how to dip the end of a tube or straw in paint and use it to print circles on large and small paper plates. Talk about the large and small plates and the large and small circles you are making.

Roll tubes in paint. Roll the large and small tubes in paint and then roll them on the paper to create trails of paint.

Paint with brushes. Paint the tubes or the large and small plates with brushes. Encourage the children to experiment with the materials in other ways.

MATERIALS

- **Book, *Mama Do You Love Me?***
- **Tubes from bathroom tissue or paper towels**
- **Drinking straws**
- **Large and small paper plates**
- **Paper**
- **Paintbrushes**
- **Paint (several different colors)**

Theme of the Day:
Large/Small

Day 2: Make-Believe Center

What to Do:

Relate the activity to the story. Remind the children that the people in the story lived in a very cold place. Say that the animals that lived there are the kind of animals that live in cold weather. Encourage the children to discuss the different kinds of animals they saw in the story. Turn to the page that shows the whale. Ask if they have ever seen a real whale. Encourage discussion. Say that whales are very large and that they live in the ocean. State that during this activity they will make a place for the whales to live.

Encourage the children to make large and small creations. Show the children how to pour water on the sand so it can be used for molding and building. Keep the pitcher with water nearby to re-wet the sand as needed. Supply the large and small containers, so that children can become involved in imaginative play centered around *large* and *small.* Show the children how to fill a container with wet sand and turn it over to form a large or small mound. Give assistance as needed. As the children work, make comments and ask questions that draw their attention to the sizes of the objects they make. "You made many hills. Are they large or small?" "Please show Danielle how to make a large tower like yours."

Discuss whales. Fill a container with water and float large and small whales in it as you talk about what the whales are doing.

Dig holes. Encourage the children to dig large and small holes in the sand and fill them with water for the whales to swim in.

MATERIALS

- Book, *Mama, Do You Love Me?* (with page marked that shows a whale)
- Sand table
- Water in pitcher
- Large and small containers, especially rounded ones from whipped topping (ideal for "igloos")
- Spoons
- Large and small toy whales (or other toy aquatic creatures)
- Other sand toys

Theme of the Day:
Cold

Day 3 Group Time: Introducing the Theme of the Day

What to Do:

Review the previous day's activities. Show the large and small artwork from the day before. Discuss which musical instruments are large and which are small. Ask a child to get a large instrument from the music center and play it. Ask another child to get a small instrument and play it. Are the sounds the same or different? Discuss what kind of objects they made in the sand table. How did they get the sand moist so they could make something?

Read the story. Put on the hat, coat, and gloves. Pick up the book. Ask the children if they can guess why you are dressing up to read the story. Elicit conversation about how the story takes place where it is very cold. As you read the story, ask children to look for signs that Mama and Dear One live where the weather is cold. Examples include: heavy parkas, ice, snow, *mukluks,* and certain animals.

MATERIALS

- **Artwork from previous day**
- **Large and small instruments used on the previous day**
- **Book, *Mama, Do You Love Me?***
- **Adult winter coat, hat, and gloves**
- **One ice cube for each child and adult, wrapped in a paper towel**
- **One ice cube on a stick, a piece of paper, and powder paint from the art center**
- **Several props from make-believe center**

Introduce the theme of the day: Cold. Give each child an ice cube in a paper towel. Encourage them to hold their ice cubes, rub them on their arms and faces, and lick them. Emphasize the word *cold* as the children feel the ice. Tell them that they will think about *cold* in the centers today.

Introduce the arts activities.

Music and Movement Center

What the children will do: Play a game to a rap and move to the cold-weather music. Clap and chant the following rap, stressing the words *coat, hat, sneeze,* and *cough.*

You <u>have</u> to wear your <u>coat</u> when it's <u>cold</u> out<u>side,</u>
You <u>have</u> to wear your <u>hat</u> when it's <u>cold</u> out<u>side.</u>
You <u>have</u> to bundle <u>up</u> when it's <u>cold</u> out<u>side,</u>
Or you'll <u>shiv</u>er and <u>shake</u> when it's <u>cold</u> out<u>side!</u>

Repeat the rap, encouraging the children to chant with you as they become familiar with the rhyme. Tell them that in music they will play a game to the rap and will move to some cold-weather music.

Art Center

What the children will do: Paint with ice cubes and paint powder. Show the children one of the ice cubes on a stick. Rub it on a piece of paper and then shake on some powder paint. Tell them they may paint with ice in the art center.

Make-Believe Center

What the children will do: Dress up for winter activities and pretend to do cold-weather activities, such as playing in the snow. Show the children some of the props from the make-believe center. Tell them they can pretend to play in the cold snow in that center today.

Have each child choose an arts activity.

Notes:

Theme of the Day: Cold

Day 3: Music and Movement Center

What to Do:

Before the activity begins, set up the cassette player with the winter music tape so that you only have to push the *start* button when the rap is finished and the children are ready to move. Use chalk or tape to make a square about 6 feet in diameter on the floor.

Relate the activity to the story. Remind the children that the little girl in the story lived where it was very cold outside. Say that whenever she went outside she had to wear a coat and mittens. Say that they will play a music game about going outside in cold weather.

MATERIALS

- Masking tape or chalk
- Cassette player
- Recording of winter music, such as "Jingle Bells"
- Container of different kinds of bells

Explain that the square is a house and it is cold outside the house. Sit with the children inside the square. Tell the children that you are pretending that the square is a house that is warm inside, and when they step out of the square they are outside the house in the cold. Tell them that they are going to pretend to get ready to go outside in the cold.

Chant the rap and show the actions to go with it. Start chanting the rap, using the following actions:

You have to wear your coat when it's cold outside (pretend to put on a coat),
You have to wear your hat when it's cold outside (pretend to put on a hat).
You have to bundle up when it's cold outside (pretend to put on boots),
Or you'll shiver and shake when it's cold outside (pretend to shiver).

Prepare the children for movement. Say, "I'm all bundled up, are you? Let's step outside the house. Isn't it cold? Brrrr! Now, let's pretend that we are going to someone's house as we move to the winter music! Where should our friend's house be?" Help the children choose a place in the room to be the "friend's house."

Start the cassette player and show movement. Move to the music with the children. Play the music through twice; once to go to someone's house and then again to come home.

Return to the square "house." Move back inside the house with the children. Sit down together and rewind the tape. As the tape rewinds, chant the following rap with accompanying actions:

You take off your coat when you come inside.
You take off your hat when you come inside.
You take off your boots when you come inside,
Or you'll be too hot when you're inside!

Play bells to music. Make bells available and encourage children to choose to play bells or to sing along (if there are words) with the tape.

Theme of the Day: Cold

Day 3: Art Center

What to Do:

To prepare ice cubes, use ice cube trays or Styrofoam egg cartons. Pour water in each section and stick in a craft stick before freezing. The sticks do not need to stand up. To prepare the paint powder, poke holes in the lids of plastic containters and put paint powder in the containers.

Relate the activity to the story. Remind the children that it was very cold where the little girl and her mother lived. Say that when it is very cold, something happens to water. Encourage discussion of water turning to ice.

MATERIALS

- Fingerpaint paper or other shiny paper
- Ice cubes with stick handles
- Powder paint, unmixed, several colors
- Containers with plastic lids
- Paintbrushes

Encourage children to experiment with materials.
Say that they will paint with ice! Encourage the children to use the materials in various ways. Provide help as needed. They might:

- Rub the ice on paper and shake on powder paint.
- Shake the powder on first and rub the ice over the powder.
- Shake the powder on the ice cube and rub the ice on paper.
- Use paintbrushes to spread the paint.

Discuss the activity. Join in and talk about what you are doing. Emphasize how cold the ice is.

Encourage the children to fold finished work in half. The children might also fold the paper in half (it is not necessary to fold accurately) after they apply the paint and talk about the changes that result.

Theme of the Day: Cold

Day 3: Make-Believe Center

What to Do:

Relate the activity to the story. Encourage a discussion of the types of activities the children like to do in the winter, or things they imagine they would like to do if they ever had any snow. Say that the little girl in the story lived where it was very cold. She had lots of snow!

Arrange a cold-weather scene. Help the children set up the materials to represent cold-weather scenes. You might:

- Drape a white sheet over a table to represent a snow mound or igloo.
- Crumple the newspaper or white paper into balls to represent snowballs.
- Make a large circle on the floor with string to form a pretend ice pond.

MATERIALS

- **Clothing for cold weather**
- **Boxes large enough for children to sit in**
- **Table (optional)**
- **White sheet (optional)**
- **Several old newspapers or white paper**
- **Piece of string long enough to make a large circle on the floor**
- **Lightweight shovels**

Pretend to play in cold weather. Encourage the children to pretend to play in the cold-weather scene they have created. Show how you can

- Push the boxes like sleds (with children in them).
- Sit on the mound of snow or in the igloo.
- Pretend to ice skate.
- Climb in the boxes, pretending they are ice caves.
- Shovel balls of "snow."
- Pretend the boxes are boats, like the *umiaks* in the story.
- Pretend to ice-fish.

Theme of the Day:
Feelings

Day 4 Group Time: Introducing the Theme of the Day

What to Do:

Introduce the day's activities with a song. Sing the song "I Love You," from day 1, to set the tone for the day's activities.

Review the previous day's activities. Discuss the activities of the previous day, showing art products, chanting the rap, and asking the children what they did when they pretended to play outside in the cold.

Read and discuss the story. Read the story, emphasizing the mother's reactions to the child's questions. Show the picture of the girl pouring water on the lamp, and discuss what the girl is doing. Then ask how the mother would feel if the little girl did that. If necessary, ask, "Would she feel happy or angry?" Show the pictures of the musk-ox and walrus, and discuss what the girl said she would do in those pictures. Ask the children how the mother would feel if the little girl turned into an animal. If necessary, ask, "Would she be happy or surprised?" Remind the children that no matter what the little girl might do, the mother still loved her.

MATERIALS

- **Art products from previous day**
- **"Getting Dressed Rap" from day 3 music and movement center**
- **Book, *Mama, Do You Love Me?* (with pages marked where the child asks about pouring water on the lamp and about turning into a musk-ox or a walrus)**
- **Pictures of angry child, sad child, happy child**
- **Two toy people from make-believe center**

Introduce the theme of the day: Feelings. Show the pictures of children's faces. (If the group includes several three-year-olds, show only one picture at a time.) Ask the children to name the feeling depicted in each picture and discuss why the child feels that way. Tell them they will think about such feelings as *angry, sad,* and *happy.*

Introduce the arts activities.

Music and Art Center
What the children will do: Practice expressing feelings by moving or painting in response to different kinds of music. Sing part of a happy song that you know well, smiling and moving to the music. (Any happy song will work well, such as "Zippity Doo Dah," or "If You're Happy.") Say that when people are happy they often sing happy songs. Say that the music and art centers will be together today and the children will move with streamers to different kinds of music or make pictures while they listen to the music.

continues . . .

Make-Believe Center

What the children will do: Practice expressing feelings as they play with toys. Show the children two toy people and act out a simple scene in which the characters express feelings. For example, have one character say, "You took my ball!" and have the other character respond, "No, I didn't!" Then have the characters argue briefly about the ball. Ask the children to tell how the toy people felt. Tell them they may play with toy people in the make-believe center.

Have each child choose an arts activity.

Notes:

Day 4: Music and Art Center

What to Do:

Be creative in your choice of music for this activity; include Dixieland, classical, pop, blues, and so on.

Relate the activity to the story. Remind the children that the mother in the story said that she would be sorry, angry, very angry, worried, sad, surprised, or scared, but that no matter how she felt she would always love her little girl. Say that they will move to music and show by the way they move whether the music makes them happy, sad, or angry.

MATERIALS

- Cassette player
- Several recordings of different types of music
- Crayons, markers, and chalk
- Large pieces of drawing paper
- Streamers
- Rhythm instruments

Introduce showing feelings by moving to music. Play a short segment of the tape. Stop the music and ask the children if they felt happy, sad, or angry when they listened to the music. Accept all reactions to the music, but encourage the children to explain their responses. For example, one child might say she felt happy because she heard bells and she likes bells. Another child might say he felt angry because he didn't like the music. Then ask the children to stand as you play another segment of the music. Tell them to move to the music and show how they feel with their faces and bodies. Join in and model moving in expressive ways. Also, look at the children's faces as they move and tell them how their faces look—happy, sad, or angry (or some other expression).

Introduce showing feelings by drawing to music. Stop the music and ask the children to help you place several large sheets of paper on the floor. Start the music and draw on the paper, talking about the music and how it makes you feel. "This music is sad. I'm making dots, like tears." Encourage the children to join you and talk about the music as they draw.

Let children choose an activity. Stop the tape and ask the children to sit around the papers on the floor. Show them the streamers and the rhythm instruments. Tell them that you will start some music again. When they hear the music, they may move to it and use streamers; if they want they may play along with instruments; or they may draw on the papers on the floor. They may use any of the materials, but they must share and take turns. They might want to draw for a while and then move around for a while, whatever the music makes them want to do. Start the tape and then join in as the children respond by moving, singing, playing instruments, or drawing. Encourage them to talk about how the music makes them feel, and encourage them to show these feelings with their faces. Introduce more emotions, such as surprised ("The music got loud. That surprised me!"), or scared ("I think this music sounds like a monster. I'm scared!").

Discuss how the children responded in different ways. After the children have responded to the music, encourage them to sit and talk about the things they did. Discuss how some children liked to move around and play instruments the most, and some children preferred drawing—everyone is different.

Theme of the Day: Feelings

Day 4: Make-Believe Center

What to Do:

Relate the activity to the story. Look through the pictures in the book. Ask the children to tell what the girl is doing and how the mother responds. Discuss the fact that the mother loves the girl, no matter how she feels about what the girl is doing. Show the children the toy people, the blocks, and the other props. Tell them they can pretend the people are doing things and feeling happy, sad, or angry.

MATERIALS

- Book, *Mama, Do You Love Me?*
- Toy people
- Building blocks
- Toy furniture or other props (optional)

Build things for the toy people with the blocks. Put out the blocks and invite the children to use them for building things for the toy people. Suggest items they might make, such as beds, tables, cars, and show how you can build different things. Younger children might only stack blocks or make lines of blocks for the toy people; older children will be able to make representational structures. If furniture and other props are available, encourage the children to incorporate them into their building structures.

Act out scenes in which toy people express emotions. Encourage the children to use the block structures and toy people to act out activities familiar to them. They might have the people ride in vehicles, go to bed, take care of babies, or go swimming. Ask questions and make comments to encourage the children to express the toy people's feelings. "The little boy is going down the slide. Does he like it? How does he feel—happy or scared?"

Theme of the Day:
Life in the Arctic

Day 5 Group Activity

What to Do:

If no pictures of icebergs are available, use the cover of the book. To make the "fish," attach a metal paper clip to each paper cutout.

Relate the activity to the story. Remind the children that people lived the way Dear One and her mama lived a long time ago. Now people in the Arctic live in houses and wear the same kinds of clothes we do.

Discuss icebergs. Show the children the picture of icebergs and explain that in the Arctic it is so cold that there are large piles of ice, called icebergs. Some piles of ice are as large as the classroom. Ask the children to name other large things; as they name things, tell them that icebergs are large like that.

Describe icebergs. Ask the children to look carefully at the picture of icebergs and tell other things about them. They might say that the icebergs are white and they look like mountains. Display the iceberg picture, so the children can refer to it during the activity to remember what icebergs look like.

MATERIALS

- Picture of icebergs
- Medium-sized and large boxes
- White paint and paintbrushes
- White paper
- White chalk
- Tape
- Piece of string long enough to form a large circle
- Magnets tied to ends of 12-inch strings (several of these)
- Large and small fish cut from construction paper or cardboard
- Large pieces of white and dark-colored fabrics to use as animal costumes

Make pretend icebergs. Show the children the boxes and tell them they may use the boxes to make pretend icebergs. (Put aside one or two large boxes to use as boats.) Let the children paint the boxes white, like icebergs. Put out the white paper, chalk, and tape. Show how to use these to create the icebergs, by tearing the paper into small pieces and gluing it to the boxes, coloring the boxes with white chalk, and taping several boxes together to form larger icebergs. Encourage the children to think of other variations for making their icebergs.

Arrange an arctic setting. When the "icebergs" are finished, encourage the children to set them up in one area. Ask them to help you form a large circle with the piece of string to make a body of water. Encourage them to put the fish in the water. Then show them one or two large boxes to use as boats.

Encourage them to play in the Arctic. See below for suggested activities.

continues . . .

Review the activity. Sit with the children to discuss the activity. Ask how they made the icebergs, what did they do? Then ask what they did to pretend to live in the Arctic. Encourage discussion.

Suggestions for Implementing "Life in the Arctic":

Show the children the cover of *Mama, Do You Love Me?* and discuss how the people are riding in a boat in the water. Look through the book and help the children label the animals they see, the pictures of icebergs, and the ice cave. Encourage them to relate these things to their own experiences. Does the boat look like one they might ride in? Invite them to use the props they created, and the pieces of fabric to pretend they are living in the Arctic, like Mama and Dear One. They might

- Dress up like animals they see in the book.
- Turn the painted boxes on their sides, and pretend to live in ice caves.
- Pretend to float in the pretend boats.
- Use the magnets on string to fish for the cardboard fish with paper clips attached. (Help them compare the fish they catch to decide which are large and which are small.)

SKILLS & GOALS MATRIX

Mama, Do You Love Me?

	Skills or Behaviors	Goals and Objectives
Cognitive	• Identify and name things associated with cold weather	• Increase concept and vocabulary development related to temperature • Increase sensory awareness
	• Identify large and small objects	• Increase concept and vocabulary development related to size • Increase visual awareness and discrimination • Increase understanding of opposites
	• Identify *in* and *out, to* and *from*	• Increase concept and vocabulary development relating to positional words • Increase understanding of opposites
	• Pretend to do cold-weather activities	• Increase ability to engage in symbolic play • Increase preliteracy skills: relate story events to real or pretend experiences
	• Compare sounds from large and small instruments	• Increase auditory-visual awareness and discrimination • Increase ability to sort objects by attributes
Language	• Discuss feeling angry, sad, happy, frightened	• Increase ability to use language to identify and express emotions
	• Learn and recite a chant	• Increase receptive and expressive vocabulary • Increase phonological awareness
	• Discuss what might be happening in a picture	• Increase receptive and expressive vocabulary • Increase ability to label expression of emotions
	• Use a name tag to label a package	• Increase preliteracy skills: awareness of letters and grapheme-phoneme connection, word recognition

SKILLS & GOALS MATRIX (CONT.)

	Skills or Behaviors	Goals and Objectives
Social	• Sing a song with others	• Increase participation as member of a group
	• Act out themes in a story by taking care of babies	• Increase understanding of point of view and feelings of others • Increase ability to imitate adult caretaking roles
	• Identify behaviors that show affection and friendship	• Increase appropriate interactions with peers • Increase appropriate expression of emotions with peers
	• Share musical instruments	• Increase ability to share and take turns • Increase appropriate interactions with peers
Fine-Motor	• Draw or paint on small papers and on large papers	• Increase bilateral coordination • Refine pincer grasp
	• Alternate rubbing and shaking materials onto paper	• Increase wrist rotation • Increase manipulation skills • Refine motor planning
	• Play musical instruments	• Increase wrist rotation • Increase hand strength • Increase bilateral coordination
	• Use wet sand to mold big and little shapes	• Increase hand strength • Increase visual-motor coordination • Increase tactile awareness
	• Wrap a small box in paper (with assistance)	• Increase finger dexterity • Increase whole hand use • Increase visual-motor coordination
Gross-Motor	• Walk by alternating big and small	• Increase gross-motor planning and steps control • Increase dynamic balance • Increase body awareness
	• Move to music with streamers	• Increase gross-motor planning and control • Increase auditory attention • Increase body awareness
	• Move in ways that express an emotion	• Increase motor planning • Increase dynamic and static balance • Increase ability to coordinate movement with auditory cues

STORY OF THE WEEK / EL CUENTO DE ESTA SEMANA

Mama, Do You Love Me?

by Barbara Joose

The Spark story this week is *Mama, Do You Love Me?* You may be able to find this book at the library. It is a story about a little girl who lives in the Arctic. The little girl wants to know if her mother will still love her even if she does something bad like breaking eggs or running away. The mother answers every question by saying that she might be worried, or angry, or sad, but no matter what happens she will still love her little girl. Ask your child to tell you about the pictures in the book. Does it look cold where the little girl lives? (Yes.) Is there snow on the ground? (Yes.) The themes to go with this story are *people who love one another, large/small, cold,* and *feelings.*

El cuento de Spark de esta semana se llama *Mama, Do You Love Me?* (Mamá ¿me quieres?). Usted puede encontrar este libro, en inglés, en cualquier biblioteca. Es un cuento sobre una niñita que vive en el Polo Artico. La niñita quería saber si su mamá la seguía queriendo cuando ella hacía algo malo, como por ejemplo, romper huevos o escaparse. Su mamá le contestó diciéndole que ella se preocupaba, se enojaba, o se ponía triste, pero que no obstante lo que pasara, ella siempre la quería. Pídale a su niño o niña que le cuente sobre las láminas del libro. ¿Parece que hace frio adonde vive la niñita? (Sí). ¿Hay nieve en la tierra? (Sí). Las ideas temáticas sobre este cuento son: *las personas que se quieren, grande/ pequeño, frío* y *sentimientos.*

© 2001 The Board of Trustees of the University of Illinois. May be reproduced for use by teachers.

The Napping House

by Audrey Wood

New York: Harcourt Brace, 1984.

Story Synopsis: *The Napping House* is a beautifully illustrated cumulative story that is highly enjoyed by preschool children. It tells about a house where everyone is sleeping. Characters are added one at a time and include animals that all children are familiar with, such as a cat, a dog, and a mouse. As each character gets in the bed, it climbs on top of the others who are already sleeping. Everything is peaceful until a flea bites a mouse. Then all the characters are startled awake and in the resulting bedlam, the bed breaks. Now no one is sleeping. The grandmother is an excellent example of an active, involved, joyous older person.

Classroom Use: This unit may be used most successfully after the children have been in school for a few weeks, as it contains more text on each page than the simpler stories and requires more maturity on the part of the listeners. Teachers can draw children into the story by encouraging them to chant the repeated lines on each page. The themes and concepts to go with this unit are very simple ones: *on/off, falling down, counting,* and *happy.* This unit may be linked with other stories and activities that focus on families.

Considerations: No special preparation is needed for this story.

Special Materials: No materials other than those typically found in preschool classrooms are needed for this unit.

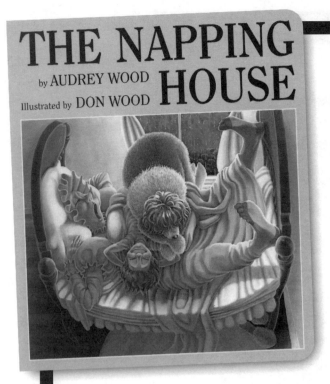

ACTIVITY MATRIX

The Napping House

Day	Concept	Music Activity	Art Activity	Make-Believe Activity
Day 1	On/Off (Cognitive, Language, Motor)	Put objects on percussion instruments and listen to sounds.	Build Styrofoam structures.	Play with balloons and parachute.
Day 2	Falling Down (Cognitive, Language, Motor)	Play music games and make crashing sounds.	Tape and glue objects together to make structures that may fall down.	Balance blocks or boxes.
Day 3	Counting (Cognitive, Language, Math)	Count meaningfully to music. Bounce animals on parachute.	Count colors in drawings.	Make a tree house for stuffed animals.
Day 4	Happy (Social)	Play kazoos and slide whistles; move to happy music.	Decide if art materials make them happy; fingerpaint.	Think of ways to make toy animals feel happy.
Day 5	Pet Store			

Theme of the Day:
On/Off

Day 1 Group Time: Introducing the Book

What to Do:

Before the activity begins, make stick puppets from character cutouts and draw a granny face on an inflated balloon.

Read the story. Read the story slowly, giving the children time to study each illustration and ask questions. Encourage them to join in as you read the repeated phrase, "a cozy bed in a napping house, where everyone is sleeping."

Introduce the theme of the day: On/Off. Spread out the old sheet or blanket and tell the children to pretend it is the bed in the story. Give each child one of the character cutouts, asking them to name their characters and make a sound that the character might make, such as a bark for the dog. Then summarize the story in simple language, as follows. As you name each character, have the child(ren) with that cutout sit on the "bed."

MATERIALS

- Book, *The Napping House*
- Character cutouts from the story glued to craft sticks—one per child
- Old blanket or sheet
- Tambourine
- Dried beans, at least one per child
- Two pieces of Styrofoam and a pipe cleaner from the art center
- Inflated balloon with a granny face drawn on it

> *A granny was on the bed. The granny was snoring.*
> *A dreaming child got on the bed.*
> *A dozing dog got on the bed.*
> *A snoozing cat got on the bed.*
> *A slumbering mouse got on the bed.*
> *A wakeful flea got on the bed. The flea bit the mouse.*
> *As everyone jumped off the bed, the bed broke! (Have everyone get off the bed.)*

Encourage the children to talk about how they got on and off the bed. Then say they will think about *on* and *off* in the centers.

Introduce the arts activities.

Music and Movement Center

What the children will do: Put different things on percussion instruments and listen to the sounds they make. Hold a tambourine with the edges facing up. Give each child a bean to put *on* the tambourine, the same way the characters in the story got *on* the bed. Wiggle the tambourine with the beans on it and encourage discussion about the sound it makes. Tell the children that they will put different objects on instruments to make sounds in the music and movement center.

continues . . .

Art Center
What the children will do: Build Styrofoam sculptures. Show the children a piece of Styrofoam. Tell them you want to put something on it. Stick a pipe cleaner into the Styrofoam and then stick another small piece of Styrofoam onto the pipe cleaner, as you prompt the children to talk about what you are doing. Tell them they may put different things on Styrofoam in the art center.

Make-Believe Center
What the children will do: Play with balloons and a parachute. Show the children the balloon with granny's face on it. Ask what granny was sleeping on. Say they will pretend that the balloon is granny and put her on the parachute in the make-believe center.

Have each child choose an arts activity.

Notes:

Theme of the Day: On/Off

Day 1: Music and Movement Center

What to Do:

Relate the activity to the story. Remind the children that the characters in the story got on the bed, and that when it broke, they jumped off the bed. Say that they will put things on and off musical instruments to see what kinds of sounds they can make.

Play instruments freely. Give the children drums and tambourines to play freely for a short time. Model tapping the instruments with different body parts. For example, say, "I'm tapping with my thumb; now I'm tapping very gently with my elbow." (Use body parts that individual children need to learn names for.)

Put beans on drums and tambourines. Put some dried beans near the children and invite them to put beans on their drums and tambourines as you did earlier. Encourage them to experiment with the beans and instruments in different ways:

- Put on one bean. What kinds of sounds can you make? How can you make the sounds? (Shaking the tambourine, tapping it, and so on.)
- Put on (five) beans. (Show how you count them.) Make some sounds. Take the beans off.
- Put on lots of beans. Make some sounds. Take off (three) beans. Can you make the same sounds?
- Put some beans on your hand. Shake your hand. Do the beans make a sound on your hand? Did the beans fall off your hand?
- Put a tambourine or drum on the beans. Can you make a sound?

Put other objects on the instruments. Give the children other small objects to put on the instruments and invite them to experiment with the sounds the objects make. Ask them to talk about what happens, especially when materials do not create sounds (cotton balls).

Put objects on other flat surfaces. Offer the other flat surfaces (cookie sheets, box lids, and so on) for the children to put the small objects on. Ask them to tell what happens, especially when objects fall off the flat surfaces.

Find other small objects to put on flat surfaces. Encourage the children to look around the room for other things to put on the instruments and other flat surfaces. Emphasize that the objects should be small. (What kind of sound does a toy car make on a tambourine?)

Make sounds to recorded music. Encourage the children to sit on the floor with you. Have them choose an object to make sounds with (whichever one they most enjoy). Play the recorded music and make sound to the music with the children. If you have time, have each child pass his object to the child on his left and play the music again, so that the children have an opportunity to play different instruments. Let children move to the music if they choose to do so.

MATERIALS

- **Cassette player**
- **Recording of music with a strong marching beat appropriate for children**
- **Several drums and tambourines**
- **Additional flat surfaces, such as paper plates, can lids, box lids, cookie sheet, metal baking pan**
- **Dried beans**
- **Several other small objects, such as dried cereal, cotton balls, crayons, small rocks, small pieces of chalk**

Theme of the Day: On/Off

Day 1: Art Center

What to Do:

Prepare for the activity by cutting some of the Styrofoam bases into triangles, circles, and squares.

Relate the activity to the story. Remind the children that first the granny was asleep on the bed, then the child got in bed on top of her, the dog got on top of the child, and every character got on top of the other one. Say that they will put things on top of other things to make an art sculpture.

Put items on bases to make sculptures. Put the Styrofoam bases where the children can choose pieces to use for their sculpture. Place the other materials where they are easily accessible. Remind the children that they are going to put items on and take items off the base to make sculptures. Show how you can insert pipe cleaners and other materials into the Styrofoam to create a free-form sculpture as you talk about what you are doing, emphasizing the word *on.* "I'm putting a stick on my base. My base is a triangle. What shape is yours? Here's another stick. I'll put it on my base too." As the children work on their sculptures, prompt them to talk about what they are doing. Encourage them to put many items on their bases. Talk about the shapes of the items, emphasizing the shapes that each child may need to work on.

Put items on pipe cleaners. Demonstrate how to string spools and other things on the pipe cleaners. "I'm putting a spool on this stick."

Take items off the sculpture. Also show how you can take things off the sculptures. "I'm taking the fork off my base."

Paint or glue paper on sculpture. Invite the children to paint their sculptures or glue paper and other things on them.

MATERIALS

- Flat pieces of Styrofoam
- Small pieces of Styrofoam in different shapes and sizes
- Pipe cleaners
- Craft sticks, clothespins, twigs, plastic forks, or other things to stick into Styrofoam
- Empty spools, large beads, dried macaroni, tissue paper, or other things to insert on pipe cleaners
- Paint and brushes (optional)
- Glue and paper (optional)

Day 1: Make-Believe Center

What to Do:

To prepare for the activity, inflate the balloons and draw the face of a character from the story on each balloon. Be sure to include a variety of colors of balloons, especially including those colors that individual children may need to learn. The balloons can also reinforce size relationships, with a fully inflated balloon representing the granny and a very slightly inflated one representing the flea.

MATERIALS

- Parachute or old sheet
- Bag of character balloons

Relate the activity to the story. Remind the children that all the characters got on top of each other on the bed and went to sleep. What happened to wake everyone up? Say that they will pretend that the parachute is the bed and they will put the balloon characters on the pretend bed.

Lift the parachute to waist height. Ask the children to help you spread the parachute flat on the floor. Have everyone stand around the parachute and hold the edge with both hands. Encourage the group to lift the parachute together to waist height.

Put one balloon on the parachute. Say, "Pretend the parachute is the bed in the story." Put a balloon on the parachute and say, "Let's pretend that this (red) balloon is the granny in the story. Granny is on the bed. Keep Granny on the bed!" Direct the group to move the parachute slowly up and down and from side to side, as you remind them to keep Granny on the bed. If the balloon falls off the parachute, ask the children to tell what happened to Granny.

Think of different ways to move the parachute. With one balloon on the parachute, encourage the children to think of other ways to move the parachute, such as by shaking their hands or walking around in a circle.

Place more balloons on the parachute, naming each character. Continue the activity with two or more balloons on the parachute, naming each balloon as a different character from the story. Also state the color of each balloon as you add it.

Pretend that the bed breaks. Put the balloons back on the parachute and suggest to the children that the bed is going to break, and all the characters will jump off. Have the children help you move the parachute up and down rapidly so that the balloons "jump off."

Review the activity. Sit with the children to discuss the activity. Which balloon stayed on the bed the longest? Which balloon fell off first?

Theme of the Day:
Falling Down

Day 2 Group Time: Introducing the Theme of the Day

What to Do:

Review the previous day's activities. Remind the children that they thought about *on* and *off* the day before. Show them the sculptures they made and invite the artists to tell how they made their sculptures. Ask them what they put on the bases. What did they take off the bases? Show them the tambourine and remind them that they put beans on the tambourine. Ask what happened when they shook it. Show the balloon character. Ask the children what they did with the balloons in the make-believe center.

Read the story. As you read the story, encourage the children to chant the repeated phrases with you.

Tell a simplified version with character cutouts and blocks. Show the children one character cutout at a time, asking them to name each one. Then make a bed out of blocks by putting two square blocks near each other on the child's chair, where everyone can see them, and placing a rectangular block across them. Tell the story using the cutouts and the bed. As you mention each character, hold it up for the children to see. Then lay it flat on the bed, stacking the characters on top of each other. To make the bed break, pull out a square block.

MATERIALS

- Sculptures from previous day
- One of the balloon characters from the previous day
- Tambourine
- Book, *The Napping House*
- Character cutouts from the story
- One rectangular and two square building blocks (or comparable boxes) from the make-believe center
- Cymbals
- Several scrap materials from the art center
- Masking tape
- Several building blocks
- Child's chair

Introduce the theme of the day: Falling down. Build a block bed again and make it fall down. Ask the children to describe what happened to the bed. Explain that the children can make things fall down in the centers today.

Introduce the arts activities.

Music and Movement Center

What the children will do: Play music games and make crashing sounds. Say that you know a song about a flea on a bed. Sing the following words to the tune of "If You're Happy," using the cymbals at the end to make a crashing sound.

Put your flea on the bed, on the bed. Put your flea on the bed, on the bed.
Put your flea on the bed, didn't you hear what I said? Put your flea on the bed, on the bed!

continues . . .

Sing the song again, encouraging the children to join you. Tell the children they will play music games and make crashing sounds in music.

Art Center

What the children will do: Make things with scrap materials. Show the children some scrap materials. Tape the objects together as you tell the children they can make things with them in the art center.

Make-Believe Center

What the children will do: Balance blocks or boxes. Place a block on the floor and tell the children to pretend it is a bed. Stack another block on the first one and say, "A granny was on the bed." Stack another block and say, "Then a child got on the bed." Stack additional blocks on the tower as you add characters from the story, continuing until the tower falls down. Ask the children to tell what happened. Then tell them they can stack blocks in the make-believe center.

Have each child choose an arts activity.

Notes:

Theme of the Day: Falling Down

Day 2: Music and Movement Center

What to Do:

Relate the activity to the story. Remind the children that at the end of the story, the bed broke and everybody fell down. Say that when things fall down they sometimes make a crashing sound. (Strike the cymbals together.) Say that they will play music games and make crashing sounds.

Sing "Ring around a Rosey"; fall down. Stand in a circle with the children, holding hands. Sing "Ring around a Rosey," and walk in a circle. When you say the last line, model falling down.

Ring around a rosey, a pocketful of posies.
Falling, falling, we all fall down.

MATERIALS

- Percussion instruments, such as cymbals, rhythm sticks, triangles, drums, tambourines, sand blocks
- Old sheet or blanket
- Character cutouts (one per child)

Repeat the song; make crashing sound with cymbals. Repeat "Ring around a Rosey," a few times until the children are familiar with the procedure. Then sing the song and let them do the movements without adult help. After you say the last line, hit two cymbals together, and say, "Crash!" Repeat this a few times.

Make crashing sounds with instruments. Let the children play freely with the musical instruments. Join in and show how you can make a crashing sound with the instruments. Encourage them to decide how to make a crashing sound with each type of instrument.

Repeat the song with children making crashing sounds. Ask each child to choose one instrument, and have them sit down with their instruments. Sing "Ring around a Rosey" again, with the children making a crashing sound with their instruments at the end.

Take turns selecting instruments for crashing sounds. Have the children put all the instruments on a table nearby. Tell them to stand in a circle for "Ring around a Rosey." Choose one instrument and stand in the middle of the circle as you sing the song. Make a crash at the end when the children fall down. Ask for a volunteer to stand in the circle as you sing the song again. Let the volunteer choose an instrument to use to make the crashing sound at the end of the song. Repeat this procedure until everyone who wants to make the crashing sound has a turn to stand in the middle of the circle.

Bring closure to the activity. Put the instruments (except the cymbals) out of sight and ask the children to help you spread a sheet on the floor. Tell them to pretend the sheet is a bed. Give each child a character cutout and ask the child to name the character. Ask the children to sit around the sheet with their cutouts, as you sing, "Put your flea on the bed." Name a different character for each verse, starting with Granny and ending with the flea. Encourage the child (or children) with that cutout to sit on the bed. After everyone is on the bed, make a crashing sound with the cymbals and tell everyone to fall over. Compliment the children for being good listeners.

Theme of the Day: Falling Down

Day 2: Art Center

MATERIALS

- Scrap materials, such as empty boxes, cans, egg cartons, plastic containers, Styrofoam meat trays, aluminum pie pans, empty spools, cardboard tubes, wood scraps
- Crayons and markers
- Tape and glue
- Paint and brushes

What to Do:

Relate the activity to the story. Remind the children that the bed in the story broke and everyone fell down. Encourage a discussion of what makes things fall down. Say that they will make structures, and sometimes structures fall down.

Put out materials. Place the scrap materials, crayons, and markers on a table and let the children experiment with them freely. Join in and show how you can draw on the scrap materials. As the children draw, ask them to talk about what they are doing. Discuss how some of the materials, such as plastic containers, are hard to make marks on.

Place glue and tape on the table. Put the glue and tape on the table and invite the children to use them to put materials together. Tape is more difficult to use than glue; encourage children to choose adhesives they are able to use successfully.

Build a top-heavy structure that falls down. Join in and put together a tall structure that is top-heavy. Stand your structure up and let it fall over. Comment that your structure fell down! Ask the children if their own structures stand up or fall down. Encourage them to experiment with ways to make their structures stand up. Encourage problem solving.

Paint the structures. Let the children paint their structures. (The paint will adhere poorly to some surfaces, such as plastic or metal.) Ask the children to tell what is happening as they paint on different types of surfaces.

Theme of the Day: Falling Down

Day 2: Make-Believe Center

What to Do:

Relate the activity to the story. Remind the children that when the bed in the story broke, everyone fell down. Ask if the characters were sad when they fell down. Did they get hurt? Did they cry? Remark that they looked as if they were having fun, didn't they? Ask the children if they have ever built anything with blocks that fell down. Encourage discussion. Say that they will build with blocks today.

MATERIALS

- Building blocks or empty boxes in various sizes

Encourage discussion as they build. Encourage the children to use position words *(on/off, top/bottom, behind/in front of)* and measurement and comparison words *(high/higher, shorter/taller, smallest/largest)* as they build. "Is your tower taller or shorter than this one?" "Do you want to make a tall tower or a short one?" "Look, my tower is taller than yours!"

Encourage conversation when a structure falls. When the children's structures fall down, ask them to describe what happened, encouraging the use of descriptive words such as *noisy, crash,* and *fast.* "What kind of sound was that?" "Did you like that sound? Why? Why not?"

Count blocks as you take turns stacking. Play a game with one child in which you stack a block and the child stacks a block, you stack a block and then the child stacks a block, continuing until the tower falls over. This is a good counting game, with the child counting the boxes as they are stacked and then counting them again after they crash: "How many boxes crashed?"

Build blocks as high as named body parts. Challenge the children to build towers that are as high as named body parts: "Build a tower as high as your chin!" As they build encourage them to label body parts by asking, "How high is your tower now? Is it up to your knees or your chest?"

Theme of the Day:
Counting

Day 3 Group Time: Introducing the Theme of the Day

What to Do:

Introduce the day's activities by singing "Put your flea on the bed." Sing the song you introduced on the previous day, "Put your flea on the bed," holding up the corresponding character cutout for each verse. Sing again, encouraging the children to sing with you.

Review the previous day's activities. Remind the children that they thought about falling down on the day before. Ask why everyone fell down in the story. Ask a child to crash the cymbals to make a falling-down noise. Then ask the other children to fall down when the cymbal crashes. Show the children the art structures they made on the previous day. Ask a volunteer to tell how she made the sculpture. Discuss how tall the structures got in the make-believe center before they fell down.

Read the story. Read the story and encourage the children to chant the repeated lines as they occur in the story.

Introduce the theme of the day: Counting. Place the piece of Styrofoam on the floor in front of the children. Then read the story, inserting the character cutouts in the Styrofoam so that they stand up as you read about them. After you read each page, ask the children to help you count the number of characters on the bed (the piece of Styrofoam). After you finish the story, thank them for helping you count, and say that they can do more counting in the centers.

MATERIALS

- Art structures from previous day
- Book, *The Napping House*
- Character cutouts from story
- Toy animals
- Flat piece of Styrofoam or bowl of sand to use for standing up character cutouts
- Several crayons and a piece of paper
- Large box with door cut out
- Three stuffed animals or hand puppets
- Cymbals

Introduce the arts activities.

Music and Movement Center

What the children will do: Count objects meaningfully to music. Show the children the toy animals. Have them help you count them. Tell the children that they will bounce the animals on the parachute in the music center as they sing a counting song.

Art Center

What the children will do: Count colors in their drawings. Show the children the crayons and paper. Draw a simple object with each of the crayons. Ask the children to help you count how many colors you used. Say that they will color beautiful pictures in the art center and then count to see how many colors they used.

continues . . .

Make-Believe Center

What the children will do: Make a tree house for stuffed animals and count how many animals can fit in the tree house. Show the children the last picture in the book and point out the tree house. Ask the children if any of them have ever seen a tree house. Elicit conversation. Place the box on the floor in front of the children. Tell them that the box is a tree house for some animals like the animals in the story. Walk the three stuffed animals through the door into the box, and ask the children to help you count how many animals are in the tree house. Say that they can make a tree house for animals in the make-believe center.

Have each child choose an arts activity.

Notes:

Theme of the Day: Counting

Day 3: Music and Movement Center

What to Do:

This activity should be limited to no more than ten children.

MATERIALS

- Parachute or sheet
- Ten toy animals
- Box to use as pretend bed

Relate the activity to the story. Remind the children that each character got on top of the last one, one at a time. Say that when the bed broke, there were six characters on the bed: the granny, the child, the dog, the cat, the mouse, and the flea. Ask them if all the characters were asleep. Help them to understand that only five of the characters were asleep; the flea was awake! Say that they will play a music counting game and pretend that the toy animals are the animals in the story.

Play freely with the toy animals. Put the toy animals where the children can play with them freely. Encourage them to name the animals and to make the sounds that the animals make. Show how to move like one of the animals as you make its sound.

Play a parachute counting game with the children. Have the children put the toy animals on the parachute while it is lying on the floor. Count the animals. Then walk around with the children as everyone holds onto the parachute. Raise the parachute up and down as you sing, to the tune of "Skip to My Lou":

One little, two little, three little animals,
Four little, five little, six little animals.
Seven little, eight little, nine little animals.
Ten little animals taking a ride.

At the end of the song, put the parachute on the floor and count the animals. How many are still on the parachute? What animals fell off? Work together to pick up the animals that have fallen off and repeat the game. Continue playing the game as long as the children are interested.

Sing "Put your flea on the bed." Show the children the box and say that you are pretending that it is a bed. Place it on the floor with the solid box bottom facing up. They will put the toy animals on the bed. Let each child choose an animal to hold. Then sing "Put your flea on the bed," using the names of the animals the children are holding. Encourage the child who is holding the animal you named in the song to put the animal on the box as you all sing. Sing about each animal in turn until all the animals are stacked up on (or falling off) the box bed.

Count the animals. Invite the children to help you count the animals that have fallen off the bed, then count the animals that have stayed stacked on the bed. Ask the children if there are more animals on the bed or off the bed. If necessary, count the animals again and compare.

Theme of the Day: Counting

Day 3: Art Center

What to Do:

MATERIALS

- Book, *The Napping House*
- Crayons (enough for each child to have access to at least six different colors)
- Paper

Relate the activity to the story. Show the children the last page in the book and encourage discussion. Ask them if it is still raining. Have them help you count the story characters that went outside after the bed broke. Point out the rainbow and ask them to count the colors in the rainbow. Say that they can color beautiful pictures and use as many different colors as they want to use.

Distribute the materials. Put out the crayons and paper and tell the children to choose a piece of paper and a crayon to start their picture. Color with them, talking about what you are drawing as you work. "I think I will make a rainbow. I'll start with a yellow crayon." "I like the big red circle you made, Justine."

Let the children color freely. Encourage the children to use many different colors. Prompt them by suggesting that they use colors that were in the picture they looked at in the book or perhaps the colors that were in the rainbow.

Count the colors used in drawings. Ask each child how many colors she used in her drawing. Encourage them to use more colors. Praise them for their colorful pictures.

Make more drawings; put out markers. If the children are interested, invite them to select another piece of paper to make another drawing. Say that they may use either crayons or markers for their drawings. Encourage them to use several different colors.

Review the activity. At the end of the activity, ask each child to count his drawings. Ask them how many colors they used in each drawing and write the number on the back of the picture. Praise them for using many colors in their drawings.

Theme of the Day: Counting

Day 3: Make-Believe Center

What to Do:

Relate the activity to the story. Remind the children that when it stopped raining the child went outside to play. Show the children the last page in the book and ask them what the child has to play with outside (a swing, a tricycle, and a tree house). Say that the cat and dog are outside too. Say that they will decorate the tree house and then see how many animals can fit in it.

MATERIALS

- Book, *The Napping House*
- Box from group activity
- Toy animals
- Markers

Decorate the tree house. Encourage the children to use the markers to decorate the tree house. Join them and remark about what you are doing. "I'm drawing a square for a window." "Can you put lines in the window?" "I think I'll put blue on the side of the window, like curtains." Praise the children for using many colors. Help them count the colors they use.

Put the animals in the tree house. Say that the tree house is so beautiful that the animals want to go in it to play. Set out the stuffed animals and encourage each child to choose an animal to put in the tree house.

Count the animals. Sit with the children in front of the tree house. Ask for a volunteer to get the animals, one by one, out of the tree house. As each animal emerges, encourage the children to count, *1, 2, 3,* and so on.

Play in the tree house. Let the children play freely with the animals and the tree house. Older children may choose to pretend to be the child in the story, playing with the animals outside after the sun comes out.

Theme of the Day:
Happy

Day 4 Group Time: Introducing the Theme of the Day

What to Do:

Review the previous day's activities. Show the children the art work from the previous day and count the colors in some of the paintings. Ask the children how many drawings they made. Ask them what they did with animals in the music center. Show the tree house box and ask how many animals fit in the house.

Read the story. Read and discuss the story. Encourage the children to chant the repeated lines as they occur in the story.

Introduce the theme of the day: Happy. Show the pictures of the child and Granny when the bed broke. Ask them to tell how the people in the picture feel and discuss how they can tell that the characters are happy. Show the pictures of the happy child and the sad child. Ask the children to select which picture shows a happy feeling. Ask them to tell about times when they have been happy. What happened? What made them feel happy? Say that they will do happy things in the centers today.

MATERIALS

- Artwork from previous day
- Book, *The Napping House*
- Pictures of happy child, sad child
- Kazoo
- Recording of happy sounding music
- Cassette player
- Stuffed animal or hand puppet
- Bright color of fingerpaint
- Piece of paper

Introduce the arts activities.

Music and Movement Center
What the children will do: Play kazoos, slide whistles, and jingle bells, and move to music. Play a short segment of the recording as you play along with a kazoo. Encourage the children to clap or sway to the beat of the music. Remind them that everyone was happy at the end of the story. Say that they will play jingle bells and move to happy music in the music center.

Art Center
What the children will do: Decide if art materials make them feel happy. Dip your finger in the fingerpaint and make a bright streak across the paper. Tell the children they may fingerpaint with different kinds of paint in the art center and make happy pictures.

Make-Believe Center
What the children will do: Think of ways to make toy animals feel happy. Pet the stuffed animal and tell the children to pretend it is one of the animals in the story. Comment that the animal feels happy when people pet it. Let each child pet the animal as you tell them they can make toy animals feel happy in the make-believe center.

Have each child choose an arts activity.

Theme of the Day: Happy

Day 4: Music and Movement Center

What to Do:

Relate the activity to the story. Remind the children that even though the bed broke and everyone fell down, all the characters were happy at the end of the story. Say that when people are happy they often make some kind of a happy sound. Encourage a discussion of what they like to do when they are happy.

MATERIALS

- **Cassette player**
- **Recording of happy music**
- **Slide whistles or kazoos**
- **Jingle bells**

Make happy sounds with slide whistles. Invite the children to find the slide whistle or kazoo that has their name on it. Show how you can make happy sounds with your slide whistle or kazoo. Encourage them to experiment to create different sounds. To prompt them you might make a sound and ask if anyone can make another happy sound.

Take turns making happy sounds as you sing a song. Ask the children to sit in a circle with their slide whistles behind their backs. Then to the tune of, "Mary Had a Little Lamb," sing the following in a cheerful manner:

We are making happy sounds,
Happy sounds, happy sounds.
We are making happy sounds,
Happy sounds today.

Then point to one child and ask her to make a happy sound with her slide whistle or kazoo. After the child makes the sound, ask if it made everyone feel happy. Encourage discussion. Then repeat the song and point to another child to make a happy sound. Continue this procedure until every child has had a turn to play a happy sound. As each child finishes playing her instrument, have her put it behind her back.

Make happy sounds with jingle bells. Collect the slide whistles. Tell them they can make more happy sounds with other instruments. Shake the jingle bells and ask them if you made a happy sound. Ask what the bells make them think of. (Older children might respond, "Christmas.") Let them experiment with the bells and then repeat the above song with the bells.

Play music for movement and instrumental accompaniment. Play the tape through and encourage the children to play their happy instruments or to get up and move to the music. Encourage creative movement, complimenting children who move in different ways.

Close the activity by singing "If You're Happy." Sit with the children to sing "If You're Happy and You Know It." Lead movements to go with various verses:

If you're happy and you know it
touch your nose
touch your ear
jump up high
lie down low
nod your head
blink your eyes

Theme of the Day: Happy

Day 4: Art Center

What to Do:

Relate the activity to the story. Remind the children that everyone was happy at the end of the story. Discuss some of the things they like to do that make them happy. Say that one of the things you like to do is to paint and that is what they will do too.

Discuss how fingerpaint feels. Help the children set up materials for fingerpainting and allow them to paint freely. As they work, ask the children to tell how the fingerpaint feels and ask them if it makes them happy. If they need prompting, ask questions such as, "Is the paint wet or dry?" "Is it rough or smooth?" "Do you like the way it feels?" "Does it make you happy?" If the children say the feeling of the paint does not make them happy, suggest that they use brushes to spread it.

MATERIALS

- Fingerpaint
- Paper
- Small bowl of cornstarch or flour
- Hand lotion (optional)
- Glue (optional)
- Shaving cream (optional)
- Paint brushes

Add cornstarch or flour. After a while put the bowl of cornstarch or flour on the table and demonstrate sprinkling some on your fingerpaint. Then rub the cornstarch or flour into the paint as you talk about how it feels. Invite the children to add some to their paint and ask them how they feel when they touch it.

Add items to fingerpaint. Show how you can add other things to fingerpaint, such as glue, hand lotion, or shaving cream.

Create textured paper. Demonstrate how to create textured paper by tearing small pieces of paper and gluing them to a larger paper. Then invite the children to fingerpaint over this homemade textured paper. Ask if making things in art makes them feel happy.

Theme of the Day: Happy

Day 4: Make-Believe Center

What to Do:

Relate the activity to the story. Remind the children that there were animals in the story. Encourage the children to remember what kind of animals there were on the bed. Say that at the end of the story the animals were happy and that they are going to pretend to make toy animals happy.

Play with stuffed animals. Let the children play with the stuffed animals, encouraging them to pet the animals to make the animals feel happy. Ask them if it makes them happy to pet the animal. Ask if anyone has a pet at home. Do they like to pet it? If any of the children has a cat, ask what the cat does when it's happy. What kind of sound does it make? Does their pet make them happy?

MATERIALS

- Stuffed animals or animal hand puppets
- Boxes large enough for stuffed animals to fit in
- Blankets or pieces of fabric
- Bowls
- Combs
- String
- Scissors

Introduce boxes and blankets. Show the children the boxes and blankets and ask how they could use them to make the animals happy. If needed, model making beds for the animals by putting blankets in them.

Feed the animals. Tell the children the animals are thirsty and hungry. Ask them to use the bowls to pretend to feed the animals to make them happy again.

Comb the animal's hair. Model combing an animal's hair and suggest that the children comb their animals too. As they comb, ask if it makes the animals feel happy or sad. They will probably differ in their opinion, so ask them to explain. Talk about how they feel when their hair is combed. Who combs their hair? Why do people comb their hair? If you have completed the *Abiyoyo* unit, ask the children if Abiyoyo combed his hair.

Walk the animals. Suggest that the children take their stuffed animals for walks around the room or through the halls. Help them tie string leashes around the animals' necks.

Discuss additional ways to make pets happy. Ask the children to think of other ways to make their animals happy. Help them gather equipment that might be needed to carry out their ideas.

Theme of the Day:
Pet Store

Day 5 Group Activity

What to Do:

Relate the activity to the story. Say that the child in the story had several pets: a dog, a cat, and a mouse. Ask the children if they think the flea was a pet. Encourage discussion. Initiate a discussion of where people get pets. Show them one of the stuffed animals. Say that this is one of the animals they took care of the day before and they made it very happy. Suggest that they will pretend to buy animals today at a pet store.

Discuss pet stores. Ask if anyone has ever been in a pet store. If so, ask them to tell what they saw there. If the children don't mention cages, state that the animals are in cages in a pet store. Put out the stuffed animals and small boxes and building blocks and ask the children to help you make some cages for the animals in the pet store. Show how to put several boxes or blocks together to make an enclosure large enough for a stuffed animal. This will become a lesson in measuring as the children use the animals to decide how big to make the cages.

MATERIALS

- Stuffed animals or animal hand puppets
- Boxes in different sizes
- Materials used for animal care in the make-believe center on the previous day, such as blankets, bowls, combs, string leashes
- Toy cash register (toy money or pieces of green paper)
- Building blocks (optional)

Set up a store. When they have completed several cages, ask the children to set them up with the animals in them and decide where to put the cash register.

Play in the pet store. See suggestions below.

Review the activity. Sit with the children to review the activity. Ask the children to tell what they did to prepare the pet store and then what part they played in the pet store.

Suggestions for Implementing Pet Store Play:

Encourage the children to participate at their own level of development. Children who are not yet ready for role-playing might take care of the animals in the pet store, petting them, combing them, pretending to feed them. Children who are ready for make-believe can decide if they want to be workers in the store or customers.

Workers in the store might run the cash register, show the animals to the customers, add pretend pet supplies to the store inventory, such as string leashes, pet food, pet blankets. You might also suggest that they set up pretend fish tanks and bird cages.

Customers will need pieces of green paper (or play money). They might take their pets home to the housekeeping area and take care of them there. They might also take dogs and cats for walks, pretend to bathe them, and pretend to teach them tricks.

SKILLS & GOALS MATRIX

The Napping House

	Skills or Behaviors	Goals and Objectives
Cognitive	• Count objects rationally	• Increase development of math concepts • Increase understanding of numbers
	• Show understanding of positional and measurement words *(on/off, smallest/largest)*	• Increase general concept and vocabulary development • Increase understanding of opposites
	• Label and point to own body parts	• Increase general vocabulary and concept development • Increase body awareness
	• Put things on surfaces	• Increase concept and vocabulary development relating to positions
Language	• Compare sounds made by different objects	• Increase auditory awareness and discrimination • Increase general concept and vocabulary development
	• Imitate animal sounds	• Increase receptive and expressive vocabulary • Increase capacity to imitate vocalizations or verbalizations
	• Chant songs and rhymes	• Increase auditory awareness and discrimination
	• Hum a song using kazoos and slide whistles	• Increase awareness of pitch and tone • Increase breath control and capacity

SKILLS & GOALS MATRIX (CONT.)

	Skills or Behaviors	Goals and Objectives
Social	• Take care of pretend animals by walking, feeding, and putting them to bed	• Increase awareness of routine self-care skills • Increase ability to follow rules in group activity
	• Sing song with others	• Increase participation as a member of a group
	• Follow rules while playing a game	• Increase appropriate interactions with peers • Increase appropriate social behaviors in supervised setting
	• Participate in a project as part of a group	• Increase appropriate verbal interactions with peers • Increase appropriate social behaviors
Fine-Motor	• Use fingerpaints and include textured materials	• Increase tactile awareness • Increase visual-motor coordination • Increase bilateral control
	• Place small objects on different surfaces	• Increase finger dexterity • Improve visually directed release • Increase hand strength and control
	• Use glue and tape to attach materials together	• Increase tactile awareness • Increase pincer grasp • Increase visual-motor coordination
Gross-Motor	• Fall down and get up again	• Increase motor planning • Increase dynamic balance • Increase arm and leg strength
	• Move arms up and down when requested	• Increase ability to initiate movements when requested • Increase awareness of body in space
	• Shake objects	• Increase motor planning and control • Coordinate gross- and fine-motor movements

STORY OF THE WEEK / EL CUENTO DE ESTA SEMANA

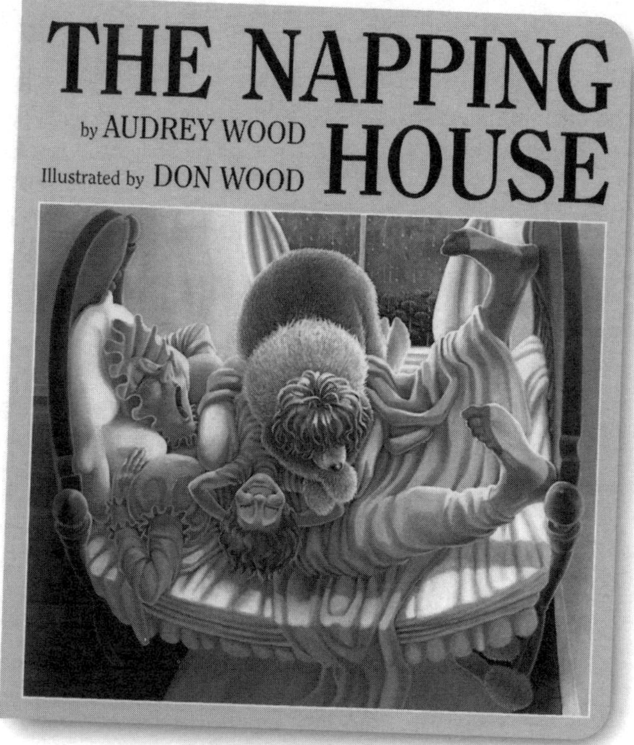

The Napping House

by Audrey Wood
Edición en español: La casa adormecida

The Spark story this week is *The Napping House*. You may be able to find this book at the library. You and your child will enjoy its beautiful pictures. The story, told in rhyme, is about a grandma, a child, and several animals that all fall asleep one on top of each other in a big bed until the flea bites the mouse. Ask your child what happened then. (The mouse scared the cat, the cat clawed the dog, the dog thumped the child, and the child bumped the granny, who broke the bed.) Did everyone keep sleeping? (No.) Did they cry? (No, they are happy.) The themes to go with this story are *on/off, falling down, counting,* and *happy*.

El cuento de Spark de esta semana se llama *La casa adormecida (The Napping House).* Usted puede encontrar este cuento en cualquier biblioteca. El mismo trata sobre una abuela, un niño y varios animales que se quedaron dormidos en una cama grande, uno encima del otro, hasta que la pulga muerde al ratón. Pregúntele a su niño o niña qué sucedió después. (El ratón asustó al gato, el gato arañó al perro, el perro le dio un empujoncito al niño, el niño chocó con la abuela quien rompió la cama.) ¿Pudieron todos seguir durmiendo? (No.) ¿Lloraron ellos? (No, ellos estaban felices.) Las idea temáticas de este cuento son: *prender, apagar, caerse, contar,* y *feliz.*

© 2001 The Board of Trustees of the University of Illinois. May be reproduced for use by teachers.

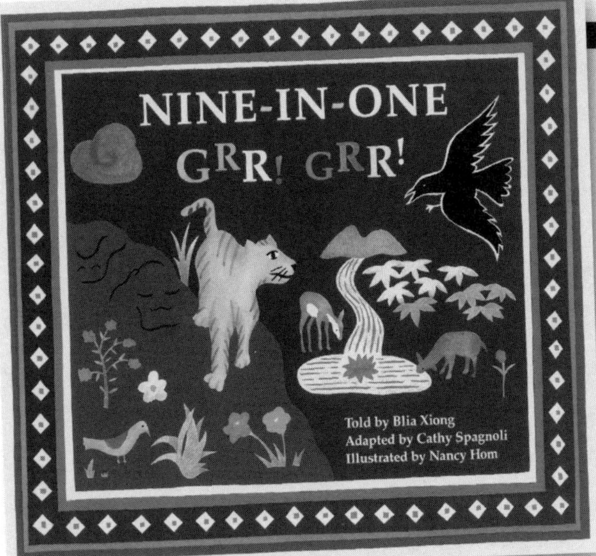

Nine-in-One, Grr! Grr!

told by Blia Xiong; adapted by Cathy Spagnoli

San Francisco: Children's Book Press, 1989

Story Synopsis: This is a Hmong folktale about a tiger that wanted to know how many cubs she would have and the black bird that tricked her. The tiger asks the great Shao how many cubs she will have. He tells her that she will have nine cubs in one year but that she must remember what he said or the prediction won't come true. The only way she can remember what Shao told her is to chant, "nine in one." The black bird does not want there to be nine new tigers every year, so he tricks the tiger into chanting "one in nine" instead of "nine in one." The illustrations contain pictures of many animals that are familiar to children.

Classroom Use: This story is one of the few preschool Hmong folktales available in this country. Children may be told that it is a story that was told long ago in Laos and that the people in the story are dressed as people dressed long ago. The *Nine-in-One, Grr! Grr!* unit may be linked with other stories that focus on animals or on Asian culture.

Considerations: This story is too complex to use with entering three-year-old children; it is more appropriate to use later in the school year. If used with entering three-year-olds, it should be told as a picture story.

Special Materials: Children's respect for another culture will be enhanced if a tape of Hmong music, Hmong art work, and rice noodles (day 4) are added to the unit. If you have access to art prints, the art print *Surprised! Storm in the Forest* by Rousseau will help children understand why tigers have stripes.

ACTIVITY MATRIX

Nine-in-One, Grr! Grr!

Day	Concept	Music Activity	Art Activity	Make-Believe Activity
Day 1	Tigers (Cognitive, Language)	Pretend to be the tiger singing her song.	Paint with brown and yellow.	Combined with music center.
Day 2	How Many (Cognitive, Language, Math)	Count how many instruments are being played.	Count drops of food coloring. Dip filters in colored water.	Sort stuffed animals into categories. Care for one animal.
Day 3	Remember (Cognitive, Language)	Remember how someone moved and move as he did.	Make a work of art. Remember how you made it.	Build block house for Shao. Tell what you did.
Day 4	Same/ Different (Cognitive, Language)	Decide which sounds are the same/different.	Make shapes out of spaghetti. How are they the same or different?	Play in the sand with toy people and animals that are the same and different.
Day 5	Butterflies			

Theme of the Day:
Tiger

Day 1 Group Time: Introducing the Book

What to Do:

MATERIALS

- Book, *Nine-in-One, Grr! Grr!*
- Yellow construction paper
- Brown paint/paintbrush

As the children gather for the group activity, play a tape of Hmong (or other Asian) music. Play the music each day as the children gather for story time to familiarize the children with the sounds of Hmong music.

Introduce the story. If you used a tape of Asian or Hmong music as the children gathered, ask the children if they liked the music you played as they got ready for the story. Had they ever heard music like it before? Tell them that the story today is about a tiger that lived in a country far away called Laos. The music they heard is the kind of music that is played in that part of the world.

Read the story. When you come to the part where the tiger sings the words, "nine in one, grr, grr," sing the words to the tune of "Ring around a Rosey." Encourage the children to join you each time you sing the tiger's song.

Discuss the story. Remind the children that the story they just heard took place in a country far away called Laos. Show them some of the pictures in the book, and ask what they see that they might see in this country. What do they see that they would not see in this country? Ask the children what the tiger in the story wanted. How many baby tigers did the great Shao tell her she would have?

Introduce the theme of the day: Tiger. Ask the children if they have ever taken a walk in the country. What kind of animals did they see? Did they see a tiger? Where would they have to go to see a tiger? If the children have been on a field trip to a zoo, remind them how big the tiger was. Say that in Laos a long time ago when this story was told, if you went for a walk in the country you might see a tiger. Say that today they will think about *tigers* in the centers.

Introduce the arts activities.

Music and Make-Believe Center
What the children will do: Pretend to be the tiger in the story as she sang her song. Ask for a volunteer to crawl around like a tiger as the others sing, "nine in one, grr, grr," to the tune of "Ring around a Rosey." Say that in the music and make-believe center they will have an opportunity to pretend to be the tiger as she sings "nine in one, grr, grr," and then they will take turns being the bird that surprises the tiger into forgetting her song.

continues . . .

Art Center

What the children will do: Paint with brown paint on yellow, like the colors of the tiger. Show the piece of yellow construction paper. Then take the brush, dip it into the brown paint and paint a stripe across the paper. Say that they will get to make their own tiger-striped paper and that after they make their tiger paper they may paint anything they want on the paper.

Have each child choose an arts activity.

Notes:

Theme of the Day: Tiger

Day 1: Music and Make-Believe Center

What to Do:

MATERIALS

- Picture of a tiger
- Picture of a cat

Relate the story to the activity. Remind the children that the story was about an animal called a *tiger* that wanted to know how many babies she would have. Say that they will make sounds like the tigers.

Discuss tigers; practice growling like tigers. Discuss pets that the children have at home. If any of the children have a pet cat, ask the child how big the cat is. Say the tiger is a cat too, a very large cat. (If possible, show them pictures of a cat and a tiger.) Meow the way a cat meows, and encourage the children to meow with you. Ask if anyone knows another sound that the cat makes. Encourage the children to make purring sounds. Say that cats make this sound when they are happy. Say that the tiger makes sounds too, but the tigers' sounds are big sounds because the tiger is a big animal. Invite the children to make the tiger's sounds. If necessary, model the sound for the children and then ask the children to practice growling and roaring like tigers.

Pretend to be tigers singing "nine in one, grr, grr!" Tell the children that they may pretend to be the tiger in the story. Remind them that the tiger was very happy as she was going home because Shao told her that she was going to have nine babies in one year. Join them and crawl around the room singing to the tune of "Ring around a Rosey": "Nine in one, grr, grr, nine in one, grr, grr." Go around several times.

Choose a sound for the bird to make. Have the children sit wherever they are and discuss the sound that the bird made when it flapped its wings and made the tiger forget her song. How do they think the bird sounded? When a sound is identified, say that you will act like the bird now and they should pretend to be surprised when you make the sound.

Act like the bird; let children take turns being the bird. Have the children start crawling around again as they sing the tiger song. As the children go past you, make the bird sound and flap your wings. Encourage the children to act surprised. Tell them that after they are surprised by the bird they should change their song to "one in nine, grr, grr, one in nine, grr, grr." Ask who else would like to be the bird. Repeat the activity as many times as the children are interested.

Sing "One little, two little, three little tigers." Praise the children for being very good tigers and birds. Ask them to sit with you, then end the activity by teaching the children the following words to the tune of "Skip to My Lou."

One little, two little, three little tigers,
Four little, five little, six little tigers.
Seven little, eight little, nine little tigers,
Nine little tigers in one year.

Sing through several times.

Theme of the Day: Tiger

Day 1: Art Center

What to Do:

Relate the activity to the story. Remind the children that the story they heard today was about a tiger. Ask if anyone knows what color a tiger is. If necessary, show them a picture of the tiger in the book. Point out the stripes on the tiger and discuss.

Paint. Put out paper and paint where they are easily accessible. Encourage the children to get a piece of paper, then paint lines on it to make tiger stripes. Encourage the children to try both brown paper with yellow paint and yellow paper with brown paint. Compare their work with the pictures in the book and discuss. Which one looks the same as the tiger? Discuss the stripes: are they long or short? curved or straight? Why do the children think tigers have stripes?

(If you have the picture *Surprised! Storm in the Forest* by Henri Rousseau, you can show the children how the stripes help the tiger hide in the grass. If the children are at an advanced developmental level, ask them why a tiger would want to hide in the grass.)

Show other things you can draw. Use a marker to make lines for such items as grass, trees, and bushes. Encourage the children to draw on their papers. Ask what else they can draw. Encourage them to discuss their pictures. Did they draw something that might be found in forests? Did they draw something that they saw in the book?

MATERIALS

- Yellow paper and brown paper
- Brown paint and yellow paint
- Paintbrushes
- Markers

Theme of the Day:
How Many

Day 2 Group Time: Introducing the Theme of the Day

What to Do:

Play Hmong or Asian music to familiarize children with the sounds.

Review the previous day's activities. Remind the children that the day before they thought about tigers because the story is about a tiger. Ask everyone to roar like a tiger. Ask them what they did in the music center. Ask the children to show how to flap their arms and make a sound like the bird in the story. Show several pieces of art from the day before and ask the children to identify their own work.

Read the story. Read the story. Encourage the children to sing "nine in one, grr, grr" as the words appear in the story. Model changing the song to "one in nine, grr, grr" after the bird startles the tiger.

Discuss the story. Ask the children why the tiger changed her song. Show them the picture in the book on page 11 that shows the tiger thinking about nine babies. Then show the picture on page 29 that shows her thinking about one baby.

MATERIALS

- **Art products from previous day**
- **Book, *Nine-in-One, Grr! Grr!* (with pages 11 and 29 marked for easy reference)**
- **Toy animals or flannelboard tigers**
- **Screen or sheet**
- **Three musical instruments (bell, drum, triangle, or whatever you have)**
- **One coffee filter**
- **Food coloring**
- **Container of water**
- **Three or four stuffed animals**

Introduce the theme of the day: How many. Ask the children how many babies Shao told Tiger she would have in one year. How many did the bird tell her? Put several toy animals on the floor in front of you (or cutouts of tigers on a flannel board). Ask a child how many animals (tigers) there are. Encourage everyone to count the animals. Ask again how many there are. Take several away and repeat the process, asking another child how many there are. Say that today in the centers they will think about how many sounds, how many drops of food coloring, or how many babies there are.

Introduce the arts activities.

Music and Movement Center

What the children will do: Identify how many instruments are being played by the sounds they make. Ask your assistant to sit behind the screen. Show the instruments to the children, then hand them to your assistant. (Before the activity begins, ask her to play only two of the instruments when she is demonstrating for the children.) After she plays the instruments, ask the children how many instruments she played. If necessary, ask her to play again. She should play one, pause, while you say "one" (holding up one finger), then play the other instrument, pause, while you say "two" (holding up two fingers). Ask the children how many instruments your assistant played. Say that in the music center they will take turns hiding behind the screen to play instruments.

continues . . .

Art Center

What the children will do: Count how many drops of food coloring they put in water and then color coffee filters by dipping them into the colored water. Squeeze drops of food coloring in the container of water. As you squeeze the container, count each drop. Then dip the coffee filter in the water. Tell the children that they will put color in water and dip filters in the water today in the art center.

Make-Believe Center

What the children will do: Sort stuffed animals into many and one, and then take care of one stuffed animal. Pile the stuffed animals one on top of another. Ask the children how many there are. Encourage the children to help you count the animals one by one. Say that today in the make-believe center they will play with the animals.

Have each child choose an arts activity.

Notes:

Day 2: Music and Movement Center

What to Do:

MATERIALS

- Folding screen, or sheet over two chairs
- Three musical instruments (bell, drum, triangle, or whatever you have)
- Ten strips of paper

Before the activity begins, set up a screen or put a sheet over two chairs.

Relate the activity to the story. Remind the children that the bird tricked the tiger into having just one baby a year instead of having nine babies each year. Discuss the fact that if you have nine of something, you have much more than someone who has one. Give one child nine strips of paper and another child one strip of paper. Ask which child has more. Say that the sound made by two or three musical instruments is more than the sound of one instrument. Say that they will listen to see how many instruments someone is playing.

Introduce the activity. Remind the children that they will each get a turn to hide behind the screen while they play instruments. Everyone else will listen and then guess how many instruments they hear. Show each of the instruments. Discuss the sound it makes, its shape, color, and so on. Give the instrument to a child and ask him to play it. Did it make a loud sound or a quiet sound? Do this with each instrument so that the children get well acquainted with the sound of each. Then play each instrument, pause, and play the next one. Ask the children how many instruments you played.

Have a hidden child play instruments; guess how many. Place the instruments behind the screen and encourage one child to go behind the screen with the instruments. The other children will sit out in front of the screen with you. Remind the children that when they are behind the screen they may play one or two or three instruments. They may choose how many they want to play. After the hidden child plays, ask the other children how many instruments she played. If they answer correntely, clap for them and praise them for good listening. If the children are older, also ask if they can tell you the names of the instruments they heard.

Take turns playing the instruments. Encourage the children to take turns playing the instruments behind the screen and continue to have the other children guess how many instruments the hidden child played. Discuss the sounds the instruments made. Did the child make loud or quiet sounds?

Sing the tiger song from the previous day. Conclude by singing the "One little, two little, three little tigers" song from the day before.

Theme of the Day: How Many

Day 2: Art Center

What to Do:

Place several paper coffee filters, containers of food coloring, and containers of water on the table before the activity begins.

Relate the activity to the story. Ask the children how many babies Shao told the tiger she would have in a year. How many did the bird say? Hold up your fingers to illustrate the number nine, then hold up one finger to demonstrate the difference between nine and one. Say that they will count drops of food coloring they put in their water and see how many they need to make a pretty shade.

MATERIALS

- Coffee filters
- Food coloring
- Containers of water
- Paper and pencil for older children

Squeeze food coloring into water and count the number of drops. Encourage each child to get a container of water, a container of food coloring, and a coffee filter from the materials on the table. Let the children choose which color of food coloring they want to add to their water, then encourage them to squeeze drops of food coloring into the containers of water. Ask them how many drops of coloring they put in their water.

Dip coffee filters into the colored water. Encourage the children to dip their coffee filters into the colored water. Let them dip several filters into different colors of water if they are interested. Hang the filters to dry.

Older children may work in teams to record each drop of food coloring. If the children are older, divide them into pairs. Encourage each team to get a piece of paper, a pencil, two containers of water, and two colors of food coloring so that each child may have a turn to do each task. As one child in each pair drops food coloring into water, the other child should record the amount by using a slash mark for each drop. After the drops are in the water, ask the recorders how many drops of food coloring their partners used.

Find things in the room the same color as the filter. After the children dip the filters into the water, have them look around the room to see how many things they can find that are the same colors as the filters.

Theme of the Day: How Many

Day 2: Make-Believe Center

What to Do:

Before the activity begins, place all the stuffed animals in the make-believe center.

MATERIALS

- Stuffed animals
- Items used for feeding and taking care of animals

Relate the activity to the story. Discuss the number of people in the children's families. Ask them if they have brothers or sisters. Does anyone have a baby sister or brother? Who takes care of the baby? State that it takes a lot of time to take care of a baby. Ask if any of the children have more than one baby at their house. Say that the tiger in the story thought that she would have nine babies every year. She would have had to work very hard to take care of that many babies. Say that they will take care of stuffed animals.

Sort the animals. Help the children sort the animals into two piles: many and one. Be sure they understand which pile has many. Ask how many it has. Help them count the animals.

Feed and take care of a stuffed animal; discuss taking care of many. Let each child feed and take care of one stuffed animal. Compare the one animal they are taking care of to the many stuffed animals. Would they rather take care of one baby or many? How many babies would they like to take care of?

Theme of the Day:
Remember

Day 3 Group Time: Introducing the Theme of the Day

What to Do:

MATERIALS

- Art products from previous day
- Two music instruments
- Book, *Nine-in-One, Grr! Grr!*
- Two to four items for children to label, such as a toy tiger and other animals
- Piece of paper and marker
- Several blocks
- Toy person or farm animal

Set the mood by playing Hmong or other Asian music.

Review the previous day's activities. Show the children the coffee filters from the day before. Ask how many drops of food color they put in the water to color the water. Whisper in a child's ear and ask him to play two instruments. Ask everyone to cover their eyes while the child plays. Ask how many instruments he played. Praise the children for good listening. Discuss what happened in the make-believe center. How did they take care of the baby animals?

Read and discuss the story. Read the story. As the tiger song occurs in the story, encourage the children to sing with you.

Introduce the theme of the day: Remember. Remind the children that Tiger had to remember what Shao told her. Ask how they remember things in their families. Suggest that some families write things down on a calendar or remind each other about activities they want to remember. Ask whether they ever try to remember something by singing it. Say they are going to practice remembering things today. Show the children two or more items (depending on the maturity of the group) and ask them to name them.

Put the items behind you. Ask who can remember what you showed them. As each item is identified, place it in front of you. Compliment the children for good remembering. After all the items have been identified, choose a child to show several items and then hide them behind her back. Ask the children what she showed them. Help them remember the items by prompting as necessary.

Praise the children and tell them that they are remembering, the way the tiger remembered what Shao told her. Today in the centers they will do activities to help them remember things.

Introduce the arts activities.

Music and Movement Center

What the children will do: Take turns showing others how to move. Hold your hands high over your head. Then clap them. (Adapt the motion to the skill development level of your group.) Ask who can remember what you did. (If no one remembers, model the actions again.) Ask the child who remembers to show everyone what you did. Have everyone do the motion. Say, "__________ remembered like the tiger tried to remember what Shao told her." Say that in the music center today, the leader will show the others how

continues . . .

to move and everyone will have to remember how the leader moved and move that way. Everyone who wants to be the leader will get a turn.

Art Center

What the children will do: Remember what they did to make a work of art. Use large motions to demonstrate picking up a piece of paper and a marker. Then draw something on the paper. Tell the children that you remember that you picked up a piece of paper and a marker and drew on the paper. In the art center today they will get to use lots of materials to make anything they want to make. Then they will tell you what they did and you will write it down.

Make-Believe Center

What the children will do: Build Shao's house out of blocks. Make a structure out of blocks, then place the toy figure in front of the house. Say that you just made Shao's house and they will get to make the place where Shao lived in the make-believe center today.

Have each child choose an arts activity.

Notes:

Theme of the Day: Remember

Day 3: Music and Movement Center

What to Do:

Relate the activity to the story. Remind the children that Tiger had to remember what Shao told her or she wouldn't have as many babies as he said. Say that they will remember how someone moved and then move like that person did.

MATERIALS

- Cassette player
- Recording of music appropriate for marching

Model a movement; have children remember and repeat it. Model a simple movement, such as jumping up and down two times. Then ask who remembers how you moved. Have that child show everyone how you moved, and let the others join in. Then ask that child to show everyone a different way to move, then have everyone move the way the child did. Praise the child for thinking of a different way to move.

Take turns leading; encourage different movements. Encourage the children to take turns leading and to move in different ways using different body parts.

Play "Follow the Leader" around the room. Play marching music as one child leads the others around the room. Encourage him to move in different ways. Everyone should move just as the leader moves.

Remember how they moved. When the march is over, have everyone sit down. Ask who can remember how they moved as they marched along. After the children have identified some of the movements, praise them for good remembering.

Sing the tiger song from the previous day. Ask who remembers the tiger song you sang yesterday. Sing "One little, two little, three little tigers" with the children.

Theme of the Day: Remember

Day 3: Art Center

What to Do:

Relate the activity to the story. Ask the children what the tiger was trying to remember. Invite them to chant "nine in one grr, grr" with you. Remark that saying something over and over can help people remember, and that they will try to remember what they are doing as they work with the art materials.

Encourage the children to use a variety of art supplies. Place many art supplies on the table and encourage the children to use them in any way they choose.

Ask each child to tell what she did. After they finish, ask each child to tell you what she did. What did she do first? Then what did she do?

Write down what the child tells you. Write down what each child tells you. Tell them they are remembering, just as the tiger remembered what Shao told her.

MATERIALS

- Paper of varying colors and sizes
- Variety of art supplies such as paint, brushes, markers, chalk, scissors, glue, glitter, yarn, etc.

Theme of the Day: Remember

Day 3: Make-Believe Center

What to Do:

Relate the activity to the story. Ask the children if they remember what Shao's house looked like. Do they remember what kinds of animals were at Shao's house? Show the children the picture on page 6 and discuss the house and the animals. Tell them to look at the picture carefully because you want them to remember what it looked like. Say that they will use blocks, toy people, and toy farm animals to build the place where Shao lived.

MATERIALS

- **Blocks**
- **Toy people**
- **Toy farm animals**
- **Book, *Nine-in-One, Grr! Grr!* (with page 6 marked)**

Start building. Set out blocks, toy people, and toy farm animals and encourage the children to start creating Shao's house. Place the book where they can use it for reference. (Depending upon the children's developmental level, they may work individually or as a group.) As they work, prompt them to remember such things as the types of animals and the number of people in the illustration.

Discuss the activity. After they finish, ask each child to tell you what he did. Praise them for the way they remembered as the tiger in the story tried to remember what Shao told her. Ask them if it was hard to remember what was in the picture.

Theme of the Day:
Same/Different

Day 4 Group Time: Introducing the Theme of the Day

What to Do:

Set the mood by playing Hmong or other Asian music. If possible, use cookies or crackers and fruit appropriate to Hmong culture.

Review the previous day's activities. Ask the children if they can be like the tiger and remember what they did the day before. Who remembers what they did in the music and movement center? Can they show one of the ways they moved? Who remembers what they did in art? Who can tell how they built the house where Shao and his family lived? What kinds of animals did Shao have?

Read and discuss the story. Encourage the children to sing with you as the song occurs throughout the story.

Introduce the theme of the day: Same/Different. Ask the children if the bird told the tiger the same thing that Shao told her. Help them understand that Shao said "nine in one year," and the bird said "one in nine years," so they said a different number. Tell the children that when one thing is exactly like another we say it is "the same."

MATERIALS

- Book, *Nine-in-One, Grr! Grr!*
- Two food items that are the same
- Two food items that are different, such as an apple and a banana
- Two musical instruments that are exactly the same
- One piece of cooked spaghetti or rice stick
- Container of paint
- Paper plate
- Towel for cleaning your hands
- Toy cow and toy person

Taste food that is the same. Show them two items that are the same, such as two crackers or cookies. Give each child a small piece of each cookie emphasizing that both pieces came from cookies that are the same. Encourage them to eat first one piece, then the other. Ask if they taste the same.

Taste food that is different. Then show them two things that are very different, such as an apple and a banana. Ask if they are the same. Help them understand that the two pieces of fruit are different shapes and colors, and even taste different. Give each child a small taste of each fruit. Emphasize that they are different from each other. (If an Asian market is available, you might choose to use cooked sticky rice and white rice for the example of two foods that are different from one another. Compare the colors of the two kinds of rice, the taste, and the texture.)

Discuss foods that the children eat at home. Ask the children what they eat at home. Brainstorm the foods and write down the children's suggestions. Point out to them the similarities in the kinds of foods they eat. Help them to see that some foods are the same, everyone eats them, and that some are different, only a few people eat them.

continues . . .

Introduce the arts activities.

Music and Movement Center

What the children will do: Decide which sounds are the same and which are different. Show the children two instruments that are the same—for example, two triangles, two tambourines, or two sets of rhythm sticks. Any two instruments that are exactly the same will be fine. Play both instruments. Ask the children if they sounded just the same, or different. Say that in the music center today they will try many instruments and decide which ones sound the same and which ones sound different.

Art Center

What the children will do: Make shapes out of spaghetti (or rice sticks) and decide how they are the same or different. Show how you can dip your piece of cooked pasta into paint, lay it on a paper plate, and move it around until it is in a curvy shape. Tell the children that in the art center they will dip spaghetti into paint the way you did and then make shapes out of it.

Make-Believe Center

What the children will do: Play in the sand table with toy people and animals and decide how they are the same and how they are different. Show the children a toy animal (for example, a cow or horse). Ask how many legs it has. Then show them a toy person. Ask again how many legs the person has. Ask if the figures are the same or different. Say that today in the make-believe center they will play with toy people and animals in the sand (or block) center.

Have each child choose an arts activity.

Notes:

Theme of the Day: Same/Different

Day 4: Music and Movement Center

What to Do:

Piped instruments and reed instruments are representative of the Hmong culture. If possible, some type of piped instrument such as soprano and alto recorders could be used for this activity.

Relate the activity to the story. Remind the children that Shao said that the tiger would have nine babies, but the bird said that the tiger would have one baby. These two things are different. Say that when two things are just exactly alike, people say they are the same, but if they aren't the same, people say they are different. Say that this is true of the way things sound too.

MATERIALS

- **Cassette player**
- **Two recordings: Hmong or other Asian music, and American (such as Dixieland jazz)**
- **Instruments such as large and small tambourines or cymbals, resonator bells, keyboard**

Move to two kinds of music; note similarities and differences. If you have a tape of Hmong or Asian music, play it and have the children move briefly to it. Then play music typical of the United States (such as Dixieland jazz) and let them move briefly to it. Ask how the music is the same, and how it is different: Do the instruments sound the same or different? Are both the recordings happy sounding? Are they both fast or are they both slow?

Experiment with a variety of instruments. Place instruments such as large and small tambourines or cymbals, large and small resonator bells, or a keyboard where they are easily accessible.

Encourage the children to play freely with the instruments, experimenting to see how sounds are the same and how they are different.

If you have resonator bells, ask one child to play a small bell and another child to play a large bell.

Ask how the sound is the same, then how it is different. If you have a keyboard, encourage one child to play a note at one end of the keyboard and another child to play a note at the other end. Ask again, how are the sounds the same? How are they different?

The same may be done with any instruments you have in different sizes. It may also be done with child-made sound makers.

Sing the tiger song. Again, finish the activity by singing "One little, two little, three little tigers."

Theme of the Day: Same/Different

Day 4: Art Center

What to Do:

Rice sticks (Banh Pho) are representative of the Hmong culture. If an Asian store is available, buy some wide rice sticks to use for this activity and tell the children that these are the kind of noodles Shao's family may have eaten or that the children might eat if they lived in Laos.

Relate the activity to the story. Remind the children that what the bird told the tiger was not the same thing that Shao told her. Say that they will be making sculptures of noodles and then looking at them to see how they are the same and how they are different.

MATERIALS

- Precooked spaghetti or rice sticks
- A few pieces of uncooked spaghetti or rice sticks
- Containers of various colors of thick paint
- Wax paper

Have materials ready on a table. Place precooked and cooled spaghetti noodles (or rice sticks), uncooked noodles, and containers of thick paint on a table. Encourage the children to compare the cooked food to the uncooked food. Discuss the similarities and differences: How are they the same? How are they different? Do they feel the same?

Dip noodles in paint and make shapes. Encourage the children to dip the noodles in paint and lay them on wax paper in various shapes. Join the children and model the activity, talking out loud about what you are doing. "I think I will dip my noodle in the red paint. Now I'll lay it down. I wonder if I can make a circle out of it."

Discuss the shapes the children have made. How are they the same, and how are they different? When they are dry, remove them from the paper and hang them.

Theme of the Day: Same/Different

Day 4: Make-Believe Center

What to Do:

Relate the activity to the story. Tell the children that the tiger lived in a country far away, but some of the things where she lived look like the kind of things we have in our country. Ask if they remember anything that was in Tiger's country that is also in this country. Say that they are going to think about the animals that were in the story.

Look through the book for animal pictures. Show the children the pictures in the book, bringing their attention to the animals. Have them help you find pictures of animals that they sometimes see where they live (same), and animals that they do not see where they live (different).

MATERIALS

- Book, *Nine-in-One, Grr! Grr!*
- Toy animals
- Toy people
- Sand table
- Large sheet of paper and marker

Play with toy animals and people, discussing things that are the same and different. Put toy animals and people in the sand table (or in an area together). Join the children as they play. Encourage the children to think about what is the same and what is different about the animals and about how the animals are the same or different from people.

Write down ideas of things that are the same/different. Write down the children's ideas. For example, how many heads do the animals have? How many heads do people have? Is that the same or different? How many legs do the animals have? How many legs do people have? How many eyes do the animals have? How many eyes to people have? How many tails do the animals have? How many tails do people have?

Theme of the Day:
Butterflies

Day 5 Group Activity

What to Do:

There are many butterflies in Laos. They fly together, touching each other, and have very positive connotations for the Hmong people. People associate them with happiness. If possible, order a cocoon that will open during this week.

Relate the activity to the story; discuss butterflies. Show the children the pictures of the stages in a butterfly's life. Ask if they think the insect is happier when it crawls around as a caterpillar or when it can fly around and be a butterfly. Say that in Laos where this story came from, the people think of butterflies when they're happy.

Ask them if they think the tiger in the story was happy. Show them the first picture when Tiger wasn't very happy. Ask how many butterflies are in the picture. Then show them page 17 when Tiger knows that she will have baby tigers. How many butterflies are in this picture? Does Tiger look happy?

MATERIALS

- Book, *Nine-in-One, Grr! Grr!*
- Pictures of butterflies and pictures of the eggs, caterpillar, pupa, and butterfly
- Tissue paper of various colors
- Prepared wing frames made of stiff cardboard or poster board
- Glue
- Scissors
- White or light-colored fabric (or old sheets)
- Markers

Show the butterfly pictures. Show the children the pictures of butterflies. Draw their attention to the colors and the designs on the wings.

Tell the children what they may do. Show them the pieces of tissue paper and posterboard wing frames. Also show them the pieces of fabric. Say that they will get to make butterfly wings. They may use either the tissue or the pieces of fabric to make wings. If they use the fabric, they may use markers on the fabric to make pretty designs. Say that you will hang up the wings when they finish, and the room will be a butterfly room so that people will be happy.

Make butterfly wings. Set the pictures of butterflies where the children may see them as they work. Then work with the children as they make their butterfly wings.

If they choose to make wings with the tissue paper, encourage them to choose a color; then lay it flat on the wing frame. (If the children are older, they may be able to work in pairs. One child can glue while another child helps press the paper into place on the frame.) When the glue is dry, help the children cut around the outsides of the frames. If they choose to use fabric, help them lay the fabric flat, glue it in place, and cut around it; then encourage them to decorate the wings with markers. Younger children may be more successful if they concentrate on making marker designs on the white fabric.

continues . . .

Review the activity. When the children have finished making their wings, sit with them to discuss what they have done. Help them remember that they have been making butterfly wings because many butterflies live in Laos, and the people in Laos think of butterflies when they are happy. Ask them why the tiger in the story was happy.

If possible, take the children outside and let them pretend to be butterflies and fly around the playground with pieces of colored tissue paper.

Notes:

SKILLS & GOALS MATRIX

Nine-in-One, Grr! Grr!

	Skills or Behaviors	Goals and Objectives
Cognitive	• Distinguish one vs. many	• Increase awareness of concept of numbers • Increase understanding of *one more*
	• Name things that are the same or different	• Increase ability to sort like objects • Increase general vocabulary development
	• Match objects by color	• Increase concept and vocabulary development relating to color • Increase general reasoning ability • Increase visual discrimination
	• Demonstrate ability to do rote counting	• Increase short-term memory • Increase vocabulary relating to number
Language	• Describe and discuss shapes	• Increase math vocabulary development • Increase expressive communication
	• Discuss characteristics of animals and insects	• Increase general vocabulary • Increase ability to sort and categorize based on verbal input
	• Discuss characters in a familiar story	• Increase preliteracy skills: link story characters to own experiences, understand story structure, and become familiar with written language
	• Match tally marks to an observed event	• Increase number vocabulary • Increase symbolic awareness
	• Chant repeated phrases	• Increase phonological awareness • Increase auditory attention and memory

SKILLS & GOALS MATRIX (CONT.)

	Skills or Behaviors	Goals and Objectives
Social	• Pretend to be happy	• Increase understanding of point of view and feelings of others • Increase ability to appropriately express feelings
Social	• Take turns being a leader	• Increase participation as member of a group • Increase ability to initiate and lead group activity
Social	• Participate in working as part of a pair	• Increase appropriate verbal interactions with peers • Increase cooperative interactions with peers
Fine-Motor	• Squeeze eye droppers/food color containers	• Increase bilateral coordination • Increase hand strength • Increase visual-motor coordination
Fine-Motor	• Apply paint with long, short, curved, straight strokes	• Increase bilateral coordination • Refine prewriting grasp and manipulation
Fine-Motor	• Dip objects in paint	• Increase general manipulation skills • Increase visual-motor coordination • Increase tactile awareness • Refine pincer grasp
Fine-Motor	• Play a variety of musical instruments	• Increase bilateral coordination • Increase visual-motor coordination • Refine grasp, hand use, and manipulation skills
Gross-Motor	• Imitate body movements	• Increase motor planning • Increase body awareness
Gross-Motor	• Move differently to different kinds of music	• Increase dynamic and static balance • Increase motor planning and control • Increase ability to coordinate body movements with auditory input
Gross-Motor	• Shake instruments	• Increase motor planning and control • Coordinate fine- and gross-motor movements

STORY OF THE WEEK / EL CUENTO DE ESTA SEMANA

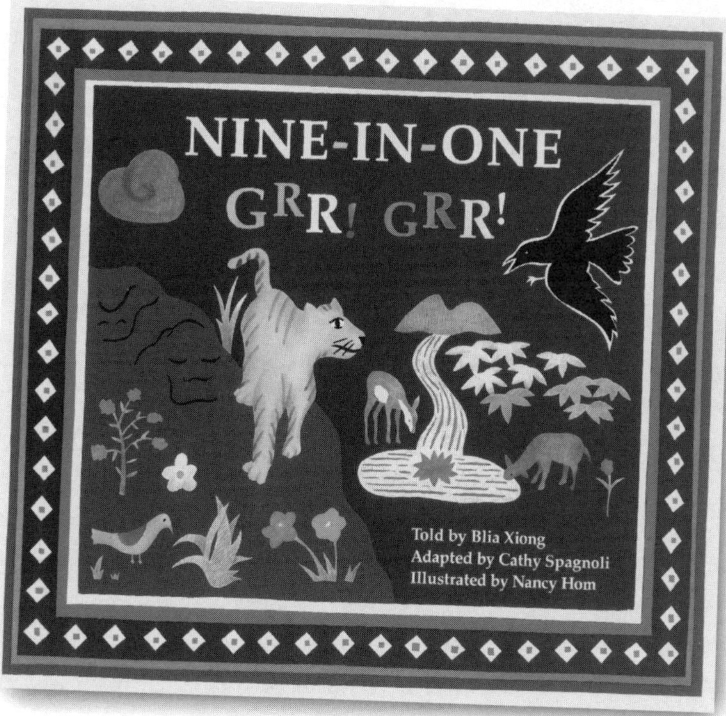

Nine-in-One, Grr! Grr!

told by Blia Xiong; adapted by Cathy Spagnoli
Edición en español: *Nueve en uno ¡Grr! ¡Grr!*

The Spark story this week is *Nine-in-One, Grr! Grr!* It is a Hmong folk tale. You may be able to find this book at the library; look in the section where they keep stories from other countries. The story is about a tiger who wants to know if she will have baby tigers. She goes to ask the great Shao. He tells her that she will have nine babies in one year, but that she will only have nine babies in one year if she remembers what he has told her. Ask your child what happened. (A bird surprised her and she forgot.) The themes to go with this story are *tiger, how many, remember, same/different,* and *butterflies.*

El cuento de Spark de esta semana se basa en una fábula folklórica Hmong y se llama *Nueve en uno ¡Grr! ¡Grr!* Usted puede encontrar este cuento en cualquier biblioteca, en la sección donde están los cuentos de otros paises. El cuento trata sobre una tigresa que quería saber si tendría bebés tigrillos. Ella fué a hacerele esta pregunta al gran Shao quien le dijo que tendría nueve bebés en un solo año, pero que los podría tener solamente si recordaba lo que él le había dicho. Pregúntele a tu niño o niña que pasó. (un pájaro la sorprendió y ella se olvidó). Las ideas temáticas que van con este cuento son: *tigre, cuántos, recordar, igual/diferente* y *mariposas.*

© 2001 The Board of Trustees of the University of Illinois. May be reproduced for use by teachers.

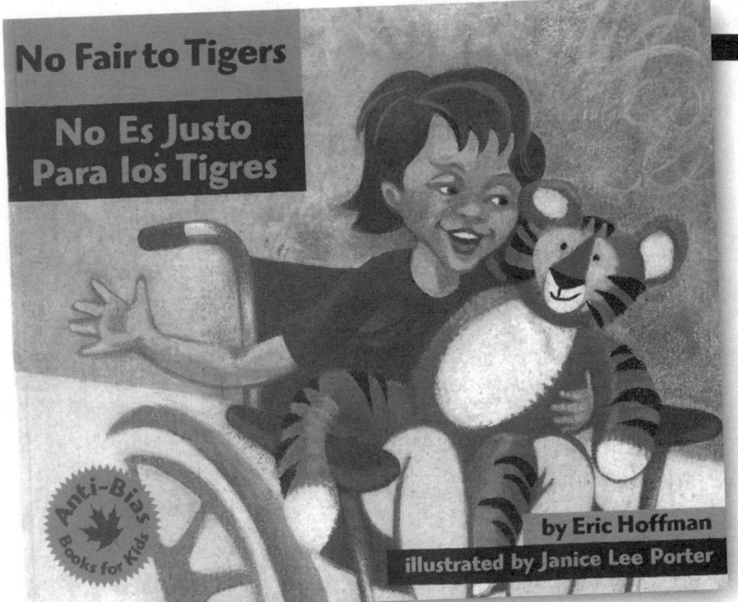

No Fair to Tigers
No Es Justo Para los Tigres
Anti-Bias Books for Kids
by Eric Hoffman
illustrated by Janice Lee Porter

No Fair to Tigers

by Eric Hoffman

St. Paul: Redleaf Press, 1999

Story Synopsis: *No Fair to Tigers* is presented in both Spanish and English. The main character in the story is a little girl named Mandy who is in a wheelchair. Mandy's disability is not the main issue in the story except when an accessibility issue arises. The story is centered on Mandy and her old toy tiger. At the beginning of the story, Mandy finds Old Tiger, who needs to be cleaned and repaired. Mandy is determined that both she and Old Tiger should be treated fairly. The illustrations show both what is actually happening in the story and what Mandy imagines.

Classroom Use: This story gently makes children aware of the problems that may be encountered by people in wheelchairs and also provides a vehicle for discussion of fair and unfair treatment. Since the text is provided in both English and Spanish, the story may be sent home to be shared with Spanish-speaking families. The story is complex for young three-year-old children. If the class includes three-year-olds who have just begun preschool, this unit will be more effective if it is implemented later in the school year. The unit will link well with stories about families or those focused on anti-bias issues. The themes and concepts for this unit are *orange/black/white, fair/no fair, ramp/stairs,* and *wheels.*

Considerations: The book is small and thus will be used most effectively with small groups of children. Many classrooms have found it helpful to have a wheelchair available to introduce children without disabilities to its use. The unit also provides an excellent opportunity for children with disabilities to discuss and demonstrate their assistive devices.

Special Materials: In addition to materials typically found in preschool classrooms, this unit suggests the use of colored cereal and an old bicycle wheel.

ACTIVITY MATRIX

No Fair to Tigers

Day	Concept	Music Activity	Art Activity	Make-Believe Activity
Day 1	Orange, Black, White (Cognitive, Kinder-garten Readiness)	Sing and perform action to Color Song sung to the tune of "If You're Happy." Move with streamers.	Mix colors using scraps of colored crepe paper stirred in water. Paint with the resulting color.	Repair and care for stuffed toys.
Day 2	Fair/No Fair (Cognitive, Social)	Decide how to use fair behavior when playing instruments. Move to music.	Decide how to distrib-ute playdough fairly. Make items with play-dough.	Act out response to unfair situations.
Day 3	Ramp/Stairs (Cognitive, Language)	Pretend to climb stairs and roll down ramps. Sing "Climb the Stairs" song.	Build stairs and ramp structures in wet sand.	Roll vehicles down ramps. Try to roll vehicles up stairs.
Day 4	Wheels (Cognitive, Language)	Decorate hub of circle and make yarn spokes of wheels. Go around to song.	Paint with wheels.	Drive vehicles along a paper road.
Day 5	The Pet Store			

Theme of the Day:
Orange, Black, and White

Day 1 Group Time: Introducing the Book

What to Do:

Introduce the story. Tell the children that the story today is about a little girl named Mandy who found her old stuffed animal tiger, Old Tiger, and then helped him in ways that were fair to tigers.

Read the story slowly. Give the children opportunities to examine the imaginary scenes that illustrate Mandy's explanations for what happened to Old Tiger and how Old Tiger would feel of he were treated in ways that were unfair. Encourage the children to become involved in the story by shaking their heads and repeating with you, "No fair. That's no fair to tigers."

Discuss the story. Ask the children to think about the story. What problems did Old Tiger have? (He was dirty. He lost his tail. He was hungry. He needed a bed.)

MATERIALS

- Book, *No Fair to Tigers*
- Three streamers: one orange, one black, one white
- Clear plastic cup of water
- Small pieces of orange crepe paper that will bleed into the water
- One craft stick
- Old stuffed toy

Introduce the theme of the day: Orange, black, and white. Show the children one of the pictures of Old Tiger. Ask them what color he is. Then show the picture of Mandy and her brother, Derek, making the tail for Old Tiger. Why are they using orange, black, and white yarn instead of white cotton?

Ask the children to look around the room for orange objects. Then have them look for black objects, and for white objects. Draw attention to any items of clothing worn by the children that are the target colors. Say that they will be doing things with orange, black, and white in the centers today.

Introduce the arts activities.

Music and Movement Center

What the children will do: Perform actions to a color song and move to music with streamers. Sing the following words to the tune of "If You're Happy and You Know It": "If you're wearing something white touch your nose, If you're wearing something white, touch your nose, If it's white and you know it, then your nose will surely show it, If you're wearing something white, touch your nose." Show the children the streamers. Ask them to label the color of each. Say that in the music center today they will move to music with the streamers and sing the color song that you just sang.

continues . . .

Art Center
What the children will do: Mix colors using scraps of colored crepe paper in water. Show the children the cup of water. Then put the colored crepe paper in the water and poke it down with the craft stick. As you stir the mixture, ask the children what is happening to the water. Is it changing color? What color is it? Say they will make colored water in the art center today.

Make-Believe Center
What the children will do: Repair and care for old stuffed toys. Show the children the stuffed toy. Suggest that the toy looks as if someone loved it very much but now it needs help. Say that in the make-believe center they will take care of the toy the way Mandy and her family took care of Old Tiger.

Have each child choose an arts activity.

Notes:

Theme of the Day:
Orange, Black, and White

Day 1: Music and Movement Center

What to Do:

MATERIALS

- Strips of construction paper (orange, black, and white)
- Orange, black, and white streamers
- Cassette player
- Recorded music appropriate for moving

Relate the activity to the story. Ask the children what color Old Tiger was. Help them to remember that he was orange, black, and white. Have them look at their clothing and then label the target colors by asking if anyone is wearing orange. Is anyone wearing black? white? Remind them that first they will sing a song and then move to music with streamers.

Distribute strips of colored construction paper. Spread the colors out on the floor. Let each child choose a color strip to hold. Ask all the children that are holding orange to hold it high. Repeat with each color until you are sure the children know what color they are holding. Ask the children to stand.

Sing a color song. Sing the following song, using the tune from "If You're Happy and You Know It." Encourage the children to follow the directions when their color is mentioned in the song. Ask the children who are not holding the specified color to help you sing as they become acquainted with the song.

If your color's black, turn around
If your color's black, turn around
If it's black and you know it
Then your turn will surely show it
If your color's black, turn around!

If your color's orange, jump up high
If your color's orange, jump up high
If it's orange and you know it
Then your jump will surely show it
If your color's orange, jump up high!

If your color's white, touch the ground
If your color's white, touch the ground
If it's white and you know it
Then your touch will surely show it
If your color's white, touch the ground!

Encourage the children to trade colors, then sing the song again. Trade colors one more time to ensure that everyone has an opportunity to identify each color by his response to the sung directions. Praise the children for good listening.

Sit with the children and distribute streamers. Ask the children to give you their color strips. Then have each child choose and label the colors of one or two streamers.

Move with the music. Start the music and join the children as they move to the music with the streamers. As you move, comment on what you and the children are doing: "Joshua is holding his orange streamer up high!" "Maria is going around and around with her black streamer!" "I'm moving my streamers up and down."

Sing a new verse. Quiet the children by singing the following verse to the previous song about colors as the children sit on the floor with you.

If you had fun say hurrah! (Hurrah!)
If you had fun say hurrah! (Hurrah!)
If it was fun and you know it,
Then your face will surely show it
If you had fun, say hurrah! (Hurrah!)

Theme of the Day:
Orange, Black, and White

Day 1: Art Center

What to Do:

Before the activity begins, cover the table with newspaper to absorb spills. Depending upon the skill level of the children, it may be more desirable to introduce each color one at a time, instead of putting them all on the table at the beginning of the activity.

Relate the activity to the story. Show the children the crepe paper and have them label each color. Ask them why they think you got out these colors. Does anyone know of anything in the story that was orange, black, and white? If necessary, show them a picture of Old Tiger.

Start the activity; make colored water. Place the crepe paper, plastic cups, and craft sticks where they are easily accessible. Model tearing the paper and putting each color into a plastic cup. As you work, talk about what you are doing. "I'm tearing the paper into little pieces so they will fit in the cup. I put all the pieces of one color in the same cup." Tell each child to take a small piece of each color of crepe paper and three plastic cups. Encourage them to tear (or cut) the paper into small pieces. Have them put each color in a separate cup.

Fill each glass partially with the water. (If the children are older, they may be able to pour their own water. In this case, you will need several pitchers of water to avoid having children waiting.) Tell the children to stir the paper and water with the craft stick. Ask what is happening to the water. Is it changing color? Which container is changing more, the one with the black paper or the one with the white paper? (Let older children make their own orange by mixing red and yellow paper scraps in the same container.)

Extend the activity. Some children may be interested in dipping white tissue, paper towels, or scraps of cloth in the water. What happens to the material when it is dipped? What happens to the water?

Paint with the colored water. Distribute the paper and brushes and model dipping your brush in colored water and painting on the paper.

Review the activity. Sit with the children to discuss the activity.

MATERIALS

- Book, *No Fair to Tigers*
- Orange, black, and white crepe paper that will bleed
- Several pair of scissors
- Clear plastic cups (enough for each child to have three)
- Pitcher of water
- Craft sticks
- Paintbrushes
- Paper

Theme of the Day:
Orange, Black, and White

Day 1: Make-Believe Center

What to Do:

The materials for this activity relate specifically to the repairs that may be needed for the toy. Include materials in the target colors whenever possible: for example, a white blanket, orange yarn. You might provide a bow to tie around the toy's neck made from one of the colors of the day.

Relate the activity to the story. Ask the children why Mandy had to help Old Tiger. What was the matter with him? If necessary, remind them that he was old and dirty and that she and her family cleaned him up and repaired him. Say that they will make (show them the toy and name it) feel better.

Brainstorm ways to help the toy and write down the suggestions. Show the children the toy again and ask them how they could help him. What does he need? Depending on the condition of the toy, the suggestions might include:

- Wash him.
- Fix his tail, ear, or eye. (If a piece is missing, ask what they could use. Show them the materials you have provided.)
- Feed him. (Show them the box of Animal Food.)
- Make him a bed. (Show them the box or basket and blanket.)

MATERIALS

- Paper/marker
- Old stuffed toy (one for each group)
- Whatever might be needed to repair the toy
- Cotton balls
- Yarn (orange, black, and white)
- Tape
- Colored cereal (orange, black, and white, if possible) in a box marked *Animal Food*
- Basket or box
- Doll blanket or soft material
- Brushes

Improve the toy's appearance. Encourage the children to brush (instead of wash) the toy, place the bow around his neck, and tape such items as a tail, leg, or ear on him.

Play with the toy. Let the children prepare food for the toy and make a bed for it. As they play, include discussion of the colors of the day.

Theme of the Day:
Fair/No Fair

Day 2 Group Time: Introducing the Theme of the Day

What to Do:

Discuss the activities of the previous day. Ask the children what they did on the previous day. What did they do in music? Sing a verse of the color song, "If your color's white, touch the ground," and ask everyone to help you sing. Show the stuffed animal. Does it look better than it did before? How did they help it? Show a painting from the art center and ask the artist to tell how she made the color.

Read the story and discuss it. Read the story, encouraging the children to join in whenever the phrase "No fair. That's no fair to tigers" occurs. Show the page again where Mandy and Derek are deciding how to fix Old Tiger's tail. Ask the children why Mandy said that Old Tiger didn't have a tail. What happened to it? (She said he was in a fight with an alligator.)

What did Mandy mean when she said that it wasn't fair to give Old Tiger a cotton tail? Why wouldn't it be fair? What did she mean? Point out the picture of Old Tiger with a cotton tail. Does it look like a tiger's tail?

Introduce the theme of the day: Fair/No fair. Say that you are going to pass out treats but they shouldn't eat their treats yet. Pass out the treats to all the children except one child. Give one to your assistant and keep one. Ask everyone who has a treat to hold it up. Stress that (Tyler) doesn't have one. Is that fair? Why isn't it fair? Will Tyler be happy when everyone else eats a treat and he doesn't have one? What can you do? (A child should suggest that you give a treat to the child.) Do so, then ask everyone who has a treat to hold it up. This time everyone should have one. Stress that it's fair now. Eat the treats. Remind the children that Mandy kept saying throughout the story that things weren't fair. Say that sometimes we do things that aren't fair and make people unhappy. Today in the centers they will think about what is *fair* or is *not fair.*

Introduce the arts activities.

Music and Movement Center

What the children will do: Decide how to use fair behavior when playing instruments. Give your assistant the empty coffee can. Keep the one filled with sound makers, such as beans or small rocks. Tell the children that you and _______ are going to see who can make the loudest sound with your cans. The one that makes the loudest sound gets a prize. Show them the prize. Shake your can. Ask your assistant to

continues . . .

MATERIALS

- Stuffed animal(s) from previous day
- Book, *No Fair to Tigers*
- Small treat (enough for each child to have one)
- Two coffee cans, one with sound makers inside, one empty
- A small wrapped box (the prize)
- Playdough

shake her can. Ask who made the loudest sound. Who should get the prize? Take the prize. Ask if what you did was fair. Did _______ have a chance to win? Pour part of your beans into the other can. Now see if the sound is fair. Tell the children that today in the music center they will play instruments and move to a song. They'll decide how to act in a way that is fair.

Art Center

What the children will do: Play with playdough. Show the children the playdough. Give a child one small piece. Give all the rest to another child. Ask if it is fair for _____ to have just a little bit of playdough and for ______ to have a big piece. Say that today in art they will divide the playdough so that each person has the same amount and make things with it.

Make-Believe Center

What the children will do: Act out how they feel in different scenarios. Ask the children how they would feel if they started to get a cookie and someone else took two cookies and they didn't get one. Ask them to show by their faces how they would feel. Ask if it is fair to take more than your share. Say that in the make-believe center they will think about how they would feel if something unfair happened to them.

Have each child choose an arts activity.

Notes:

Theme of the Day: Fair/No Fair

Day 2: Music and Movement Center

What to Do:

The intention of this activity is to help children understand how their behavior can affect others. The poem or fingerplay that you use should be particularly enticing to children, and you should present it in a very quiet voice so the children will begin to understand that it is unfair to others to be noisy in the classroom. If the children are not already familiar with the poem or fingerplay, "Little Cabin in the Woods," or a similar song-story complete with gestures, would work well.

Discuss the activity; relate it to the story. Remind the children that all through the story, Mandy said, "No fair." Suggest that people are unhappy when they think something is not fair. Say that you have a very special poem (or fingerplay) to read to them, and that everyone will get to hear it, but not at the same time. While they are waiting their turn to hear the poem, they may play with cans and rocks.

MATERIALS

- Rocks and empty cans with lids (enough for each child to have one)
- Tape
- Strikers
- A poem or fingerplay that is especially appealing to children
- Cassette player
- Recorded music that children enjoy moving to

Make sound makers. Place the cans and rocks where the children have easy access to them. Join the children in placing rocks in the cans and taping the tops securely in place.

Divide the group. Divide the group and give group 1 the strikers. Have group 2 place their cans behind them on the floor. Tell group 1 to play their cans. Say that they may use the strikers or just shake the cans while you read to the other children. Do not ask them to play quietly.

Read to one small group as the other group plays. As group 1 plays with their rock-filled cans at will, present the poem or fingerplay very quietly to group 2. Use facial expressions and gestures to make your presentation as enticing as possible. Reverse the groups and read to group 1 without comment about the loudness of the instrument players.

Discuss the activity. Ask the children if they liked the (fingerplay) that you told them. Ask them if they could hear it. Why couldn't they hear? Was it fair for the group that was playing the instruments to play so loudly the other group couldn't hear? What would make it better? What should they do in the room if some children are trying to hear something special? Is it fair to be so loud that other children can't hear? Present the fingerplay for all the children.

Move to music. Play a music tape that is a classroom favorite. Say that only the children with (choose an article of clothing such as white shoes, certain hair color, or color of eyes) can move to the music. Everyone else should sit with pretzel legs and hands in their laps. Let the chosen children move any way they wish to move. Praise their movement.

When the music stops, ask if it was fair for only some of the children to be allowed to move. Ask if the seated children were happy when the other children got to move and they didn't. Play the music again, and let all the children move. When they finish, ask if it was fair this time.

Discuss the activity. Remind the children that it makes people sad to have something unfair happen to them. Encourage discussion.

Theme of the Day: Fair/No Fair

Day 2: Art Center

What to Do:

Discuss the activity; relate it to the story. Tell the children that Mandy didn't think it was fair to give Old Tiger a cotton tail, wash him in the washing machine, or feed him a peanut butter sandwich. She wanted him to be treated like a tiger. Say that they will get to make things with playdough and they should try to be fair with their playdough.

MATERIALS

- Playdough
- Playdough accessories such as rollers, stamps, plastic knives

Distribute playdough unfairly. Give part of the children large pieces and other children very small pieces of playdough. Ask if the way you passed out the playdough is fair. What can they do to make it fair? Encourage the children to divide the playdough more evenly.

Distribute presses to make designs, rollers, and plastic knives. Place the playdough accessories on the table where they can be reached easily. Ask if it's fair to have the equipment where everyone can reach it. Help them to understand that it's fair as long as everyone can reach it, and as long as no one takes something and doesn't share it.

Play with the children with the playdough. Stress what is fair or not-fair behavior as the children share materials.

Theme of the Day: Fair/No Fair

Day 2: Make-Believe Center

What to Do:

Act out the scenarios with hand puppets and then let the children play with the puppets.

MATERIALS

- Book, *No Fair to Tigers*
- Hand puppets
- List of scenarios

Relate the activity to the story. Remind the children that after Mandy found Old Tiger things happened all day that she said were no fair. What happened to Mandy that she said was no fair? Turn to the page in the book where Mandy encountered the steps outside the pet store. Ask the children to look at Mandy's face. How did Mandy feel? Why did she say it wasn't fair? Say that they are going to show how they would feel if unfair things happened to them.

Relate a scenario and discuss it. Tell the children that everyone in your family got to go to McDonald's and you had to stay home. Say that you were mad! Model the body language that displays anger. Say that you are going to tell them some things and they should pretend that these things have just happened to them and show how they feel. Read one of the provided scenarios or tell something that is specifically appropriate for your group of children. For example, if you have children who do not speak English or children who are disabled, tailor the scenarios to fit them.

> **Scenario #1:** *Lia wanted to paint, but all the paint aprons were gone. Carmen was wearing all the paint aprons. Was this fair? How would you feel if you were Lia? Have the children show by their expressions how they would feel if this happened to them. What could Lia do?*
>
> **Scenario #2:** *Nakio wanted to play cars with the other boys, but they made fun of him when he tried to play and said he was too little to play with them. Was this fair? How would you feel? What could Nakio do?*
>
> **Scenario #3:** *The children were playing hide-and-seek. When it was Toby's turn to hide his eyes, he peeked and watched where the other children hid. Was this fair?*
>
> **Scenario #4:** *When all the children went outside, they started running around and having fun. Malika wanted to swing, but Kylie pushed her out of the way and took the last swing. Was that fair?*

Share experiences. Ask the children if anything has ever happened to them that they didn't think was fair. Discuss the incident. Ask how they felt.

Theme of the Day:
Ramp/Stairs

Day 3 Group Time: Introducing the Theme of the Day

What to Do:

Review the previous day's activities. Remind the children that on the previous day they thought about what was fair and what was not fair. Ask them if they could hear what they wanted to hear when someone else was being noisy. Ask them how they should play the instruments if someone else is involved in a quiet activity. Show them the playdough. Ask a child how to divide the playdough so that it's fair. Ask them to show you how they would feel if someone did something to them that wasn't fair.

Read and discuss the story. Read the story, encouraging the children to chant the "no fair" phrase and shake their heads when the phrase occurs in the story. Ask the children why Mandy and her sister went to the pet store. What did Mandy want to get at the store? Why didn't she give Old Tiger a peanut butter sandwich?

MATERIALS

- Playdough
- Book, *No Fair to Tigers*
- Enough blocks of varying lengths to make steps
- Large piece of sturdy cardboard
- Two toy cars
- Toy or puppet
- Flat box with sand
- Glass of water

Introduce the theme of the day: Ramp/Stairs. Show the children the picture of Mandy when she first sees that the only way into the pet store is a set of stairs. What is the matter? Help the children understand that Mandy couldn't get into the store by herself because the store did not have a ramp. How did she feel when she saw the stairs?

Make stairs from the blocks by putting the longest block on the bottom and placing the next longest on top of that. Continue in this manner until you have stairs. Then make a ramp from the piece of cardboard. Ask a child to roll a toy car down the ramp. Ask another child to roll the car up the ramp. Ask a child to roll a car down the stairs. Ask another child to roll the car up the stairs. State that if you can't walk, it's very difficult to get up or down stairs, but that you can roll a wheelchair up and down a ramp. Say that they will think about *ramps* and *stairs* in the centers today.

Introduce the arts activities.

Music and Movement Center

What the children will do: Pretend to climb stairs and roll down ramps to directions sung in a song. Sing the following words to the tune of "Skip to My Lou" as you move a toy or a puppet as if it is following the directions to the song.

continues . . .

Climb, climb, climb the stairs
Climb, climb, climb the stairs
Climb, climb, climb the stairs
Oh climb the stairs today.

Tell the children that in the music center they will pretend to climb stairs and roll down ramps.

Art Center

What the children will do: Build stairs and ramp structures in wet sand. Show the children the sand. Moisten it by pouring the water on it, then show them how to make a hill. Use the piece of cardboard to flatten one side of the hill to create a ramp. On the other side of the hill, create stairs. Ask the children to label the ramp and the stairs. Say that they will make ramps and stairs in wet sand in the art center.

Make-Believe Center

What the children will do: Roll vehicles down a ramp. Remind the children that the cars can roll down cardboard ramps, but can't roll down stairs. Tell them that in the make-believe center they will roll cars down ramps.

Have each child choose an arts activity.

Notes:

Theme of the Day: Ramp/Stairs

Day 3: Music and Movement Center

What to Do:

Before this activity begins, ensure that there is plenty of room for movement by clearing space if necessary.

Relate the activity to the story. Ask the children why Mandy was upset when she got to the pet store. Why couldn't she get into the store? Tell them that they will pretend to climb stairs and roll down ramps.

Teach the song. Remain seated with the children and sing the following words several times to the tune of "Skip to My Lou." Encourage the children to sing with you.

Climb, climb, climb the stairs
Climb, climb, climb the stairs
Climb, climb, climb the stairs
Oh climb the stairs today!

Roll, roll, roll down the ramp
Roll, roll, roll down the ramp
Roll, roll, roll down the ramp
Oh roll down the ramp today!

Demonstrate movements. Ask a child to show you how to pretend to climb stairs. Praise the child for moving well, and join in the movements. Exaggerate the movement, lifting one leg at a time and pretending to climb. Ask all the children to join in the movement. Talk about how high you're getting! Ask another child to demonstrate how to pretend to roll down a ramp the way wheelchairs do. Again, praise the child and let the other children roll on the floor with her.

Move to the song. Tell the children to listen to the song and do what it tells them to do: pretend to climb the stairs, or roll down a ramp. Sing the song as the children perform the actions. If there's a set of stairs near the classroom, take the children to the stairs and encourage them to climb up, then climb down the stairs as you all sing the song together.

Theme of the Day: Ramp/Stairs

Day 3: Art Center

What to Do:

Relate the activity to the story. Remind the children that Mandy could not go into the pet store because it did not have a ramp. Say that they can make ramps and stairs in the sand.

Try to build with dry sand. Join the children and try to build hills with the dry sand. Ask them what the problem is. Help them to understand that the sand has to be wet before it will keep its shape well enough for them to use it for building.

Add water and form shapes. If the children are older, encourage them to pour water on the sand. If not, help them with the water. Make a sand mound, then form stairs and a ramp. Talk about what you are doing as you work: "I made a big, smooth hill. I wonder how I can make stairs. Maybe if I start at the top and make little shelves. One side of the hill could be my ramp. How can I make my ramp smooth?"

Praise the children as they use the cardboard to smooth off the ramp or scoop sand out to make stairs. Pretend to walk up the stairs with your fingers or slide down the ramp with your hand or a toy.

MATERIALS

- Sand
- Pitcher of water
- Small pieces of heavy cardboard
- Toys

Theme of the Day: Ramp/Stairs

Day 3: Make-Believe Center

MATERIALS

- Several large pieces of strong cardboard
- Masking tape
- Toy cars and/or trucks
- Blocks

What to Do:

Relate the activity to the story. Remind the children that Mandy couldn't go into the pet store because wheelchairs can't go up stairs. She thought the pet store should have a ramp because wheelchairs can go up and down ramps. If you have a toy wheelchair, demonstrate with it. Otherwise, say that you don't have a toy wheelchair but that other toys like cars and trucks have wheels and can go on ramps the way wheelchairs do.

Have the children help you set up the activity. Make several ramps of varying heights and help the children build a set of block stairs.

Experiment with the cars. Encourage the children to decide whether stairs or ramps work best for vehicles with wheels:

- Encourage them to attempt to roll the cars down the stairs.
- Would cars have accidents if they tried to go down stairs?
- Let them roll the cars down the ramps.
- Do cars have accidents when they roll down the ramps?
- Which ramp makes them go the farthest?
- Will they roll up the ramps?
- Can they roll up the stairs?

Let the children play freely with the blocks, ramps, and vehicles.

Theme of the Day:
Wheels

Day 4 Group Time: Introducing the Theme of the Day

What to Do:

Review the previous day's activities. Remind the children that on the previous day, they thought about ramps and stairs. Ask them why Mandy couldn't go into the pet store. Sing the "Climb the stairs" song as the children demonstrate the motion. Ask them to describe how they made ramps and stairs in the sand. Discuss the make-believe activity. Ask them if the cars could go up the stairs. Ask what else they did in the make-believe center.

Read and discuss the story. Read the story and encourage the children to shake their heads and chant the "No fair to tigers!" phrase whenever it occurs in the story. Discuss how the wheels on the wheelchair helped Mandy go around the house and to the pet store.

MATERIALS

- Book, *No Fair to Tigers* (with page marked when Mandy tells Allie that Old Tiger is hungry)
- Toy vehicle
- A bicycle wheel (if possible)
- One piece of heavy yarn from the music center
- Tray of paint from the art center
- Piece of paper

Introduce the theme of the day: Wheels. Show the children the picture in the book where Mandy is telling Allie that Old Tiger is hungry. Point to the wheel on the wheelchair. Hold up a toy vehicle and have a child point to the wheel (or if you have a bicycle wheel, show it to the children). Ask the children to think of things they could do with a wheel. Encourage them to think of ideas, even unusual or impossible things, such as, "Roll it to the moon." Thank the children for their great ideas. Tell them they will do things with wheels in the centers today.

Introduce the arts activities.

Music and Movement Center

What the children will do: Make a wheel. Show the children the picture of the wheelchair again (or the bicycle tire) and say that the lines that go across the wheel are called *spokes.* Show the children the heavy yarn. Have two children stand up. Give each one of them an end of the yarn. Ask them to go around in a circle, making the spoke go around with them. Sing to the tune of "Mary Had a Little Lamb":

Round and round they're making a wheel,
Making a wheel, making a wheel.
Round and round they're making a wheel,
Making a wheel today.

Say that in music they will get to make the spokes of a wheel and go around and around.

continues . . .

Art Center

What the children will do: Paint with wheels. Dip the wheels of the toy vehicle in the tray of paint, and then roll the vehicle along the piece of paper. Show the children the tracks the wheels made on the paper. Tell the children that the paper in the art center will cover the whole table. Say they can paint with wheels in the art center.

Make-Believe Center

What the children will do: Drive vehicles along a paper road. Discuss the fact that Mandy's wheelchair had wheels so she could move around. Ask the children to name some things they ride in that have wheels (cars, buses, tricycles, wagons). Then move a toy vehicle along the floor and tell them they may pretend they are driving vehicles in the make-believe center.

Have each child choose an arts activity.

Notes:

Theme of the Day: Wheels

Day 4: Music and Movement Center

What to Do:

Make a wheel. Have the children sit in a circle with you on the floor and show them the picture of the wheel. Ask what shape it is. Tell them that they can make a big wheel that looks like the wheel on Mandy's wheelchair. After they make the wheel, they can move it to music. Show the children the cardboard circle, and explain that this will be the middle (hub) of the wheel. (Point to the hub of the wheel in the picture.) Let them choose markers, glue, and glitter and work together to decorate the circle any way they choose.

Show the children the pieces of yarn and discuss their color. Point to the spokes on the wheel in the picture and explain that they will use the yarn for the spokes of the wheel. Then use the stapler to fasten one end of a piece of yarn to the edge of the wheel. Fasten a piece of yarn to the hub of the wheel and encourage the children to follow your example.

MATERIALS

- Book, *No Fair to Tigers*
- Cardboard circle, approximately 24 inches in diameter
- Markers
- Glue
- Glitter
- Heavy yarn of several colors that have been cut into 3-foot strips
- Stapler

Practice moving in a circle. Ask the children to stand up and form a circle. (Have them leave the yarn and the decorated hub on the floor in the middle of the circle.) Practice going around in a circle, singing to the tune of "Mary Had a Little Lamb":

Round and round, we're going around
Going around, going around.
Round and round, we're going around.
Going around today.

Move the wheel. When the children are moving smoothly around in a circle, have them each pick up a piece of yarn, then move around in a circle again, this time singing,

Round and round, we made a wheel,
Made a wheel, made a wheel.
Round and round, we made a wheel,
Made a wheel today.

Vary the activity by singing, "our wheel goes fast," and "our wheel goes slow" and moving appropriately.

Ask for suggestions and follow them. Ask the children for other suggestions as to how to move the wheel, and move according to their suggestions. When you are finished with this part of the activity, put the wheel aside.

Roll like wheels. Tell the children to pretend they are wheels. Ask them to think of ways they can roll around like a wheel, such as rolling sideways or doing a forward roll (older children). Sing the first verse of the song again, and invite the children to roll like wheels while you sing.

Theme of the Day: Wheels

Day 4: Art Center

What to Do:

Before the activity begins, cover the entire tabletop with butcher paper and tape it securely in place. Older children might mix the paint themselves by combining equal parts of liquid paint and water.

Relate the activity to the story. Remind the children that Mandy couldn't walk and that she moved around in a wheelchair. Say that a wheelchair is a chair on wheels, and when the wheels go around, the person in the chair moves from place to place.

Paint with vehicles. Have the children sit around the table. Place trays of watery paint in several places on the table (away from the edge!) and join in the activity with the children. Show how you choose a vehicle and dip the wheels in paint. Then roll the vehicle along the paper to make trails and designs. Encourage the children to paint with several different vehicles and compare the tracks they make on the paper.

Paint with spools. You might also show the children how to make their own wheel by pushing a pencil through the hole in a spool. They can roll this kind of wheel by holding the ends of the pencil and rolling the spool on the paper. As the children paint with the spools, have them compare the spool tracks to the vehicle tracks. Can they tell them apart? How are they different? How are they the same?

Wash the vehicles. When the children are finished painting, tell them to take their vehicles to the car wash (the container of water). Let them wash the paint off the vehicles.

Trace and decorate trails. Let the children use pencils or other writing utensils to trace or decorate the trails they made with paint.

MATERIALS

- Table
- Masking tape
- Butcher paper
- Watery paint in Styrofoam trays
- A variety of toy vehicles
- Empty thread spools and pencils (optional)
- Tub of water for washing the vehicles
- Pencils, markers, crayons, or chalk

Theme of the Day: Wheels

Day 4: Make-Believe Center

MATERIALS

- Small toy vehicles
- One strip of paper per child and adult, approximately 17 inches by 2 inches
- One or more pieces of paper per child, approximately 17 inches by 11 inches
- Scissors
- Several red circles and black marker pens to make stop signs (optional)
- Building blocks (optional)

What to Do:

On each full-sized piece of paper, use a black marker to draw lines the length of the paper, about 3 inches apart. These will be cutting guides for the children.

Relate the activity to the story. Remind the children that wheels made it possible for Mandy to move around. Say that wheels help us to get around too, because there are big wheels on cars, and cars can't move without them. Mandy needed a ramp for her wheelchair just as cars need ramps and roads.

Play with toy vehicles. Let the children choose toy vehicles and drive them around on the floor.

Make a road for vehicles with precut paper strips. Show the children the paper strips and invite them to make a road for the vehicles to drive on. When they have made the road, show how you can drive a vehicle without going over the edges of the road.

Cut additional strips for a longer road. If the children want to make the road longer, let them cut additional strips of paper by cutting along the lines on the paper you prepared. Encourage them to make a long road system for their vehicles to drive on.

Add block structures and stop signs. If the children are interested, introduce building blocks, so they may make structures along the sides of the road or bridges for the vehicles to drive over. They might also print *STOP* on the red circles, and place the stop signs along the road. Show how you stop your vehicle whenever you come to a stop sign along the road.

Theme of the Day:
Animal Hospital

Day 5 Group Activity

What to Do:

As you set up this activity, include both the types of animals that might be found in a small-animal hospital and ones that are more appropriate for farms and zoos.

If a local veterinarian is available, a field trip to the clinic or a visit by the veterinarian to the classroom would add to the educational value of this activity.

Relate the activity to the story. Remind the children that when Mandy found Old Tiger, he needed help. Say that when real animals need help that their owners can't give them, their owners take them to the animal hospital.

Discuss animal hospitals in general. Ask if anyone has ever been to an animal hospital. Discuss the visit and ask them why they went. Encourage the children to brainstorm all the reasons why animals might have to go to the animal hospital. Discuss the fact that animal doctors are called *veterinarians* and their helpers are called *veterinarian assistants.*

MATERIALS

- Small toy animals or pictures
- Items used for pet care such as feeding dish, brush or comb, bed
- Paper and marker
- Small and large boxes
- Open baskets
- Blankets
- Various kinds of cereal to make pretend food (or playdough and cut-up paper)
- Markers
- Masking tape
- Long piece of paper for sign

Discuss the types of animals treated in most animal hospitals. Show the children the toy animals. Ask which of these animals they might see in an animal hospital. Discuss which of the animals make good pets. Help them understand that the types of animals they might see in a zoo usually aren't in small-animal hospitals. They are usually too big.

Ask if any of the children have a pet. Discuss the pets by asking such questions as what type of animals they are and what they do with their pets. If you have a pet, tell them about your pet to encourage them to relate their own experiences.

Discuss pet health. Ask the children how they keep their pets healthy. Discuss such actions as providing appropriate food, water, a place to sleep, and exercise.

Brainstorm items used in animal hospitals. Discuss with the children the kinds of things they think the veterinarian might use to check the animals and take care of them. Brainstorm the items and list their suggestions.

continues . . .

Plan to make animal hospital items. Tell the children that they may use the materials you brought to make things for the animal hospital. Show them the small boxes, baskets, blankets, and cereal. Say that they can use the little boxes for food dishes, make beds out of the baskets and blankets, and pretend the cereal is pet food. Tell them that you want them to tell you what they are going to make. Ask each child what he plans to make and write his name down beside the item on the list the children brainstormed.

Encourage the children to make the items as planned. Work with the children to help them in any way they wish. Help them to understand that they need more than one item of each kind because animal hospitals have many animal beds, food dishes, and so on. Encourage them to gather stuffed animals to use in the animal hospital.

Arrange the animal hospital. When the children are finished assembling the items, let them set up the animal hospital. With your help, older children might make and decorate a large sign that says *ANIMAL HOSPITAL.*

Encourage animal hospital play. See suggestions below.

Review the activity. Sit with the children to discuss the activity. Invite each child to tell you what he/she made for the hospital. Check the list with the children to see if they did what they originally planned to do.

Suggestions for Implementing Animal Hospital Play:

Invite the children to use the props they created to pretend to be workers or people who bring their sick or hurt animals to the animal hospital.

- They could take turns being the veterinarian and veterinarian assistants.
- They could pretend to examine the animals.
- They could bandage the animals.
- They could feed the animals.
- They could groom the animals.
- As animal owners they could bring their pet to the hospital.
- As owners they could visit their sick pet.

SKILLS & GOALS MATRIX

No Fair to Tigers

	Skills or Behaviors	Goals and Objectives
Cognitive	• Recognize and name colors	• Increase color concept and vocabulary development • Increase visual awareness and discrimination
	• Discuss ramps and stairs	• Increase concept and vocabulary development relating to energy and force
	• Discuss *rolling* vs. *non-rolling*	• Increase observation skills • Increase ability to sort like events
	• Recall events in a story	• Improve recall memory skills • Increase preliteracy skills: awareness of sequencing and structure in stories
Language	• Imitate sounds from a familiar story	• Increase auditory discrimination • Increase oral-motor coordination
	• Learn and recite a chant	• Increase receptive and expressive vocabulary • Increase phonological awareness
	• Identify objects with wheels	• Increase receptive and expressive vocabulary • Increase ability to associate words and objects
	• Use road signs with pretend roads	• Increase preliteracy skills: become familiar with written language, identify environmental print and words

SKILLS & GOALS MATRIX (CONT.)

	Skills or Behaviors	Goals and Objectives
Social	• Sing a song with others	• Increase participation as member of a group
	• Discuss what makes others feel angry or sad	• Increase understanding of point of view and feelings of others • Increase ability to recognize and label emotions
	• Practice sharing with peers in equal amounts	• Increase appropriate verbal interactions with peers • Increase ability to play cooperatively with peers • Increase understanding of *equal* for all
Fine-Motor	• Tear paper into small pieces	• Increase bimanual coordination • Refine pincer grasp • Increase hand strength
	• Pour water into glasses	• Increase wrist rotation • Increase visual-motor coordination • Refine motor planning
	• Cut paper with scissors	• Increase manipulation skills • Increase hand strength • Increase bimanual coordination
	• Roll cars and other toys through various materials	• Increase visual-motor coordination • Increase tactile awareness
Gross-Motor	• Do a standing jump	• Increase gross-motor planning and control • Increase dynamic balance • Increase awareness of body in space
	• Move to music	• Increase gross-motor planning and control • Increase auditory attention • Increase awareness of body in space
	• Roll like wheels in different directions	• Increase motor planning and control • Increase understanding of directionality of movement • Increase mobility and agility skills

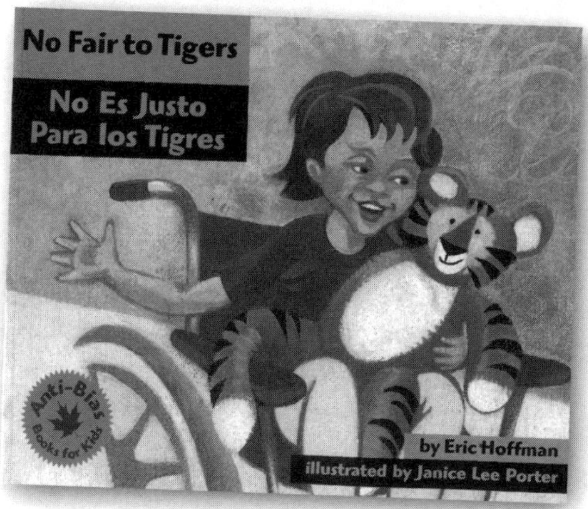

No Fair to Tigers/No es justo para los tigres

by Eric Hoffman
(bilingual edition/ edición bilingüe)

The Spark story this week is *No Fair to Tigers/No es justo para los tigres*. You may be able to find this book at the library. It is the story of a little girl named Mandy who has found her old stuffed tiger. Old Tiger is dirty and has lost his tail. Her father and brother help Mandy clean Old Tiger up and repair him in ways that are fair to tigers. Then she and her sister go to the pet store to get some tiger food for him to eat. When they arrive, Mandy, who is in a wheelchair, can't go in the store because the only way to get into the store is by climbing steps. Ask your child what happened. How did Mandy get food for Old Tiger? (The pet store man came out of the store to talk to Mandy.) The themes to go with this story are *orange/black and white, fair/no fair, ramp/steps,* and *wheels.*

El cuento de Spark de esta semana se titula *No Fair to Tigers/No es justo para los tigres.* Usted puede encontrar este libro en cualquier biblioteca. Este cuento es sobre una niñita llamada Mandy que encontró a un viejo tigre de peluche, el Viejo Tigre. El mismo estaba sucio y se le había perdido la cola. El padre y el hermano de Mandy la ayudaron a limpiar y a arreglar al Viejo Tigre de la manera más justa para el tigre. Luego, ella y su hermana fueron a una tienda que venden productos para animalitos a fin de conseguir comida de tigre para que él pudiera comer. Cuando llegaron a la tienda Mandy, que está sentada en una silla de ruedas, no pudo entrar. La única manera de hacerlo era subiendo los peldaños. Pregúntele a su niño o ninna qué pasó. ¿Cómo fue que Mandy consiguió la comida para el Viejo Tigre? (La persona a cargo de la tienda salió para hablar con Mandy). Las ideas temáticas que discutiremos esta semana serán las siguientes: *anaranjado/negro y blanco, justo/injusto, rampa/escaleras* y *ruedas.*

© 2001 The Board of Trustees of the University of Illinois. May be reproduced for use by teachers.

Polar Bear, Polar Bear, What Do You Hear?

by Bill Martin Jr.

New York: Henry Holt, 1991.

Story Synopsis: This simple story is by the same author as the beloved story, *Brown Bear, Brown Bear, What Do You See?* In the Polar Bear story, each page shows a different animal and the question is asked, "(name of animal, name of animal) what do you hear?" At the end of the story, the zookeeper is asked what he hears, and all the animal sounds are repeated.

Classroom Use: *Polar Bear, Polar Bear, What Do You Hear?* is an excellent story to use to reinforce children's listening skills and to introduce wild animals. It may be used successfully any time of the year, although many teachers choose to use it as part of a winter theme. The illustrations are simple and colorful, and the text is one that children enjoy whether they are entering three-year-olds or older preschool children. Children enjoy chanting "What do you hear?" and making the sounds of the animals as each one is introduced. Many teachers encourage individual children to create the sounds that the animals make. This unit may be successfully linked to other stories about animals or winter. The themes and concepts for this unit are *animal sounds, sounds around us,* and *listening* (two days).

Considerations: This is a story that is accepted without reservation by children. It has no cultural or anti-bias considerations.

Special Materials: In addition to the materials typically found in preschool classrooms, this unit also suggests using a tape of farm animal sounds if one is available, as well as face paint, feather duster, measuring cups, and a toy cash register.

ACTIVITY MATRIX

Polar Bear, Polar Bear, What Do You Hear?

Day	Concept	Music Activity	Art Activity	Make-Believe Activity
Day 1	Animal Sounds (Cognitive, Language, Social)	Sing animal songs and make animal sounds.	Make sounds like animals make while using various art materials.	Dress up like animals and imitate them.
Day 2	Sounds Around Us (Cognitive, Language)	Identify instruments that make sounds.	Make different sounds with art tools.	Listen to sounds in the school and pretend to be the objects that made the sounds.
Day 3	Listening (Cognitive, Language, Social)	Follow directions in songs.	Follow directions to make playdough.	Talk and listen with toy telephones.
Day 4	Listening (Cognitive, Language, Social)	Take turns being the leader of the band and tell other children when to play their instruments.	Tell each other what art tools to use.	Continue phone play.
Day 5	Pizza Parlor			

Theme of the Day:
Animal Sounds

Day 1 Group Time: Introducing the Book

What to Do:

Read the story. Read the book and make the animal sounds as they occur. It is not necessary to make accurate sounds for the animals, but try to make them appealingly dramatic, such as a lion's loud roar and a mysterious boa's hiss.

Ask children to imitate animal sounds in the book. Show the children the pictures of the animals in the book again and encourage them to make the sounds with you.

Introduce the theme of the day: Animal sounds. Tell the children that you have some other animal sounds for them to listen to. Encourage them to listen carefully as you play one animal sound on the farm animal tape. (If you do not have access to a tape of farm animal sounds, make the sound yourself.) Stop the tape and ask the children to guess what kind of animal made that sound. If they name the correct animal, show them the matching picture, and ask them to repeat the animal's name. If they do not name the correct animal, show the matching picture to help them. If needed, name the animal and ask the children to repeat the animal's name. Allow time for the children to talk about the animal. Repeat this procedure with the other animal sounds. Tell the children that they can make and listen to animal sounds in the centers today.

MATERIALS

- **Book, *Polar Bear, Polar Bear, What Do You Hear?* (with pages of lion and boa constrictor marked)**
- **Cassette player**
- **Recording of farm animal sounds (optional)**
- **Animal pictures (matching animal-sounds tape)**
- **One half of a potato**
- **Paper**
- **Small container of paint to dip potato in**
- **Long cardboard tube**

Introduce the arts activities.

Music and Movement Center

What the children will do: Sing songs with animal sounds. Hold up a picture of a lion. Model roaring like a lion and encourage the children to join you. Then hold up the picture of the boa constrictor. Model hissing and have them join you. Tell them they will sing animal songs and make animal sounds in the music center.

Art Center

What the children will do: Make sounds like animals make when they move through the forest. Ask the children what kind of a sound an elephant might make when it walks through the forest. Show them the potato half. Dip it into the paint, then stamp it loudly on the paper. Say that they will use art materials to make sounds like animals make in the art center.

continues . . .

Make-Believe Center

What the children will do: Use props to dress up like animals and imitate them. Tell the children you are going to pretend to be an elephant. Hold a long cardboard tube to your mouth and make an elephant sound through it, as you walk slowly. Ask the children, "Children, children what do you hear?" When they have identified the elephant, tell them they will pretend to be different animals in the make-believe center.

Have each child choose an arts activity.

Notes:

Theme of the Day:
Animal Sounds

Day 1: Music and Movement Center

What to Do:

Relate the activity to the story. Ask the children where the animals in the story lived. If they don't respond, prompt them by saying that the man in the story was called the zookeeper. How did the animals know that other animals lived in the zoo? Help them to understand that the animals heard the other animals make sounds. Say that they will think about the sounds that farm animals and zoo animals make.

MATERIALS

- Pictures of farm and zoo animals
- Book, *Polar Bear, Polar Bear, What Do You Hear?*

Introduce "Old MacDonald." Show the children a picture of a cow and ask them to make the sound a cow makes. (Model the sound if necessary.) Say that you know a song about animal sounds and that you want them to help you make the sounds of the animals and to sing with you if they know the song.

Sing "Old MacDonald Had a Farm," displaying the picture of each animal as you sing about it. Encourage the children to make the animal sounds. Encourage them to be creative in the way they make the animal sounds.

Sing "Old MacDonald Had a Zoo," displaying the animals in the book. Encourage the children to create sounds for the animals and help you sing as they become familiar with the song.

Categorize pictures by farm and zoo animals. Ask the children to help you separate the pictures into two categories—zoo animals and farm animals.

Encourage the children to take turns leading. Tell the children that it is their turn to decide which animal to sing about. They will take turns to be the leader. Ask for a volunteer to lead the activity first. Provide help if needed as the leader chooses farm or zoo animals and selects an animal picture. (Encourage older children to name both the category and the animal.) Encourage the children to sing "Old MacDonald" and make animal sounds as the leader holds up the pictures of different animals from the category she chose.

Theme of the Day:
Animal Sounds

Day 1: Art Center

What to Do:

Relate the activity to the story. Ask the children if all animals make the same sounds. Encourage them to roar like a lion, crow like a rooster, quack like a duck. Say that animals even make different sounds when they are walking. Ask them how they think an elephant would sound as it moved through the jungle. Would it make big, loud sounds? Ask someone to demonstrate how an elephant walks. Praise the child for good moving. How do they think a kangaroo would sound as it jumped along? Ask someone to demonstrate how a kangaroo moves. Praise the child. Say that that snakes are very quiet when they move. Does a snake have feet to make big stamping sounds? Can a snake jump like a kangaroo? Ask for a volunteer to show how a snake moves. Say that they will make sounds that animals might make when they are moving.

Distribute materials and demonstrate the activity. Arrange the supplies, except the toy animals, where they are easily accessible. Show the children how to put the sponges into the watery paint until they are squishy. Dab them on the paper. Say that you made the sound of a frog jumping in the water. Ask what other animal might make that sound. They might answer "duck" or "fish." Praise creative thinking. Demonstrate how to dip the potato in the paint. Jump the potato across your paper. Say that you are a kangaroo jumping across the paper.

Encourage the children to use the materials freely. Tell the children to use the materials as they wish. As they work, ask them what animal sounds they are making. Join the activity and dip a snake in the paint. Draw it across the paper. Say that your snake didn't make any sound at all! If children are interested in the crayons, say that the crayons might be chickens pecking at the ground. Strike the crayons on the paper. Ask what other sound the crayons might make.

Label the drawings. As the children finish a drawing, ask them what animal sound they made. Write their response on their paper.

Make animal footprints; elicit conversation. To extend the activity, let the children walk the plastic animals across their paintings to make "footprints" on them. Encourage them to talk about the animals: "Where is the bear going?" "The bear is walking, and what does she see?"

MATERIALS

- Sponges for painting
- Watery paint (for sponge painting)
- Potatoes, cut in half
- Several colors of paint of usual consistency, in wide containers (for potato prints)
- Toy rubber snakes
- Crayons
- Brushes
- Paper of several sizes and colors
- Small toy animal figures

Theme of the Day:
Animal Sounds

Day 1: Make-Believe Center

What to Do:

If possible, have a camera ready to take pictures of the children in their costumes.

Relate the activity to the story. Show the children the pictures at the end of the book where the children pretend to be animals. Say that the children are dressed up and they will dress up like animals too.

Help the children dress up like animals. Let each child look through the book to choose an animal to pretend to be. Show each child the props and ask the child to think of ways to make animal costumes. Provide suggestions, but allow the children to make the final decisions. Encourage talking by asking the children what they need for their costumes. Some possible suggestions might be:

- Polar bear: Use markers to make fingernails black like claws; paint face white.
- Lion: Make fingernails black like claws; paint face yellow.
- Hippopotamus: Paint face blue/gray.
- Flamingo: Paint face pink and tape feather duster to back of pants for a tail.
- Zebra: Paint black and white stripes on face.
- Boa constrictor: Use markers to make circles on the pillowcase and wear it like a tunic.
- Elephant: Paint face gray and use a long cardboard tube like a trunk.
- Leopard: Paint face yellow with black circles.
- Peacock: Color fan-shaped paper with markers and tape to back of pants like a tail.
- Walrus: Paint face purple or gray and hold two cones extending from the corners of the mouth like tusks.

Encourage the children to pretend to be animals. If they need prompting, describe things for the different animals to do, such as:

- Polar bear: A polar bear walks slowly. How could you walk like a big, slow polar bear? Make a sound like a polar bear. Now lie on your back in the snow and wiggle. That feels so good! What else could you do in the snow? You see a fish in the water. You eat fish. How could you get that fish? How would you eat the fish?

MATERIALS

- Book, *Polar Bear, Polar Bear, What Do You Hear?* (with pages marked of children dressed like animals)
- Face paint
- Washable markers
- One or more feather dusters
- One or more old pillowcases with holes cut for head and arms to fit through to wear like a tunic
- Long cardboard tubes
- Old long socks (to stuff for tails)
- Newspaper or other material to stuff socks
- Several pieces of paper folded into fans
- Two or more small cones made from white paper
- Masking tape

continues . . .

- Lion: You are a big lazy lion lying in the sun. Wag your tail slowly, slowly. Stretch your long legs. What else could you stretch? You are sleepy. How could you look sleepy? But now you are hungry. What do you do? Walk around and look for an animal to catch and eat. Where could you look? You see something! Run! Run! Catch it! What happened?
- Hippopotamus: You like the water. What could you do in the water? How do you drink the water? How do you eat the weeds in the water? Get in the water and float around. What kind of sound do you make? You sound like a happy hippopotamus!
- Flamingo: Hold your head up high. You have a long neck! Make a flamingo sound. Flamingos like to stand on one foot in the water. How could you do that? Flamingos walk around slowly in the water. They have long legs. Try to walk on your tiptoes. How would you bend over and take a drink? What could you do with your pretty tail?
- Zebra: There are flies on your back. You don't like those flies! How could you get the flies off your back with your tail? What kind of sound do you make? You eat grass. How could you pretend to eat grass like a zebra? Uh-oh, a lion is coming! What do you do? Why are you running? Don't let the lion get you!
- Boa constrictor: How could you crawl like a snake? Try to keep your tummy on the floor! Make a snake sound. A snake curls up to go to sleep. How could you curl up like a snake? Now wake up. You are hungry. You want to eat a mouse. Catch a mouse and curl your body around it. Yum! Show how you eat that mouse.
- Elephant: How could you make the tube look like an elephant trunk? What kind of sound does an elephant make? Walk around slowly and make your elephant sound. You are by some water. How could you use your trunk to take a drink?
- Leopard: Pretend this chair is a tree. Leopards sit in trees to look for food. How could you look like a leopard in a tree? What else could you use for a tree? Look down. What kind of animal do you want to eat? You jump on your food to catch it. There's a little animal! What do you do?
- Peacock: Hold your head up high. You have a long neck. Yelp, like a peacock. Call the other peacocks. You like to walk slowly and show everyone your pretty tail.
- Walrus: You like to sit on rocks in the warm sun. What could you use for a rock? Make a walrus sound. Now you are hungry. How could you dive in the water and look for some fish to eat? Swim, swim, swim. Show how you catch a fish with your mouth. Eat it up! Get out of the water and climb back on your rock. You need a nap.

Encourage the children to share their ideas with each other. They might act out their animals for each other to watch, or pretend to be animals together, giving each other suggestions for the animal movements.

Theme of the Day:
Sounds Around Us

Day 2 Group Time: Introducing the Theme of the Day

What to Do:

Discuss previous day's activities. Remind the children that the day before they thought about the sounds that animals make. Sing "Old MacDonald" and hold up the picture of the animal you choose to sing about. Encourage the children to sing and make the sound of the animal with you. Show the children the drawings they did on the previous day, and encourage them to talk about the way they pretended to be animals in the make-believe center.

Read the story. Read the book and ask the children to make the animal sounds after you, encouraging them to make up their own variations.

MATERIALS

- Fingerpaintings from previous day
- Book, *Polar Bear, Polar Bear, What Do You Hear?*
- Drum
- Crayon and piece of paper
- Picture of animal for "Old MacDonald"

Introduce the theme of the day: Sounds around us. Explain that the polar bear heard many animal sounds in the zoo. The children can hear different sounds in the classroom if they listen carefully. Tell them to be very quiet and listen to the sounds around them. After a short time, name an adult, and repeat the question from the story: "Marie, Marie, what do you hear?" The adult should name an object, imitate the sound it makes, and point to the object (if possible). An example might be a car or a fire engine. Tell the children to pretend they are that object and make the sound it makes.

Tell the children to be quiet and listen again. Repeat the question from the book, naming a child to answer it: "Lorenzo, Lorenzo, what do you hear?" The child may either name the object that makes a sound, or imitate the sound. When the child responds, show everyone the object that makes that sound (if possible). Then tell them to pretend they are the object and make the sound it makes. Allow for discussion about the object as well. Continue, giving several children turns to name sounds. Conclude by telling the children they will be listening to sounds in the centers.

Introduce the arts activities.

Music and Movement Center

What the children will do: Identify instruments that make sounds. Tap a rhythm on a drum and repeat the question from the book, "Children, children, what do you hear?" When they correctly name the drum, tell them they will play a listening game with instruments in the music center.

continues . . .

Art Center

What the children will do: Make different sounds with art tools. Tell the children to listen carefully as you tap a piece of paper with a crayon to make dots. Show them the marks the crayon made on the paper and ask them to imitate the sound the crayon made. They might make verbal sounds or tap the floor with a finger. Tell them they can make many different sounds with art tools in the art center.

Make-Believe Center

What the children will do: Listen to sounds in the school building and pretend to be the objects that made the sounds. Tell the children they will go for a walk in the building for a make-believe activity today and listen to sounds.

Have each child choose an arts activity.

Notes:

Theme of the Day:
Sounds Around Us

Day 2: Music and Movement Center

What to Do:

MATERIALS

- Musical instruments
- Large box or other object to hide things behind

Relate the activity to the story. Remind the children that the animals in the story heard sounds around them and that the sounds they heard were other animals. Say that they will hear sounds around them too, but the sounds they hear will be musical instruments.

Introduce the drum activity. Tell the children that the drum can talk to them. Say "Children, children, what do you hear?" and play a steady walking rhythm on the drum (♩ ♩ ♩ ♩ ♩ ♩ ♩ ♩). Ask them what the drum told them. Did it suggest a way to move? Ask someone to show you how the drum said to move.

Move to different drum rhythms. Tell the children that you will play the drum and they may do what it says; when you stop, they should freeze. (Explain what this means.) Say "Children, children what do you hear?" and play a walking rhythm. After an appropriate amount of time, stop. Say, "Children, children, what do you hear?" and play a running pattern. Stop. Keep changing the pattern, stopping each time and waiting until all the children freeze before you start the next pattern. Each time, chant "Children, children, what do you hear?" before you start the new rhythm. Include an uneven pattern (♩. ♪ ♩. ♪ ♩. ♪). (Teachers often have all the children move in the same direction and end the activity with a slow, measured pattern.)

Imitate the sounds of instruments; play and move freely. Invite the children to sit with you near the instruments. Tell them they will listen to the sound of an instrument and make a sound like it. As you show each instrument, discuss its size, shape, and color. Place the instruments behind you so that they will not distract the children. Show them one instrument and play a short rhythm or tune on it. Then repeat the question from the book, "what do you hear?" Compliment them for imitating the sound of the instrument; encourage them to name it. Then put it behind you and repeat with another instrument until the children are familiar with the procedure. Let each child get an instrument to play freely for a while. Encourage the children to move to the sounds they create.

Hide the instruments behind your backs. Ask the children to sit in a circle again. Tell them to hide their instruments behind their backs so you can play a game.

Take turns playing instruments. Name one child to take his instrument from behind his back and play it. Compliment the child if he plays a regular beat or creates a harmonious sound. If the child plays the instrument in an inappropriate way, show how to make a more musical sound. After the child makes the musical sound, ask, "Children, children, what do you hear?" When they name the instrument, tell the child to put it behind his back again. Repeat until everyone has had a turn.

Play instruments behind a screen. If the children are very familiar with the instruments, put all the instruments behind some type of screen, such as a large box. Ask one child to go behind the screen to play one instrument. Then ask the children, "Children, children, what do you hear?" When they name the instrument, let someone else have a turn. Praise them for being good listeners.

Theme of the Day:
Sounds Around Us

Day 2: Art Center

What to Do:

Relate the activity to the story. Remind the children that the sounds the animals heard were the sounds of other animals. Say that the sounds around them will be the sounds they make while they are drawing.

Encourage discussion of sounds made with crayons and paper. Put out crayons and paper for the children to use freely. As they draw, encourage them to talk about the sounds they are creating: "You are making big circles. What kind of sound is your crayon making? Is it a quiet sound or a loud sound?" "You're making dots. Tap, tap, tap. What other sound can your crayon make?"

MATERIALS

- Crayons
- Paper
- Materials with textured surfaces, such as sandpaper, screening, graters
- Other art materials, such as chalk, markers, scissors, glue

Show how to make marks and sounds. Join in and model other types of marks and sounds to help the children discover additional ways they can use crayons. Talk about the different ways you use the crayons, and imitate the resulting sounds: "These are zigzags (swish, swish)." "I can make lines fast (quick swishes)." "This is a winding path (r-r-r)." "I'm pressing hard."

Introduce textured materials. Introduce textured materials for the children to put under their papers. Encourage them to try to make the same types of marks on these surfaces. Prompt the children to talk about the resulting sounds and marks. Comment on what they are doing, using the words *rough* and *bumpy* often.

Encourage experimentation with surfaces throughout the room. Let the children walk around the room to find other types of surfaces to work on (both textured and smooth), such as carpeting, wood, vinyl, and windows. As they work, ask them to imitate and describe the sounds they are creating. Help them discover that rough surfaces create different sounds from smooth surfaces.

Use additional art materials. Let the children choose chalk, markers, scissors, and other art tools to work with at the table. Ask them to describe or imitate the sounds they make with these art materials. They will discover that some materials make more noise than others.

Theme of the Day:
Sounds Around Us

Day 2: Make-Believe Center

What to Do:

MATERIALS

- Pencil and paper

Relate the activity to the story. Remind the children that each animal in the story heard another animal. Say that the animals were careful listeners. Say that they will go for a walk and listen to discover what kinds of sounds they can hear.

Go for a walk. Take the children for a walk (outside, if possible), telling them to listen carefully to the sounds they hear. Ask one child at a time to name or imitate a sound that everyone can hear. Write down each sound source the children name.

Return to the classroom; imitate the sound sources. Return to the classroom and read the list of things the children heard, encouraging them to pretend to be each object when you name it. Encourage them to imitate the sound and/or pantomime it.

Theme of the Day:
Listening

Day 3 Group Time: Introducing the Theme of the Day

What to Do:

Discuss the previous day's activities. Remind the children that they listened to many different sounds on the previous day. Play a walking rhythm on the drum. Say, "Children, children, what do you hear?" Ask a child to move to the drum beat. Praise the child for listening to the drum and moving as it said. Ask the children to name things they heard on their walk and to discuss the animal sounds they made in art.

Read the story. Show the cover of the book and talk about how the polar bear used his ears and listened to the other animals. Then read the book.

Play "Do What I Say." Tell the children that you have a game for them to play. They will need to stand up and listen carefully to play this game:

Make sure everyone is looking at you. Then move your hands and describe what you are doing. "Put your hands on your head." Invite the children to do what you did. Repeat this procedure several times with other movements.

When the children are familiar with the procedure, tell them that now they must listen carefully.

Describe additional movements, but do not demonstrate the movements. If any of the children are interested, let them take turns describing movements for the others to do. If a child needs assistance as leader, an adult might whisper a movement into the child's ear for him to repeat to the others.

Introduce the theme of the day: Listening. Tell the children that they will listen in the centers today, as they did in the game.

Introduce the arts activities.

Music and Movement Center
What the children will do: Follow directions in songs. Sing "Let Ev'ry One Clap Hands Like Me," encouraging the children to do the actions you model. Include, "stamp feet," "jump high," and so on. If you are unfamiliar with this folk song, sing the words to the tune of "Skip to My Lou": "Clap, clap, clap your hands." Tell the children they can listen and move in the music and movement center.

MATERIALS

- List of things the children heard in the make-believe center on the previous day
- Book, *Polar Bear, Polar Bear, What Do You Hear?*
- Sample materials for making playdough from the art center
- Toy telephone
- Drum

continues . . .

Art Center

What the children will do: Follow directions to make playdough. Show the children some of the materials from the art center and tell them they can make their own playdough.

Make-Believe Center

What the children will do: Talk and listen with toy telephones. Show the children the toy telephone and make a ringing sound. Answer the phone and pretend to listen to someone briefly. Then say good-bye and hang up. Tell the children that the person on the phone told you they can play with toy telephones in the make-believe center.

Have each child choose an arts activity.

Notes:

Theme of the Day: Listening

Day 3: Music and Movement Center

What to Do:

MATERIALS

- Big circle on the floor (made with tape, string, or chalk)

Relate the activity to the story. Remind the children that the animals listened to the other animals and that is how they knew what other animals were in the zoo. Say that it is important to be a good listener and that it is especially important when they play music games.

Give directions for several actions. Remind the children to listen carefully as you give them several directions in relation to the circle, such as:

- Stand on the circle like a peacock.
- Walk around the circle like a polar bear.
- Stand in the circle like an ostrich.
- Stand outside of the circle like a hippopotamus.
- Jump into the circle like a kangaroo.

Ask the children to suggest other movements for everyone to do. Praise them for being good listeners.

Sing song, "In and out the Circle." Tell the children to listen carefully as you sing a song. The song will tell them things to do with the circle. Sing the following words to the tune of "London Bridge Is Falling Down" and move to the words with the children:

Let's sit in the circle
In the circle, in the circle
Let's sit in the circle
Now stand up!

Let's walk around the circle
Around the circle, around the circle
Let's walk around the circle
Now step in!

Let's jump in the circle
In the circle, in the circle
Let's jump in the circle
Now sit down!

Step out of the circle (spoken)

Repeat the song and have the children try to follow the words without an adult modeling the movements. Stress that they need to listen to know what to do. Include different words to the song. Verses: *Walk all around the circle; Run all around the circle; Jump in the circle; Stand on the circle; Now sit in the circle.*

Sing, "If You're Happy," using motions. Ask the children to stand for this song. (If a child is unable to stand, adapt the words accordingly.) Sing "If You're Happy" and clap with the children. Then tell the children to listen carefully as you sing additional verses describing other movements. Do not model the movements unless the children have trouble following your directions. Some movements might include: turn around; shake your head; close your eyes; jump up high; touch your toes; stamp your feet. Ask the children to suggest other movements.

Theme of the Day: Listening

Day 3: Art Center

What to Do:

Relate the activity to the story. Remind the children that if the animals hadn't listened, they wouldn't have known there were other animals in the zoo. Listening to what other people say is very important, so they will listen to what you tell them and make their own playdough.

Encourage each child to help make playdough. Name a different child to do each of the following steps, giving help whenever a child needs it:

- Measure 2 cups flour and put it in the bowl.
- Measure 1 cup salt and put it in the bowl.
- Everyone put your hands in the bowl and mix the flour and salt.
- Put about 5 drops of food coloring in the water.
- Stir the water and food coloring with the spoon.
- Pour the water into the bowl with the flour and salt mixture in it.
- Everyone put your hands in the bowl and mix the dough. (If it is too dry, add water.)

As the children work, prompt them to talk about what they are doing, how it feels to wait for a turn, what the playdough feels like at different steps of the procedure, what colors they would like to make the playdough, and what they could do with the playdough.

Encourage discussion as the children play with the playdough. Let each child remove a piece of playdough from the bowl and use it, again encouraging them to talk about what they are doing.

MATERIALS

- Measuring cups: 1 cup and ½ cup
- Salt (at least 1 cup)
- Flour (at least 2 cups)
- Water in a pitcher (½ cup)
- Food coloring
- Large bowl
- Spoon

Theme of the Day: Listening

Day 3: Make-Believe Center

What to Do:

MATERIALS

- Two or more toy telephones
- Housekeeping center
- Paper and pencil
- Old phone books (if available)

Relate the activity to the story. Ask the children how the zoo keeper knew that the children were acting like animals. Help them to understand that he listened. Say that they are going to pretend to listen to someone talking on the telephone.

Show how you talk on the telephone. Put the phones in different locations in the housekeeping center. Tell the children they can use them to talk to each other. Model this by making a ringing sound and answering one of the phones. Answer by saying, "Hello, this is (your name)." Then hand the phone to one of the children and say, "It's for you." When the child takes the phone, pick up the other phone and initiate a conversation: "Hi, Carla, can you come to my house? We can play outside. What else could we do?" Encourage the child to say something in response. If the child needs prompting, suggest something for her to say. Then hand the receiver to another child and invite him to say something.

Encourage the children to play in the housekeeping center and talk to each other on the phones. As they play, join in again and show how to write information on paper: "Tell me where you live. I will write it down." Encourage the children to pretend to write information and phone messages.

Give directions over the phone. Encourage careful listening by giving directions over the phone, such as, "Hello, Jana, please give Jorge a broom to use." Encourage the children to give each other directions over the phones too.

Pretend to look up phone numbers. If old phone books are available, show how you use them to look up phone numbers. Then ask the children to pretend to look up phone numbers: "Brian, whose phone number do you want to look for in the phone book?"

Theme of the Day:
Listening

Day 4 Group Time: Introducing the Theme of the Day

What to Do:

Review the previous day's activities. Talk with the children about the listening activities they did on the previous day. Show them the playdough they made by listening to directions. Ask them to tell how they made the playdough. Sing, "If You're Happy," telling them to listen and do what the song says. Show them the telephones they used for listening in the make-believe center, and encourage them to describe what they did.

Read the story. Before you turn each page, ask if the children can tell you what sound the animal heard.

Introduce the theme of the day: Listening. Give one of the children a two-part direction such as, "Tyler, go to the toy shelf and bring me back a red car." When the child returns to the circle with the car, thank him for being a good listener. Ask the other children how Tyler knew what to do. Help them to understand that he listened. Remind them that the animals in the book listened carefully, and that's how they knew what animal was next to them. They can do more listening activities in the centers today.

MATERIALS

- **Playdough from the previous day**
- **Toy telephone**
- **Book, *Polar Bear, Polar Bear, What Do You Hear?***
- **Large appliance box from make-believe center**
- **Stick to use as a baton**
- **Container of art materials**

Introduce the arts activities.

Music and Movement Center
What the children will do: Take turns being the leader of the band to show the other children how to play their instruments fast and slow. Show them the stick. Say that you are pretending that it is a baton and that is what music leaders use. Have them sing a song they know well as you wave the baton. Say they will use the baton to show the other children how to play their instruments fast or slow in the music center.

Art Center
What the children will do: Tell each other what art tools to use. Place the box of art materials where the children can see it. Have another adult tell you which one to use: "Make a mark on the paper with the piece of chalk." Inform the children they can tell each other what art tools to use in the art center.

Make-Believe Center
What the children will do: Continue phone play, adding a phone booth. Show the children the appliance box and tell them they can use it in the make-believe center.

Have each child choose an arts activity.

Theme of the Day: Listening

Day 4: Music and Movement Center

What to Do:

MATERIALS

- Cassette player/blank audio tape
- Musical instruments
- Podium (box or stool)
- Stick, to use as a baton

Relate the activity to the story. Remind the children that the animals in the story listened to each other. Ask what the zookeeper heard at the end of the story. Praise them for listening to what you asked and for knowing that the zookeeper heard the children. In the music activity they will listen to sounds you make and then make the same sounds. They will be like the children in the story who listened to the animals and then made the same sounds the animals made.

Copy the sounds. Tell the children to listen while you make another kind of sound. Slap your thighs fast with the palms of your hands. Ask the children to make the same sound. After they have made this fast sound, slap your thighs very slowly, and ask them to make that slow sound. Make this into a game by asking one child at a time to slap his thighs fast or slow for the others to copy.

Repeat this procedure with another movement, such as clapping your hands, tapping your chest, or tapping the floor with your feet while sitting.

Identify the sounds by listening. After several rounds of clapping, tapping your feet, and/or slapping your thigh, invite the children to close their eyes. Say that you want them to listen and then tell you how you made a sound. Clap your hands. Ask if anyone can tell what you did to make the sound. Repeat with several of the other movements.

Discuss *conductor;* select instruments. Have the children sit on the floor with you. Tell the children that people often play musical instruments together for other people to listen to, but that when people play music together they need a leader. This leader is called the *conductor.* The conductor usually stands on something (a podium) so everyone can see him. He uses a stick called a *baton.* Encourage the children to get an instrument to play. Have them put their instruments on the floor in front of them.

Take turns being conductors. Stand on the podium and lift up the baton. Tell them that when you do this, they should pick up their instruments. Practice several times. Then move the stick fast (they should play fast) and move the stick slowly (they should play slowly). Let each child who wishes to participate have a turn being the leader of the band.

Record the sounds and play them back for the children to listen to.

Theme of the Day: Listening

Day 4: Art Center

What to Do:

Relate the activity to the story. Ask the children if they have ever listened to sounds at a zoo. What do they think they would hear at the zoo? Suggest that the children in the story were playing a game. They listened to the animals and then pretended to be the animals. Say that they will play a drawing game. They will listen so they know what to do.

Play a drawing game. Prompt each child to get a piece of paper. Remind them to listen carefully. Then name a type of art tool for them to find in the box to use. For example, you might say, "Find a red crayon in the box. Draw with the red crayon on your paper."

MATERIALS

- Paper
- Box containing three or four types of art supplies, such as crayons, chalk, glue, pieces of yarn
- Large piece of butcher paper for children to decorate together

Continue the game using different art tools. After a short time, tell them to put the art tool back in the box and take out a different tool. "Put your red crayon in the box. Now find a green marker." Continue in this way with several art tools.

Allow children to take turns giving instructions. When the children are familiar with the procedure, invite them to name things for each other to take out of the box to use. To avoid confusion, let one child at a time name an art tool, and have the children put the tools back in the box each time.

Add items that the children name. Ask the children to name other things they might add to the box. Help them find the things they named (or explain why they cannot use any inappropriate things they named). Continue the game with these additional art tools.

Work on a large piece of paper using items that the children name. Extend the activity by letting the children use the art tools to work on a large piece of butcher paper together, following the above procedure. Let one child at a time name a type of art tool for everyone to use on the paper.

Theme of the Day: Listening

Day 4: Make-Believe Center

What to Do:

Relate the activity to the story. Remind the children that the way the children in the story knew what kind of sounds to make was by listening to the animals. Say that when people talk on the telephone, they have to listen to know what the other person is saying, but sometimes when they are away from home they have to find a special telephone to use to call the person. Show the children the picture of the phone booth. Discuss where they might see a phone booth and ask them to share their own experiences with phone booths. Tell the children they will make a phone booth and then pretend to make calls on the telephone.

MATERIALS

- Materials used for phone play on previous day
- Large appliance box with one side removed
- Child-sized chair
- Markers or crayons
- Picture of phone booth (optional)

Decorate a pretend phone booth. Stand the appliance box with the open side facing the children and tell them they can make it into a pretend phone booth. Show them how they can go in and out of the box through the open side. Invite them to use the markers to decorate the box before they set it up as a phone booth.

Place a phone and a chair in the booth. After the phone booth is decorated, place the phone and chair in it and pretend to call one of the children.

Make calls from the phone booth. Put the phone booth near the housekeeping center and encourage the children to pretend to call each other.

Encourage pretend play involving telephones. Encourage the children to expand play in this center by pretending to drive a car or take a bus or cab from the phone booth to the housekeeping center after you make a call home: "Hello, Jill, I am coming home now. What should I buy at the store? Okay, good-bye." (Children may enjoy setting up chairs like a bus and pretend to ride home on the bus.)

Theme of the Day:
Pizza Parlor

Day 5 Group Activity

What to Do:

Set up the materials on a table that is off to one side of the room.

Relate the activity to the story. Remind the children that they have been hearing a story about a zoo all week. Ask if anyone has ever been to a zoo. Encourage discussion of their experiences. Ask if they ate anything when they were at the zoo. Did they take food with them, or did they buy something? State that some zoos have food for people to eat while they are there. Say that they are going to pretend that there's a place to get pizza at the zoo.

Discuss pizza. Sit with the children and ask if they have ever eaten pizza. Let them discuss pizza—what kinds they like, what toppings they like, experiences they have had ordering or making pizzas.

MATERIALS

- **Setting for telephone play used in make-believe center on previous days**
- **Red paper circles, about the size of pizzas**
- **Construction paper**
- **Scissors**
- **Glue**
- **Stuffed wild animal, any kind**
- **Toy cash register**

Sing a song about pizza. Teach the children the following words to the tune of "Apples and Bananas":

I like to eat, eat, eat, eat.
I like to eat pepperoni pizza.
I like to eat, eat, eat, eat.
I like to eat pepperoni pizza.

Add other verses to the song, based on the types of pizza the children mentioned during the discussion.

Make pretend pizzas. Show the children the paper circles and tell them they can pretend to work in a pizza parlor at the zoo and make pizza. Demonstrate cutting shapes out of construction paper and pasting them to a circle to add toppings to a pizza.

Add the telephone to the pizza parlor. Suggest that the zoo is very large and if you get hungry in one part of the zoo, you can go into a telephone booth to call to order your pizza. Use a toy telephone in the telephone booth and pretend to order a pizza over the phone. Say that you are near the elephants and are very hungry. Then ask one of the children to deliver the paper pizza.

continues . . .

Suggestions for Implementing Pizza Parlor:

Ask the children to choose whether they would like to work in the pizza parlor, making and delivering pizzas, or go to the place where the (name a stuffed animal) is and order pizzas.

In the pizza parlor:

- Have a toy telephone available for the children to take pizza orders.
- Let them cut free-form shapes to add to the red paper circles as they wish. If they are not yet able to cut with scissors, children can tear off small pieces of paper to glue to the pretend pizzas.
- Put in a cash register for walk-in customers.
- Suggest that children pretend to deliver pizzas to homes.

From somewhere in the zoo:

- Model ordering a pizza on the phone to be delivered.
- Invite children to seat dolls at a pretend picnic table and serve them pizza.
- Suggest that they pretend to clear away their paper plates and napkins and throw them in the trash after eating.
- Model getting ready to go to the place that sells pizza. Purchase the pizza and eat it there.

Notes:

SKILLS & GOALS MATRIX

Polar Bear, Polar Bear, What Do You Hear?

	Skills or Behaviors	Goals and Objectives
Cognitive	• Show understanding of *fast* and *slow, loud* and *quiet, rough* and *smooth*	• Increase general concept and vocabulary development • Increase understanding of opposites
	• Match sounds to pictures of animals and to instruments	• Increase ability to combine like objects • Increase auditory discrimination • Increase visual discrimination
	• Predict actions and sounds in a familiar book	• Increase general reasoning and problem-solving ability • Increase understanding of story structure
	• Sort animals into zoo vs. farm animals	• Increase ability to sort objects by categories • Increase rational counting ability
Language	• Identify and imitate animal sounds from a familiar story	• Increase auditory discrimination • Increase oral-motor awareness and coordination • Increase awareness of environmental sounds
	• Follow directions involving two different actions	• Increase receptive vocabulary • Increase ability to follow two-step directions
	• Use reading and writing in routine activities and in play	• Increase receptive and expressive vocabulary • Increase awareness of functional use of language • Increase exposure to reading and writing process
Social	• Have pretend conversations on the telephone	• Increase appropriate conversational skills in routine social situations • Increase turn-taking abilities
	• Sing a song with others	• Increase participation as member of a group
	• Take turns leading a group action	• Increase ability to assume group leadership role • Increase turn-taking ability • Increase appropriate social behaviors with adult supervision
	• Participate in making suggestions for group activity	• Increase ability to speak up in a group setting • Increase appropriate verbal interactions with peers

SKILLS & GOALS MATRIX (CONT.)

	Skills or Behaviors	Goals and Objectives
Fine-Motor	• Copy clapping sounds made by others	• Increase bimanual coordination • Increase ability to imitate movements
	• Work with playdough	• Increase hand strength, wrist rotation, manipulation skills • Increase tactile awareness
	• Pat, scratch, clap, tap with hands and art tools	• Increase wrist rotation • Increase visual-motor coordination • Refine manipulation
	• Paint with sponges, potato halves, brushes	• Increase bilateral coordination • Increase visual-motor coordination • Increase tactile awareness
Gross-Motor	• To move different body parts when given directions in a song	• Increase motor planning and control • Increase dynamic balance • Increase awareness of body parts
	• Move to different drum rhythms	• Increase gross-motor planning and control • Increase auditory attention • Increase body awareness
	• Imitate the movement of animals in a story	• Increase motor planning and control • Increase dynamic and static balance • Increase ability to imitate movement
	• Follow directions for doing different animal actions	• Increase motor planning and control • Increase movement repertoire • Increase awareness of body in space

STORY OF THE WEEK / EL CUENTO DE ESTA SEMANA

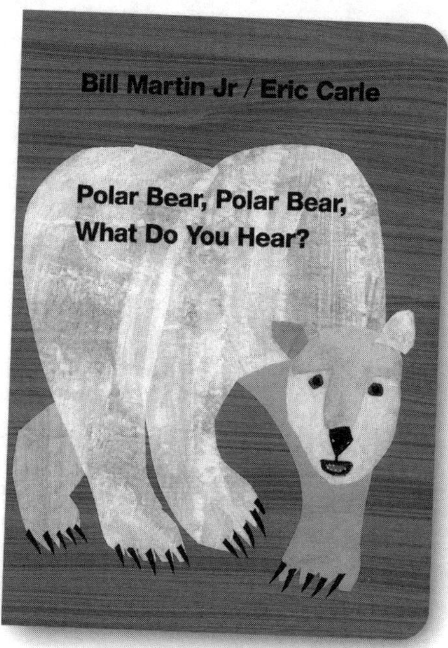

Bill Martin Jr / Eric Carle
Polar Bear, Polar Bear,
What Do You Hear?

Polar Bear, Polar Bear, What Do You Hear?

by Bill Martin

Edición en español: *Oso polar, oso polar ¿qué es ese ruído?*

The Spark story this week is *Polar Bear, Polar Bear, What Do You Hear?* This book has many colorful illustrations of animals and may be available at the library. Each animal in the story is asked what it hears. Then at the end of the book, children dressed like animals make the animal sounds. It is very important when getting children ready for kindergarten to develop their listening skills. These skills are the main focus of the week. Ask your child to name some of the animals in the story (polar bear, lion, hippopotamus, flamingo, zebra, boa constrictor, elephant, leopard, peacock, and walrus). The themes to go with this story are *animal sounds, sounds around us,* and *listening.*

El cuento de Spark de esta semana se llama *Oso polar, oso polar ¿qué es ese ruído?* Este libro tiene muchas ilustraciones de colores sobre los animales. En el cuento se le pregunta a cada animal qué escucha. Luego, al final del libro, los niños vestidos como animales hacen los sonidos de los animales. Es muy importante cuando los niños se están preparando para el jardín de infancia, que los mismos desarrollen sus habilidades para escuchar. En esta semana nos concentraremos en estas habilidades. Pídale a su niño o niña que nombre algunos de los animales del cuento (un oso polar, un león, un hipopótamo, un flamingo, una cebra, una culebra, un elefante, un leopardo, un pavo real y una foca). Las ideas temáticas de este cuento son: *sonidos de animales, sonidos en nuestro ambiente* y *escuchar.*

© 2001 The Board of Trustees of the University of Illinois. May be reproduced for use by teachers.

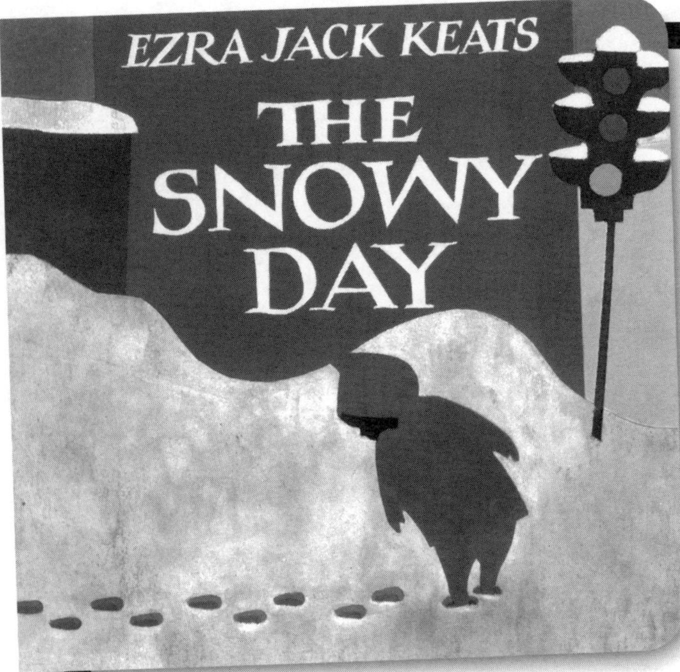

The Snowy Day

by Ezra Jack Keats

New York: Viking Press, 1962

Story Synopsis: *The Snowy Day* is a children's classic. It is a very simple story about a little boy named Peter who awakened one day to find that snow had fallen during the night. Peter went outside to play in the snow and did many things. He saw older children playing and wished he could play with them. He made a snowball and tried to save it for another day. Children can easily relate to this story since they also are too young to play some of the games older children play and wish they could save snow for another day.

Classroom Use: This unit is most successful if there is snow outdoors. If you live in a region of the country that seldom has snow, you can still use this unit with your children by substituting shaving cream, frost from a freezer, and/or shredded paper for snow. Teachers in the southern states have reported that the unit is an excellent way to increase southern children's understanding of the concept of snow. This unit may be linked to other stories about cold weather or families. The themes and concepts for this unit are *snow, covered, melt,* and *making a story.*

Considerations: This story is simple and easy to understand. It is a story to which children can easily relate.

Special Materials: In addition to the materials typically found in the preschool classroom, this unit suggests the use of Epsom salts for one of the art activities.

ACTIVITY MATRIX

The Snowy Day

Day	Concept	Music Activity	Art Activity	Make-Believe Activity
Day 1	Snow (Cognitive)	Make and tape quiet sounds.	Squirt paint or food coloring on snow.	Walk on footprints and make tracks in pretend snow.
Day 2	Covered (Cognitive, Language)	Pretend to cover body with outdoor clothing to song. Tape song.	Cover things with Epsom salts snow.	Play in pretend snow.
Day 3	Melt (Cognitive, Language, Science)	Pretend to be melting snowman, sing songs about melting snow.	Paint with melting ice.	Play with frozen and melting snow.
Day 4	Making a Story (Cognitive, Language, Preliteracy)	Tell stories that they hear in songs.	Make a book.	Make up stories about toy people.
Day 5	Snowy Fun			

Theme of the Day:
Snow

Day 1 Group Time: Introducing the Book

What to Do:

This unit is most successful if there is snow outdoors. If there is no snow outdoors, scrape frost from a freezer or shred ice in a blender or food processor to make artificial snow.

Read the story. Read the story, then go back through the book to look at the pictures with the children and ask them to describe the things that Peter saw outdoors—piles of snow, tracks in the snow, trees without leaves, snowballs, hills, the shining sun, snow falling.

Compare the illustrations to the view out the window. Ask the children if what they see outside the school looks the same as the scenes in the book. Let them look out windows and describe things they see. Emphasize the word *winter* as the children make their observations. If there is no snow, explain that sometimes there is snow in the winter and sometimes there isn't. Encourage them to name things they see that look the same as the illustrations in the book, such as bare trees, and things that look different. Encourage careful observations—ask them to describe how the grass looks, name animals they see, describe what the sky looks like and how people are dressed.

Introduce the theme of the day: Snow. Let the children feel the snow in the container. Ask them to tell how it feels and looks. Does it have an odor? Does it make a sound? Emphasize the cold feeling of the snow. Tell the children they will think about *snow* in the centers today.

Introduce the arts activities.

Music and Movement Center
What the children will do: Make very quiet sounds like the ones made by falling snow. Show the page from the book that displays Peter and his friend going out into the falling snow and discuss the fact that snow is falling from the sky. Give some shredded paper to each child, and tell the children to pretend that it is falling snow. Show them how to hold the paper up high and drop it as if it were snow falling to the ground. Suggest that they stay very quiet as they drop the snow again. Ask what kind of sound the pretend snow made as it fell. Say that real falling snow is very quiet. Tell them that they will make quiet sounds in the music and movement center, like the ones made by falling snow.

MATERIALS

- Book, *The Snowy Day*
- Container of snow for children to feel
- Shredded paper
- Squirt bottle filled with paint or food coloring mixture from the art center
- Piece of "footprint paper" from the make-believe center

continues . . .

Art Center
What the children will do: Use squirt bottles to paint snow. Demonstrate forming some snow into a ball and then squirting paint (food coloring) on another clump of snow; tell the children they can make clumps of snow and squirt paint or food coloring on it in the art center.

Make-Believe Center
What the children will do: Pretend to walk in footprints in the snow. Show the children a sheet of "foot-print paper," and tell them to pretend that the marks are footprints in snow. Ask one child to walk along the footprints on the paper, and tell everyone to pretend the child is Peter walking in the snow. Say that they can walk on the footprints in the make-believe center.

Have each child choose an arts activity.

Notes:

Theme of the Day: Snow

Day 1: Music and Movement Center

What to Do:

MATERIALS

- Small amount of shredded paper for each child
- Cassette recorder and blank tape
- Assorted musical instruments
- Recorded music that is quiet, such as the Pachelbel Canon in D

Relate the activity to the story. Ask the children if they have ever been outside when it is snowing (if they live in a geographic area where snow is commonplace). Encourage them to discuss their snow experiences. Say that falling snow is very quiet and that they will make quiet sounds like the snow.

Record quiet sounds of shredded paper falling. Place the shredded paper where it is easily accessible, telling the children to get a handful of paper. Join the children in the activity. Model holding the paper high and then dropping it and watching it flutter to the floor. Say that you are pretending that the paper is snow falling. Use the cassette recorder to record the sounds of the paper falling. Play the tape and ask the children to tell what they hear. Discuss why they cannot hear the paper falling—it is very quiet, like falling snow.

Find items around the room that fall quietly; record sounds. Ask the children to look around the room for other things that might make quiet sounds when they fall. Let them experiment with the objects they find to discover whether or not they make a sound when they fall. Help them record the sounds. Listen to the tape and compare the sounds to the quiet of the falling paper. Is anything else as quiet as the paper?

Experiment with the sounds of the musical instruments. Play musical instruments with the children, saying such things as, "I just made a very quiet (or loud) sound!" Show how to make a sound with an instrument so quietly that it can barely be heard. Tell the children that you are playing quietly, like falling snow. Invite them to play quietly the way you did.

Invite the children to use the cassette recorder to record sounds they make. Encourage them to make sounds that are so quiet the tape recorder does not record them.

End the activity by moving quietly to music. Ask the children to show you how they can move very quietly. Encourage creative movement. If no one tiptoes, model the movement. Tell the children that you will play some quiet music, and you want them to move as quietly as they can to the music.

Theme of the Day: Snow

Day 1: Art Center

What to Do:

This activity can take place indoors, using containers of snow, or outdoors in a snow-covered area.

Relate the activity to the story. State that Peter played outside in the snow. Ask if they remember what Peter made in the snow (footprints, tracks, a snowman, and an angel). They will make things with snow, as Peter did.

MATERIALS

- Containers filled with snow
- Brightly colored watery paint or food coloring in squirt bottles
- Styrofoam trays

Make shapes with snow. If you are indoors, invite each child to get a handful of snow and a Styrofoam tray. If you are outdoors, tell each child to pick up some snow. Show how to use the snow to make balls and other shapes, both recognizable (triangles, "snakes," and so on) and free-form shapes. As you work, talk about how the snow feels and why it is melting.

Squirt snow with paint. If you are indoors, give the children more snow to put on their trays. If you are outdoors, have them spread out to work with the snow on the ground. Show the children how to squirt the paint directly on the snow to make art creations. Join in and model using the squirt bottles to create different effects:

- Squirt streams of paint by squeezing a long time.
- Squirt short spurts of paint by squeezing and releasing quickly.
- Shake the bottle to create drips of paint.

Outdoors, paint with your whole arm. If you are outdoors, show how to move your arm in different ways as you squirt the paint:

- Move your whole arm in a big circular motion.
- Move your whole arm in a small circular motion.
- Rotate your wrist to move only your hand.
- Move your arm from side to side, crossing the midline of your body.
- Move your arm forward and back—away from your body and toward your body.
- Move your arm up and down.
- Hold a bottle in each hand and squirt both of them.

Discuss painting. As the children paint, encourage them to talk about the figures they are creating. Do not expect them to make representational figures (a dog, a house). Rather, prompt them to talk about the different kinds of lines and visual effects they are making:

"You made wiggly lines. How did you do that?"

"You made circles here. What kind of shape did you make here?"

"What happened when you stepped on your painting?"

"You made dots. How could you make lines?"

If you are outdoors, ask the children to name other things they would like to squirt with the paint. Tell them whether or not it is all right to paint each thing they name, and allow them to paint the appropriate objects.

Theme of the Day: Snow

Day 1: Make-Believe Center

What to Do:

On one sheet of butcher paper, use the marker to make a trail of child-sized footprints before the activity begins.

Relate the activity to the story. Remind the children that when Peter walked in the snow, his feet made footprints. Say that they will walk on footprints and make tracks in pretend snow.

Walk along footprints on paper. Place the butcher paper with the footprints on the floor and tell the children to pretend it is a trail of footprints in the snow. Walk along the trail, matching your steps to the footprints on the paper and inviting the children to join you. Tell them to pretend that they are Peter walking in the snow. Remind them that Peter also walked with his toes pointed out and then his toes pointed in. Model these movements. Have the children walk around with their toes pointed out or in.

Make additional footprint trails to walk along. Spray shaving cream on another large piece of butcher paper. Remind the children that Peter also made marks by dragging his feet in the snow. Show them the illustrations in the book that display Peter dragging his feet in the snow. Ask how many tracks there were after he found the stick. Ask the children to help you make more footprints in the snow by walking on the piece of butcher paper on which you have sprayed shaving cream. Tell them you will drag a marker behind them to make the third track. Encourage them to walk along the paper as you drag the marker. Let them decide where to walk, making twisting and straight paths on the papers.

Have the children outline each other's footprints. Encourage the children to make their own footprint trails by outlining each other's feet on fresh sheets of butcher paper. Do not expect the children to outline the footprints accurately. Assist them as needed.

Walk along the footprint trails. When you have completed several footprint trails, ask the children to arrange them on the floor, and walk along them.

Rearrange the footprint trails. After the children have walked on the original trails, suggest that they rearrange the footprint trails in different ways and walk along them.

MATERIALS

- Book, *The Snowy Day*
- Shaving cream
- Black markers
- Large sheets of white butcher paper

Theme of the Day:
Covered

Day 2 Group Time: Introducing the Theme of the Day

What to Do:

Review the previous day's activities. Play the tape of quiet sounds the children recorded on the previous day, and talk about how they made the sounds. Discuss the quiet sounds; compare them to falling snow. Ask the children how they painted snow in the art center. Discuss the footprint trails that they walked on in the make-believe center.

Read the story. Read the story, asking the children to name things that are covered with snow in each picture.

Take an outdoor walk to name things covered with snow. Tell the children that you will take a walk outside to see things that are covered with snow. (If you live in an area without snow, ask the children to suggest items that would be covered with snow if you had snow.) As the children put on outdoor clothes, ask them why they need warm clothes in winter. Then during the outdoor walk, encourage the children to use all their senses (safely!) to learn about winter. Ask them to tell how the wind feels on their faces, what colors they see, what sounds they hear, what they see in the sky, what smells they notice. Also have them look around and name things that are covered with snow, such as the ground, bushes, trees, steps, cars. (If you do not go outdoors, have the children look out windows and name things that are—or could be—covered with snow.)

Introduce the theme of the day: Covered. Go indoors (or have the children move away from the window), and have everyone sit down. Ask them to name all the things they can remember that were covered with snow outdoors. Tell them they will cover things in the centers today.

Introduce the arts activities.

Music and Movement Center

What the children will do: Pantomime getting dressed to go outside in cold weather. Get in a huddled position and pretend to shiver. Tell the children that you are pretending to be cold, and you need to cover yourself to feel warm. Pantomime putting on a coat as you explain that a coat will make you feel warm when you play in the snow. Then place the sheet on the floor, and tell the children to pretend it is snow covering the ground. Tell them they can pretend to put on outdoor clothes to a song in the music and movement center today.

MATERIALS

- Tape of quiet sounds recorded by the children on the previous day
- Book, *The Snowy Day*
- White sheet or large piece of white fabric
- Container with Epsom salts and glitter mixture from the art center
- Piece of paper
- Paintbrush
- Several handfuls of shredded paper

continues . . .

Art Center

What the children will do: Cover paper and box houses with pretend snow. Dip a brush in the Epsom salts and glitter mixture and shake the paint brush so that the mixture spatters on the paper. As you work, talk to the children about how the snow is falling on the ground and covering the ground. Tell them they can cover paper and other things with pretend snow in the art center.

Make-Believe Center

What the children will do: Cover the floor with paper snow and pretend to be Peter in the story. Drop some shredded paper on the floor and walk through it with your toes pointing in, as Peter did in the story. Remind the children that Peter walked like this, and ask them to walk this way too. Tell them that in make-believe they can cover the floor with paper snow, and do some things that Peter did.

Have each child choose an arts activity.

Notes:

Theme of the Day: Covered

Day 2: Music and Movement Center

What to Do:

Relate the activity to the story. Remind the children that Peter went outside to play in the snow, but that when he first saw the snow he was wearing his pajamas. Did he go outside in his pajamas? Why not? What did he put on when he went outside? If necessary, refer to the cover of the book. Say they will pretend to get ready to go outside in the snow.

Pantomime to a song. Ask the children to pretend to put on a coat while you sing the following words to the tune of "Skip to My Lou," pantomiming the actions with the children.

Putting on coats to go outside,
Putting on coats to go outside,
Putting on coats to go outside
'Cause it is cold outside!

MATERIALS

- Book, *The Snowy Day*
- Coat, hat, gloves, boots, or other outdoor clothes
- Cassette player
- Blank tape

Name outdoor clothes. Ask the children to name other things they wear when it is cold outside. If they need reminders, show them the outdoor clothes. When they name each article of clothing, ask them to tell what part of their body they cover with it.

Pantomime children's suggestions to the song. Sing the "Putting on coats" song several times, using outdoor clothes the children named. Sing about a different piece of outdoor clothing each time, and encourage the children to pantomime putting on that type of clothing along with you.

Tape the song. Show the children the cassette player/recorder and explain that they can make a tape of the song using the coat words first. Invite them to sing along with you if they choose to do so. Whenever you hold up the coat during the song, they should shout, "coat," as loudly as they can. After the children sing a verse about the coat, play the tape for them to hear.

Listen to the tape and pantomime putting on clothes. Record several verses of the song, using the other outdoor clothes, with the children shouting the names of the clothes as they occur in the song. Play the tape for the children to listen to, inviting them to pantomime putting on the clothes as they listen.

Theme of the Day: Covered

Day 2: Art Center

What to Do:

To make the Epsom salts solution, dissolve 1 cup of Epsom salts in 1 cup of water.

Relate the activity to the story. Remind the children that when Peter looked out of his window he saw snow all over everything. It covered the ground and the roofs of houses. Say that they will cover objects with pretend snow.

Add glitter to the Epsom salts solution. Show the children how to add glitter to the Epsom salts solution and stir it with paintbrushes. The mixture needs to be stirred well. (The Epsom salts will sparkle when the mixture dries; glitter causes the mixture to sparkle right away.)

MATERIALS

- Containers of Epsom salts solution
- Glitter
- Paper
- Large brushes
- Small boxes
- People figures
- Toy cars (optional)
- Measuring cup

Cover papers with Epsom salts mixture. Have each child get a piece of paper and a brush. Show how to shake a brush to spatter the mixture on paper and how to spread the mixture with the brush. As the children work, talk about how they are covering their papers with pretend snow.

Spatter "snow" on the box buildings. Prompt the children to get boxes, and tell them to pretend the boxes are buildings and spatter "snow" on them. Tell them to cover their buildings with snow.

Play with toy people and cars around the buildings. When the buildings dry, show how to move the toy people around, pretending that they find snow on their houses. The children may want "snow" to fall on toy cars and other objects. (This mixture is washable.)

Make more Epsom salts solution. You can also help children make more of the Epsom salts solution if they run out.

Theme of the Day: Covered

Day 2: Make-Believe Center

What to Do:

Relate the activity to the story. Remind the children that Peter got dressed in very warm clothes and then went outside to play in the snow. Say that they will dress up and pretend to play in snow as Peter did.

Cover the floor with pretend snow. Give the children paper and show how to tear it up to make more snow. Have them sprinkle the shredded paper on the floor, as you talk about how they are covering the floor with pretend snow. As they work, state that real snow is very cold.

Dress up in winter clothes. Have the children choose dress-up clothes and pretend to get dressed for playing in the snow. Talk about the types of clothes they need for snow play, such as coats, hats, mittens, and scarves. Have them pretend to put on any items they do not have in the dress-up clothes.

Walk in pretend snow like Peter. Tell the children to pretend to go outdoors to look at the snow covering the ground. Then have them walk in the pretend snow as Peter did. Demonstrate some of the things Peter did in the snow for the children to try:

- Walk with toes pointing out.
- Walk with toes pointing in.
- Drag feet through the snow.
- Pretend to drag a stick in the snow.
- Make a pile of snow, like a snowman.
- Make snow angels.
- Make a snowball.

Move in other ways in the pretend snow. Put out the dolls, pretend sled, shovels, and other available props. Encourage the children to use the props to find more ways of moving around in the snow. Model some actions if the children need prompting:

- Pull dolls on pretend sleds.
- Shovel the snow into piles and sit in the piles.
- Roll around in the snow.
- Crumple together lots of paper to make a large ball.

As the children participate, ask questions that will promote conversation: "How did you make that big pile of snow? Tell Tina how you did that." "You covered the chair with snow. What else can you cover with snow?"

Remove outdoor clothes. After the children have played for a while, show how you go indoors and remove outdoor clothing to do indoor activities.

MATERIALS

- Some shredded paper (either white scrap paper or newspaper)
- Additional paper for children to tear apart for more snow
- Dress-up clothes or scraps of fabric (if possible, include such items as hats, scarves, mittens)
- Large heavy piece of cardboard with rope tied to one end, like a sled
- Dolls
- Other props for pretend snow play, such as shovels

Theme of the Day:
Melt

Day 3 Group Time: Introducing the Theme of the Day

What to Do:

Review the previous day's activities. Ask the children to tell about things they saw on their walk and to name some things they saw that were covered with snow. Sing "Putting on coats" from the music and movement center activity, and show the papers and box houses that they covered with snow in the art center. Encourage discussion of the way they covered the floor with paper snow in the make-believe center.

Read the story. Then discuss what happened to Peter's snowball. Why wasn't it still in Peter's pocket? Where did it go? Tell the children that the snow melted, and discuss what that means.

Go outdoors, and put snow in bags. If possible, take the children outdoors and give everyone a paper bag. Let each child put some snow in his paper bag, and print the child's name on the bag. Then return to the classroom. (If it is impossible to go outdoors or if there is no snow, put some snow or ice shavings in a bag for each child.)

Place the bags around the room. When you are all back indoors, tell the children to pretend the bags are Peter's pockets. Remind them that Peter put snow in his pocket and it melted. Ask them to think of different places to put the bags of snow, encouraging a variety of storage conditions—sunny, shady, cold (refrigerator), very cold (freezer), very warm (heating vent). Emphasize the terms *cold, hot,* and *melt,* and encourage the children to use these words too. The concept of melting is difficult for young children to understand, so do not expect the children to be fully aware of what will happen to the snow. However, by drawing their attention to melting snow, you will help them become more familiar with this natural occurrence.

Introduce the theme of the day: Melting. Tell the children to leave their bags of snow in the storage areas while they go to the centers. Say that while they are in the centers, they will think about *melting,* and maybe the snow in their bags will melt too. (After they finish working at each center, let the children check their bags and compare the rates at which the snow is melting under the different conditions. During the rest of the day have them check the bags every 15 minutes or so. Before they leave for the day, encourage them to look at all the bags and describe the results. If necessary, comment that the warm samples melted and turned to water, but the samples in cold places stayed the same.)

MATERIALS

- Snow-covered paper or house from previous day
- Book, *The Snowy Day*
- One paper bag per child
- Marker
- Hat
- Broom
- Ice cube on a stick from the art center
- Handful of shredded paper from the make-believe center
- Small amount of snow on Styrofoam tray
- Toy person

continues . . .

Introduce the arts activities.

Music and Movement Center

What the children will do: Sing songs about melting snow. Put on a hat and scarf and hold a broom in front of you. Tell the children to pretend that you are a snowman. Sing the following words to the tune of "I'm a Little Teapot":

I'm a little snowman, white and cold,
I'm made of snow and chunks of coal
Put a warm hat and a scarf on me
I'll make you happy when you see me.

Say that when the sun shines on a snowman, it melts! Slowly lower yourself to the floor as you say, "I'm melting!" Tell the children they can pretend to be melting snowmen and sing other melting songs in the music and movement center.

Art Center

What the children will do: Paint with ice. Hold out the ice cube on a stick for everyone to touch. Encourage the children to describe how the ice cube feels, and whether or not they like the feeling. Explain that it is cold outdoors in winter, like an ice cube. Then tell the children they will use ice cubes in the art center.

Make-Believe Center

What the children will do: Play with frozen and melting snow. Sprinkle a small amount of snow on a Styrofoam tray and talk about how snow is falling from the sky. Then walk a toy person across the snow, and tell the children to pretend it is Peter. Walk the toy person around on the snow until it starts to melt. (If necessary, press your fist on the snow as you manipulate the toy to make the snow melt faster.) When water becomes evident, have the toy person look at it and comment that the snow is melting. Let the children feel the water as you tell them they can play with real snow and toy people in the make-believe center, and watch the snow melt.

Have each child choose an arts activity.

Notes:

Theme of the Day: Melt

Day 3: Music and Movement Center

What to Do:

Relate the activity to the story. Ask the children what happened to the snowball that Peter put in his pocket. Why did it melt? Remind them that Peter made a snowman and that when the sun shines on snowmen, they melt, just as the snowball melted in Peter's pocket. Say that they will think about things melting while they sing songs and play music games.

MATERIALS

- Hat
- Broom
- Small container of snow
- Large bag filled with shredded paper

Repeat the "little snowman" song and take turns being the snowman. Let the children take turns putting on the hat and holding the broom to pretend that they are the snowman as you sing the song from group time. Encourage the children to sing along with you, especially after you have repeated the song several times.

Melt snow and sing "snow is falling." Invite the children to sit in a circle and hold out one hand (palm up). Go around the circle, sprinkling a small amount of snow (from the container of snow) on each child's hand as you sing the following words to the tune of "Skip to My Lou."

Hooray, hooray, snow is falling.
Hooray, hooray, snow is falling.
Hooray, hooray, snow is falling.
We'll have fun today.

When all the children have snow on their hands, show them how to tap the snow with a finger until it melts. As they melt the snow, sing the next verse to the song:

Oh no, the snow is melting.
Oh no, the snow is melting.
Oh no, the snow is melting.
We can't play today.

Discuss the changes in the melted snow. Talk about what happened to the snow when it melted. What did the snow look like? How did it feel? How did it change when it melted? What does it look like now? How does it feel?

Sprinkle shredded paper and sing a song. Let the children get handfuls of shredded paper and drop it on the floor like falling snow. Then model walking around in the shredded paper as you sing, to the tune of "Farmer in the Dell":

Walking in the snow,
Walking in the snow,
Walk and walk and walk and walk,
Walking in the snow.

Change to a faster tempo and sing another verse: "Running in the snow," for the children to move to. Remind them to stay in the area with the paper snow. Slow down the tempo and sing, "Sliding in the snow," demonstrating how to slide, if necessary. End the song with a very slow tempo: "Crawling in the snow," and then, "Sitting in the snow."

Pick up the paper and sing a melting song. Comment that the snow is melting and tell the children to put all the paper snow back in the bag, as you sing, "Oh no, the snow is melting . . . "

Theme of the Day: Melt

Day 3: Art Center

What to Do:

Prepare ice cube paint sticks a day ahead of time: Pour watery paint into ice cube trays and stick a craft stick in each section. Freeze them overnight.

Relate the activity to the story. Remind the children that the snowball that Peter put in his pocket melted. When snow or ice gets warm, it turns to water. Say that they will paint with ice and watch it melt.

MATERIALS

- Ice cube paint sticks
- Fingerpaint paper or other paper with a glossy finish
- Paintbrushes and sponges

Paint with ice sticks. Place the materials where they are easily available. Join the children in spreading paint on the paper by using the frozen cubes. As they work, encourage them to feel the cold cubes and to talk about how it is cold outside in winter, like the ice cubes are cold. As the cubes begin to melt, discuss the fact that they are turning to colored water because they are melting. Encourage experimenting with the materials by modeling different techniques:

- Rub the paper with the ice, both quickly and slowly.
- Press hard as you move the ice cube around on the paper.
- Tap the paper with the ice.
- Hold the ice cube in one spot for a while.
- Make circles, lines, squares, and zigzags.

Encourage talking. As the children work, ask them to talk about what they are doing: "Manuel, is your ice moving fast or slow?" "Devon, what shape are you making? How do you do that?"

Apply melted paint with brushes. Show how to use brushes and/or sponges to spread the paint after it is applied to the paper with the cubes. Talk about how the cubes melted, so now you have wet paint.

Paint with ice cubes in different ways. Praise the children for good thinking when they make up new ways to use the materials, and make suggestions to prompt further experimenting:

- Rub the sponge on your ice cube. What happened to the sponge? What happened to the ice cube? Rub the paper with the sponge. What do you see?
- Put your finger on the ice cube. Press hard. How does that feel? Rub your finger on the paper. What do you see?
- Rub the paper with the ice cube. What do you see? Now rub it with the ice cube stick. Does it look the same?

Melt ice cubes in different ways. Encourage the children to try to melt the ice cubes fast, by blowing on them, holding their hands around them, or placing them in the sunlight. Praise them for thinking of other ways to melt the cubes.

Theme of the Day: Melt

Day 3: Make-Believe Center

What to Do:

Relate the activity to the story. Remind the children that Peter went outside to walk and play in the snow. They will play with toy people in snow.

Put snow on trays and describe its characteristics. Put the trays and snow where they are easily available, encouraging the children to get a tray and a handful of snow. Show them how to sprinkle the snow on the tray, like snow falling. Talk about the snow as the children handle it. How does it feel? What color is it? Can they smell it? Does it make a sound?

Use props in the snow. Let the children choose toy people and other props to use on their snow. Join in and make hills of snow for people and animals to walk on, drive toy cars through the snow, and place blocks on the snow as pretend houses for the toy people to go into. Praise the children for creating different ways to use the snow and the props.

Describe melting snow. As the snow melts, encourage the children to talk about how it is changing. "What is happening to the snow?" "Is your snow the same or different now?" "Your snow melted! How does it feel now? What color is it? Can you smell it?"

Add more snow. After their snow melts, let the children pretend it is snowing again and get more snow to use.

MATERIALS

- **One Styrofoam tray for each child**
- **Large container of snow**
- **Toy people and other props—cars, animals, blocks**

Theme of the Day:
Making a Story

Day 4 Group Time: Introducing the Theme of the Day

What to Do:

Review the previous day's activities. Ask the children to sing the snowman song and pretend to melt the way they did the day before in music. Show the children the ice paintings they made and discuss how the ice melted as they painted. Then talk about how the snow melted in the make-believe center while they played with the toy people.

Observe paper bags from the previous day. Let the children get the paper bags they stored in different locations on the previous day. Ask them to tell how the bags have or have not changed. Ask what happened to the snow in the bags. Show the picture in *The Snowy Day* of Peter looking in his pocket for his snowball. Ask the children to tell what happened to it. (Do not expect a clear understanding of "melting." To many children the disappearance of the snow will seem like magic.)

Review incidents in the story. Show the book, and say that this is a story about some things that a little boy did. Show the pictures in the book, and ask the children to tell what is happening and to imitate what Peter is doing.

Write down activities that the children recall doing. Remind the children that they have done some things too. Ask them to describe activities they have done in the classroom on this day, and write down what they say, encouraging everyone to make one contribution. To help the group focus on the conversation, let the children show everyone objects related to the activities they describe. For example, if a child says he played with blocks, he can get a block to show the group.

Introduce the theme of the day: Making a story. Explain to the children that they have just made up a story about their day so far in school. Read their descriptions to them, beginning with the phrase, "Once there were some children who had a busy day at school. . . . " Continue by incorporating the children's suggestions into the story. For example, "Cora and Tarell pretended they were doctors. They gave medicine to the babies and put them to bed." Let the children hold up the objects for the activities as you read about them. Tell the children they can tell more stories in the centers today.

MATERIALS

- Hat
- Broom
- Ice paintings from the previous day
- Paper bags still in various locations from the previous day
- Book, *The Snowy Day*
- Large piece of paper and marker
- Several pieces of paper stapled together along one side, to resemble a book
- Container of sand (or other substance), twigs, and toy people from the make-believe center
- Shredded paper

continues . . .

Introduce the arts activities.

Music and Movement Center

What the children will do: Tell stories that they hear in songs. Sing the "Snow is falling" song from the previous day, inviting the children to join in.

Hooray, hooray, the snow is falling.
Hooray, hooray, the snow is falling.
Hooray, hooray, the snow is falling.
We'll have fun today.

Tell the children that this song tells a story: The snow is falling, and everyone is happy! Tell them they can sing songs and tell stories in the music center.

Art Center

What the children will do: Make a book. Show the children some papers stapled together along one side like a book, and tell them that they can make their own books in the art center.

Make-Believe Center

What the children will do: Make up stories about toy people in a wintery setting. Show the children the container of sand, and tell them to pretend the sand is the ground outdoors. Stand up some twigs in the sand and say that they are trees in winter with no leaves on them. Sprinkle shredded paper on the sand for snow, and then have some toy people jump in the snow, as you say, "One day some children jumped in the snow. It was fun!" Tell the children they can play with these things in the make-believe center and tell more stories.

Have each child choose an arts activity.

Notes:

Theme of the Day: Making a Story

Day 4: Music and Movement Center

What to Do:

Relate the activity to the story. Remind the children that the books we read are stories that someone wrote down. Say that they can make up stories too. Say that they will sing songs that tell stories.

Sing and pantomime a song. Sing the following words to the tune of "Farmer in the Dell" as you pantomime playing in the snow. Sing the song again, inviting the children to act as if they are playing too.

Playing in the snow,
Playing in the snow,
Play and play and play and play,
Playing in the snow!

Tell a story about a song. Say, "There is a story for this song: One day a little boy named Peter went out to play in the snow. He played and played. He had a good time."

Have the children tell a story for a song. Show the toy cows. Then sing the following words to the tune of "Skip to My Lou," reminding the children to listen carefully to the story.

Cows in the snow, moo, moo, moo.
Cows in the snow, moo, moo, moo.
Cows in the snow, moo, moo, moo.
Cows in the snow today.

Afterward, ask them to tell the story in the song. (Cows are in the snow. They said *moo, moo, moo.*) If the children need prompting, begin the story and prompt them to continue it. "One day some cows were in the snow. What happened?" Sing the song again if they need reminders. Encourage creativity by praising the children for changing the story or adding to it.

Use props and pantomimes to continue with other songs. Continue the procedure with other songs, using props and actions to help the children visualize each simple story. Encourage each child to contribute at her own level. Some may only say one or two words for a story. Others will be able to use full sentences to express complete thoughts. You might use the following props and actions to introduce each song:

- "Mary Had a Little Lamb"—Show a toy girl and a toy lamb.
- "Playing in the Snow"—Show a picture of a child playing in the snow.
- "Old MacDonald"—Show a toy man and a toy farm animal.
- "The Bear Went Over the Mountain"—Use a toy bear to act out the song.

MATERIALS

- **Toy props to help the children visualize the story (such as a plastic spider for "Eensy Weensy Spider")**

Day 4: Art Center

What to Do:

Relate the activity to the story. Ask the children what story they have been hearing this week. Who is the story about? What did Peter do? Say that stories happen to them too, and they will make their own story.

Draw in booklets. Place the materials where they are easily available, inviting the children to make drawings in their books. The pictures need not be representational drawings depicting stories with a plot; rather, allow the children to decorate the pages freely, using crayons, markers, and pencils.

MATERIALS

- **Several pieces of paper stapled together along one side**
- **Drawing paper**
- **Stapler**
- **Drawing tools—crayons, black and colored pencils, markers**

Print "stories" in books that children dictate. Ask each child if he would like to add words about the pictures for an adult to record on the pages. When recording, print only a few words or sentences on each page. The stories can cover any topics, not necessarily things the children have done. The stories will probably consist of short thoughts, without a definite beginning, middle, or end. As you record a child's story, stop from time to time and read the book from the beginning, to help the child decide what else to add. Allow a child to elaborate or to be as brief as she wishes.

Read booklets. When a child is finished, offer to read the entire story; some children will enjoy pretending to read their own stores. As they "read," they might remember many parts of the written story, or they might make up entirely new stories.

Day 4: Make-Believe Center

What to Do:

Relate the activity to the story. Remind the children that the story they have been hearing this week is about a little boy who went out to play in the snow. Say that they do things that are stories too. They will do things that could be stories while they play.

Play freely with the materials. Let the children play freely with the props. Join in and show how to play with the materials in different ways to suggest winter activities:

- Mark roads in the sand for the vehicles to drive on. Drop snow on the roads for toy trucks to push out of the way, like snow plows.
- Make sand hills and cover them with paper snow. Then have toy people slide down them.
- Lay a toy person in a pile of paper or real snow. Wiggle the person as if to make a snow angel.
- Put small boxes in the sand like houses and garages for people and vehicles to go into.

Make up stories about the materials and the children's actions. As the children play, encourage them to talk about what they are doing. Help them make their descriptions into stories: "What is your truck doing, Kaitlin?" ("Pushing snow.") "What happened to the snow over here on the road?" ("It's all gone.") "You made a story: A truck was pushing snow. Now the snow on the road is all gone."

MATERIALS

- **Large containers filled with sand or other materials, such as rice or beans**
- **Shredded paper or real snow (gloves are needed for play with real snow)**
- **Twigs from trees or bushes and evergreens**
- **Toy people**
- **Toy vehicles and other props for a small-scale snowy setting**
- **Small boxes, large enough for toy people and vehicles to fit in**

Theme of the Day:
Snowy Fun

Day 5 Group Activity

What to Do:

Relate the activity to the story. Remind the children that Peter went outside to have fun in the snow. Say that they are going to have fun in pretend snow.

Remind the children of some things they did in the snowy setting in the make-believe center on day 2. Tell them they can pretend to play in the snow again today, and there will be more things to do.

Sing "Putting on coats" and pretend to get dressed for outdoors. Tell everyone to pretend to dress for outdoor play as you sing the song, "Putting on coats," introduced on day 2. For the first verse, sing about putting on a coat. Ask the children to name other outdoor clothes for the additional verses.

Introduce the new props for the setting. Show the containers of snow or Styrofoam pieces. Tell the children they can play in the snow, using shovels, buckets, and other things they would like to add.

Make a circle on the floor with the string. Slide around on it and tell the children they can pretend it is ice. (If the room is carpeted, wrap wax paper around the children's feet and tie it in place around their ankles with string.)

Show the children the kitchen props in the housekeeping area. Tell them that people like to drink hot chocolate after they play in the snow. Invite them to discuss their own experiences with hot chocolate. Tell them they can pretend to make hot chocolate with the materials.

Implement "Snowy Fun" play. See suggestions below.

Review the activity. Sit with the children to discuss what they did during the activity.

MATERIALS

- Make-believe props for playing in the snow used on day 2
- Large containers of real snow (gloves needed) or Styrofoam pieces
- Shovels, buckets, and other containers
- Housekeeping area with cups, toy stove, cooking pot, large spoon
- Long piece of string or yarn to make a large circle on the floor
- Wax paper and string (if the classroom is carpeted)

Suggestions for Implementing Snowy Fun:

Let the children continue the play they began in the snowy setting on a previous day. Encourage them to think of new ways to play in the pretend snow and to look around the room for other props to add to the setting.

continues . . .

Let the children play with the containers of snow or Styrofoam pieces as in a sandpile. Join in and show how to shovel, fill buckets and empty them, and make mounds of snow or Styrofoam.

Pretend to skate on the make-believe ice, sliding your feet, turning around, and standing on one foot. If the "skaters" begin to get wild, ask one child at a time to perform on the ice for the others to watch (and applaud), as you sing the following words to the tune of "Farmer in the Dell":

Skating on the ice;
Skating on the ice.
Slide and slide and slide and slide.
Skating on the ice.

If the children need help when they pretend to make hot chocolate, describe the steps for them to follow: pour milk in a pan; add cocoa and sugar; put the mixture on the stove to heat up; stir; pour the hot chocolate into cups; serve it to dolls and other children. Ask the children to name other things to pretend to cook. Give assistance as needed.

Notes:

SKILLS & GOALS MATRIX

The Snowy Day

	Skills or Behaviors	Goals and Objectives
Cognitive	• Identify things that fall quietly	• Increase concept development relating to physical properties of objects • Increase ability to group like objects
	• Discuss change from snow to water	• Increase concept and vocabulary development • Increase awareness of qualitative change
	• Plan and then build a pretend environment for play people	• Increase problem-solving ability • Increase ability to set and achieve goals
	• Identify indoor and outdoor clothing	• Increase classification skills • Increase semantic understanding
	• Pretend to be outside in the cold, walking and playing in snow	• Increase use of imaginative play • Increase development of imaginative vocabulary
Language	• Listen for and label very quiet sounds	• Increase auditory discrimination • Increase receptive and expressive vocabulary
	• Learn, and sing, a song	• Increase receptive and expressive vocabulary • Increase phonological awareness
	• Identify quiet and loud sounds	• Increase auditory discrimination
	• Help create a story by providing parts of the story for an adult to record	• Increase preliteracy skills: increase sequencing skills, understand grapheme-phoneme connection, become familiar with written language
	• Say words with a group when cued by an adult	• Increase oral-motor coordination and control • Increase ability to respond to a request

SKILLS & GOALS MATRIX (CONT.)

	Skills or Behaviors	Goals and Objectives
Social	• Sing a song with others	• Increase participation as member of a group
	• Pretend to be a character in a story	• Increase understanding of point of view and feelings of others • Increase ability to speak in a group
	• Participate in supervised pretend play as part of a small group	• Increase appropriate verbal interactions with peers • Increase appropriate social behaviors with adult supervision
Fine-Motor	• Tear paper into small pieces	• Increase bilateral coordination • Refine pincer grasp • Increase visual-motor coordination
	• Form small piles of snow into specific shapes	• Increase tactile awareness • Increase hand strength • Refine motor planning
	• Play musical instruments quietly	• Increase wrist rotation • Increase bilateral coordination
	• Squeeze, shake, and paint with squirt bottles in large and small movements	• Increase bimanual coordination • Increase visual-motor coordination • Increase postural stability
Gross-Motor	• Move quietly to music on tiptoe	• Increase gross-motor planning and control • Increase dynamic balance • Increase awareness of body in space
	• Move whole arm in circular motions	• Increase ability to perform motor task after demonstration • Increase and/or maintain range of motion in shoulder • Increase awareness of body in space
	• Walk with toes in and then with toes out	• Increase motor planning and control • Increase body awareness
	• Walk on a trail of footprints	• Increase motor planning and control • Increase dynamic balance • Increase body awareness

STORY OF THE WEEK / EL CUENTO DE ESTA SEMANA

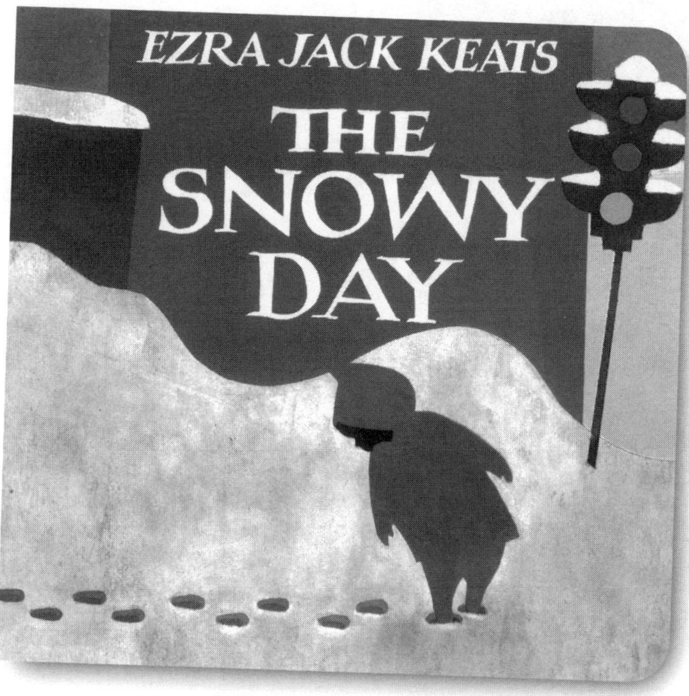

The Snowy Day

by Ezra Jack Keats
Edición en español: ***El día nevado***

The Spark story this week, *The Snowy Day,* has become a children's classic. It is available in most libraries. You may remember this story from when you were little. It is the story of a little boy named Peter and the fun he has playing in the snow. One thing Peter does is make a snowball and put it in his pocket to save. Ask your child what happened to the snowball (it melted). Also ask your child what Peter did outside in the snow (made tracks in the snow, knocked snow off a tree with a stick, made a snowman, watched a snowball fight, made angels, and climbed a hill of snow). The themes to go with this story are *snow, covered, melt,* and *making a story.*

El cuento de Spark de esta semana se llama *El día nevado.* Usted puede encontrar este libro, que es un clásico infantil, en cualquier biblioteca. Es probable que usted lo recuerde de su infancia. El cuento trata sobre un niñito llamado Peter y cómo se divertía jugando en la nieve. Un día Peter hizo una bola de nieve y la guardó en su bolsillo. Pregúntele a su niño o niña qué le sucedió a la bola de nieve (se derritió). También pregúntele qué hizo Peter afuera en la nieve (hizo huellas en la nieve con sus piés, tumbó la nieve de los árboles con un palo, hizo un muñeco de nieve, vió una pelea de bolas de nieve, hizo ángeles en la nieve y se subió a una montaña de nieve). Las ideas temáticas de este cuento son: *nieve, cubierto, derretido,* y *haciendo un cuento.*

© 2001 The Board of Trustees of the University of Illinois. May be reproduced for use by teachers.

Tree of Cranes

by Allen Say

Boston: Houghton Mifflin, 1991

Story Synopsis: This story provides an opportunity through its illustrations and story line to gently introduce traditional Japanese culture. The Japanese mother in the story, who grew up in the United States but now lives with her son and husband in a traditional house in Japan, explains the Christmas holiday to her son. As she and her son decorate a tree with silver cranes and candles, she explains that Christmas is a day of love and peace.

Classroom Use: This story is the most complex one in the curriculum. It has two story lines: one is concerned with the boy's disobedience, and the other introduces the custom of Christmas as a day of peace and love. The illustrations are excellent for use in the preschool setting. In clear, distinct lines and brilliant colors, they depict a traditional Japanese home. The bathtub is made of wood; the boy eats with chopsticks and sleeps on a pallet on the floor. The mother is dressed in traditional Japanese clothes. This unit is most effective when used in December. It may be linked to other winter, Christmas, Asian, or family units.

Considerations: Due to the complexity and length of the story, *Tree of Cranes* must be adapted for young preschoolers. It is best to use the book as a picture story. It is a valuable addition to the preschool curriculum since it offers an opportunity to introduce Japanese culture and also discusses Christmas as a day of peace and love.

Special Materials: In addition to the materials typically found in preschool settings, this unit suggests playing a recording of Japanese or Asian music each day while the children gather for group time. An Autoharp or keyboard is suggested but not necessary to implement the unit. The materials for some activities need to be prepared the day before the activity is implemented. These preparations include freezing ice cube sticks, ice cubes, and wet plastic bags (for ice boots).

ACTIVITY MATRIX

Tree of Cranes

Day	Concept	Music Activity	Art Activity	Make-Believe Activity
Day 1	Feelings (Social)	Play musical instruments and decide how the sounds make them feel.	Make a mural of things that make them smile and things that make them frown.	Actions that others are pretending to do, and the feelings that they are pretending to feel.
Day 2	Hot/Cold (Cognitive, Language, Science)	Investigate cold and hot sounds by playing ice drums, swishing ice strikers through warm water, and walking in ice boots.	Uses ice cubes and warm water in sand play.	Pretend to prepare hot and cold foods.
Day 3	Open/Close (Cognitive, Language)	Experiment with a jingle bell in an open and closed bag.	Put playdough and food coloring in plastic bags and mix them together.	Prepare pretend gifts to give away.
Day 4	Quiet (Cognitive, Language)	Play bells quietly. Play a quiet music game.	Use quiet materials for making sculptures.	Create a quiet place for doing quiet things.
Day 5	Decorating Trees			

Theme of the Day:
Feelings

Day 1 Group Time: Introducing the Book

What to Do:

Create the setting each day by playing recorded Japanese or Asian music as the children gather for the activity.

Briefly discuss the music you played. Tell the children that the music they have been hearing is the type of music the little boy in today's story might hear in his country. Say that he lived in a faraway country called *Japan.* Suggest that they look for things that are different from what they have at home while they listen to the story and look at the pictures.

Read and discuss the story. Read or tell the story, commenting about the characters' feelings after you complete each page. For example, after page 4, you might say that the boy's mother will probably feel angry, because she told him not to play in the cold water, but he did it anyway.

Ask what things they saw in the pictures of the boy's home that were different from what they have in their homes. What did they see that was the same as it is in this country? If appropriate with your group of children, encourage them to realize the similarities to their lives. The boy was just like them in many ways. He lived in a house with his family, he had rules to follow, he ate food, took baths, and made a snowman.

Discuss feelings. Turn to page four and ask the children to tell what the boy is doing (playing in cold water). Remind them that the boy's mother told him not to play in the cold water. Then ask, "How will the boy's mother feel when she finds out he played in cold water—happy or angry? Why?"

Turn to page 12. Remind the children that the boy is going to bed because he is sick. Ask, "Does the boy want to go to bed?" "How does he feel—happy or sad?" "Is he smiling or frowning?" "Why?" "How would you feel?"

Turn to page 24. Ask the children to tell what the boy and his mother are doing (looking at the tree full of lights). Ask, "How does the boy feel—angry or happy? Why?" "How would you feel?"

Turn to page 28. Explain that the boy's mother and father gave him a kite. Ask, "How does he feel—happy or sad? Why?" "How would you feel?"

Teach the song; discuss frowning and smiling. Comment that most people frown when they are angry or sad, and smile when they are happy. Ask the children to frown and smile. Tell the children to pretend they are the boy's mother. He played in the cold water after she told him not to. How does she feel? Should they smile or frown? As the children frown sing the following to the tune "If You're Happy and You Know It":

MATERIALS

- Book, *Tree of Cranes*
- Autoharp (or keyboard)
- Magazine picture of something that you like
- Magazine picture of something that you don't like
- Mural from the art center
- Masking tape

continues . . .

If you're angry and you know it, frown with me.
If you're angry and you know it, frown with me.
If you're angry and you know it, then your face will surely show it,
If you're angry and you know it, frown with me.

Finally tell the children to pretend they are the boy when he sees his new kite. How does he feel? Should they smile or frown? As they smile, sing to the same tune:

If you're happy and you know it, smile with me.
If you're happy and you know it, smile with me.
If you're happy and you know it, then your face will surely show it,
If you're happy and you know it, smile with me.

Introduce the theme of the day: Feelings. Name one incident that would make you feel angry or sad, such as spilling your milk, and ask everyone to frown with you. Tell the children to name things that would make them feel angry or sad, encouraging everyone to make at least one suggestion and allowing them to name things that have already been mentioned. After each child names something, tell everyone to frown.

Repeat the procedure, asking the children to name things that would make them feel happy, and encouraging them to smile after each suggestion. Afterward, tell the children that they will think about *feelings* in the centers.

Introduce the arts activities.

Music and Movement Center

What the children will do: Play musical instruments and decide how the sounds make them feel. Ask the children to listen as you play a sound on the Autoharp or play several notes together on a keyboard. If you have an Autoharp, strum loudly, without holding down any keys. (Any discordant sound will suffice, such as several instruments played loudly and simultaneously.) Ask how the sound made them feel—did they want to smile or frown? Why? The children may react in either way, saying that they frowned because they didn't like the sound, or they smiled because it sounded funny. Explain that they can make music with slide whistles, kazoos, and the Autoharp in the music center, and decide how the sounds make them feel.

Art Center

What the children will do: Make a mural of things that make them smile and things that make them sad. Show the children the picture of something you like. Explain that this picture makes you want to smile, because you like it. Ask them to tell how the picture makes them feel, reminding them that it is okay for everyone to feel differently about it. Tape the picture to the mural under the smiling face. Then show the picture of something that makes you unhappy and ask the children how it makes them feel. Explain why the picture makes you feel sad and tape it to the mural under the sad face. Say they can find pictures that make them feel happy or sad in the art center and make two big murals of pictures—a happy mural and a sad mural.

Make-Believe Center

What the children will do: Guess actions that others are pretending to do and the feelings they are pretending to feel. Ask a volunteer to stand near you. Tell everyone that the child will pretend to do something, so they should watch carefully and guess what the child is doing. Whisper to the child that she should pretend to fall down and get hurt. When the others guess what the child is pretending to do, ask them to tell how the child feels. Say that they can pretend to do things for each other to guess in the make-believe center.

Have each child choose an arts activity.

Theme of the Day: Feelings

Day 1: Music and Movement Center

MATERIALS

- Autoharp or keyboard (optional)
- A variety of musical instruments
- Cassette player and blank cassette
- Tape marked *Crying, Laughing*

What to Do:

Make sure you have a wide variety of musical instruments available, including slide whistles, jingle bells, drums, Autoharp (to be played with supervision), and kazoos; also include such items as pans with spoons and a grater with a spoon.

Relate the activity to the story. Ask the children how the boy felt when he had to go to bed. Was he happy or sad? Discuss what they do when they're sick. Do they eat special food and rest as the boy did in the story? Say that one of the ways that people let other people know how they are feeling is by the sounds they make. Encourage them to make a crying sound, a laughing sound, an excited sound (hooray!), and so on.

Play the instruments freely. Place the instruments where the children have easy access to them. Let the children experiment with the instruments, encouraging them to exchange them often, so that they may try each one. Discuss the color, shape, and size of each instrument: "What color is your drum?" "What shape is the tambourine?" "Is the bell big or little?"

Make angry or sad sounds with instruments. Say that instruments can sound happy or sad too. Ask the children to make sounds that make them feel sad or angry (because they don't like the sounds), such as banging or grating sounds. Let them practice making these "frowning" sounds for a while, and then tell everyone to stop playing. Ask each child to play a sad or angry sound for the others to hear. Ask the children to frown or smile when they hear each sound to show how they feel. If some children smile instead of frowning when they hear a sound, discuss how things make some people happy and some people angry or sad.

Make happy sounds with instruments. Tell the children to practice with their instruments again and try to make happy or funny sounds, sounds that make them smile. Repeat the above procedure with the children playing their sounds for each other and reacting with smiles or frowns.

Tape sounds. Show the children the tape recorder and ask them to say, "happy sounds," all together as you record their voices. Then encourage the children to play happy sounds and tape the sounds. (You might tape older children one child at a time.) Do the same thing for "sad sounds." Repeat this procedure a few times, so that you have a tape with several happy sounds, followed by several sad sounds, followed by several happy sounds, and so on. Collect the instruments.

Move to the taped sounds. Play the tape the children made and move your body to the recorded sounds, making corresponding facial expressions and moving differently to happy and angry or sad sounds. For example, you might hunch your shoulders and shuffle your feet for sad sounds, and jump around for happy sounds. Encourage the children to join you and react to the sounds in any way they wish as long as the movement is appropriate.

continues . . .

Sit with the children to sing. Have the children join you on the floor. Sing "If You're Happy" with them the way it was sung in group time, encouraging the children to frown or smile. Add a verse, "If you're unhappy and you know it, look sad."

Theme of the Day: Feelings

Day 1: Art Center

What to Do:

Tape the large sheets of paper to a wall at a height that the children can reach. Draw a smiling face at the top of one paper, and a sad face at the top of the other paper. For children not yet using scissors, precut the pictures before the activity or encourage the children to tear the pictures out of the magazine.

Relate the activity to the story. Remind the children that the boy was sad when he had to go to bed, but happy when he received a new kite. Say that they will make murals of happy and sad pictures.

MATERIALS

- Two large sheets of paper
- Magazines for cutting
- Scissors
- Tape
- Markers

Look for pictures that make children feel emotions. Look through a magazine with the children, until you come to a picture that might make them feel an emotion, such as an adult holding a child or an animal. Ask each child to tell how the picture makes him feel and discuss how it is all right for them to react differently to the picture. Then cut out the picture and let someone tape it to one of the sheets of paper, under the appropriate face. Repeat this procedure until the children seem to be familiar with it.

Cut out pictures and tape them to the murals. Let the children cut out pictures and tape them to the murals independently. As they work, ask the children to tell how the pictures make them feel and explain why. This might lead to discussion about other emotions, as children find pictures of things that make them feel scared, worried, and so on, and decide whether those pictures should be under the smiling or the frowning face.

Decorate the murals. If the children want to decorate the murals, let them use markers. Younger children will probably scribble on the murals, using the markers freely; older children might draw pictures of things that make them feel like smiling or frowning.

Theme of the Day: Feelings

Day 1: Make-Believe Center

What to Do:

MATERIALS

- Book, *Tree of Cranes*

Relate the activity to the story. Ask the children how they think the boy felt when his mother held him on her lap and told him about the Christmas tree. Suggest that he probably was very happy when he was sitting on his mother's lap. Say they are going to pretend to do things that make them happy.

Have a child perform an action for others to guess. Ask for a volunteer to take the first turn. Whisper an activity for the child to act out, such as eating an ice cream cone. Tell the other children to guess what the child is pretending to do. When they guess correctly, ask them to tell how the child might feel and to make their faces show how the child feels.

Invite the children to take turns acting; name feelings. Let one child at a time act out an activity that you whisper to him. If needed, suggest what the child can do to act out the activity. Also, remind the child not to tell the others what he is pretending to do. Have the others guess what the child is doing, tell how he probably feels, and show that feeling with their faces. Activities that you whisper to the children might include:

- Take a bath.
- Roller skate.
- Swim.
- Get into bed.
- Blow up a balloon until it breaks.
- Dance.
- Beat a drum.

Have children suggest activities for everyone to act out. Encourage the children to name other activities to act out. After each suggestion, ask everyone to pretend to do the activity and show their feelings with their faces. After they stop pretending to do each action, ask two or three children to tell how they were pretending to feel.

Theme of the Day:
Hot/Cold

Day 2 Group Time: Introducing the Theme of the Day

What to Do:

The day before you do this activity, place wet plastic bags, ice cubes, and ice strikers in the freezer. (Ice strikers may be made by filling ice cube trays and placing a craft stick in each section to use as a handle.) Place the frozen items in a cooler before the activity begins.

Suggestion: Set the mood by playing recorded Japanese music.

Review the previous day's activities. Show the children the cover of the book and explain that the boy's parents have given him a kite, but he can't fly it because it's snowy outside. Ask the children if they think the boy feels happy or sad. After a brief discussion, remind the children that they thought about feelings on the previous day. Show them the mural they made in the art center and ask them to identify things in the mural that make them feel happy and things that make them feel sad. Ask them to make their faces look happy and then sad. Play the tape that they made in the music center and tell them to smile or frown when they hear the different sounds. Suggest that the children pretend that they are eating an ice cream cone as they did in the make-believe center and to show with their faces how they feel.

Read the story. Read the story, making comments when the words *cold* and *hot* occur, to help the children be aware of these concepts in the story: The water in the pond was *cold.*

MATERIALS

- Book, *Tree of Cranes*
- Mural from the previous day
- Cassette player
- Tape of sounds from the previous day
- Bowl of cold water (use ice cubes to keep it cold)
- Bowl of warm water
- Two ice strikers (see "What to Do") and empty tin can
- One frozen plastic bag
- Bowl of sand
- Ice cube
- Small container of warm water
- Mixing spoon
- Cooking pot

Feel cold water and discuss experiences with it. Put out the bowl of cold water and tell the children to pretend it is the pond in the story. Remind them that the water in the pond was very cold, and let them take turns putting their hand in the water to find out how cold it is. Encourage them to tell about their own experiences with cold water, such as in a swimming pool or lake, splashing in a puddle of water on the ground, or drinking cold water. Ask them to tell how cold water makes them feel, whether they want to smile or frown when they are in cold water. Allow for different reactions.

Feel the warm water and discuss it. Put out the bowl of warm water and tell the children to pretend it is the tub of hot bath water from the story. Let them take turns feeling the water in the bowl, as you explain that it is hot, but not too hot. Say that hot water, like the water in the bowl, is nice for a

continues . . .

bath. Ask them if taking a bath in nice hot water makes them want to smile or frown. Then explain that very hot water can hurt them, and give examples of very hot water, such as water boiling on the stove. Discuss how they should not touch very hot water. Ask them to tell how they would feel if they did touch very hot water.

Introduce the theme of the day: Hot and cold. Tell the children that in the centers today they will do things with different kinds of cold things and hot things (but not too hot!).

Introduce the arts activities.

Music and Movement Center
What the children will do: Investigate cold and warm sounds by playing ice drums, swishing ice strikers through warm water, and walking in ice boots. Use the ice strikers to tap gently on the bottom of the tin can. Let the children take turns touching the ice. Discuss the way the ice feels and the sound it makes. Show them the frozen plastic bag and slip it over your foot like a boot. Say that in the music center they will play music with the ice sticks and walk in ice boots like yours.

Art Center
What the children will do: Use ice cubes and warm water as they build with sand. Pass around the ice cube and talk about how cold it feels. Then put the ice cube in the bowl of sand and roll it around, so that sand begins to cling to it. Remove the ice cube from the sand and talk about what happened to it. Then put it in the sand again, and pour some warm water over it. Let the children look in the bowl as you discuss what happened to the ice cube, emphasizing the word *melt.* Tell them they will make things with ice, sand, and warm water in the art center.

Make-Believe Center
What the children will do: Pretend to prepare hot and cold food. Show the children the picture on page 15 and tell them that the boy's mother made him some hot food to eat. Ask them how they think she made the food hot. Then stir a mixing spoon in a pot, as you explain that you are making pretend soup. Tell them that they may pretend to make hot and cold food in the make-believe center.

Have each child choose an arts activity.

Notes:

Theme of the Day: Hot/Cold

Day 2: Music and Movement Center

What to Do:

Relate the activity to the story. Ask the children what the boy did to get his mittens wet. Ask if they have ever played in cold water. If appropriate, encourage them to share their experiences by asking if adults got angry when they played in cold water. Say that they will make sounds with very cold things in this activity!

Strike cans with the ice strikers. Distribute the ice strikers and cans. Play the "ice drums," with the children and show how to gently hit the strikers together like rhythm sticks and gently hit the can with them. Discuss how cold the strikers are and ask what happens to the strikers as the children hold and play them. (They're melting.) If the children know the song "Jingle Bells," encourage them to sing the song as they tap their cans.

MATERIALS

- Ice strikers, enough for each child and each adult to have two (see Day 2: Group Time)
- Empty tin cans, enough for each child and each adult to have one
- Frozen plastic bags to go over children's shoes
- Container of warm water
- Book, *Tree of Cranes*

Experiment with warm water. Encourage the children to swish their ice strikers around in the warm water, listen to the sounds and discover what happens when ice is in warm water. Encourage them to discuss what is happening to the ice. If you live in an area of the country where winter brings snow and ice, compare their ice to the icicles that form when snow melts and refreezes.

Walk around in frozen plastic bags. Distribute the frozen bags and encourage the children to put them over their shoes. Talk about the sounds made by the cold bags as the children handle them. Encourage the children to walk around in the bags, making sounds with their feet. As the bags get warm, discuss how the sound is changing.

Sing a song. Show the children page 32 in the book, drawing their attention to the snowman. Ask if they think the snowman is hot or cold. Sing the following words to the tune of "I'm a Little Teapot":

I'm a little snowman, I'm so cold,
I'm made of snow and chunks of coal.
Put a big hat and scarf on me,
I'll make you happy when you see me.

Theme of the Day: Hot/Cold

Day 2: Art Center

What to Do:

Relate the activity to the story. Remind the children that when the boy went outside to play with his kite, he discovered that it had snowed during the night. He had to wait until the snow melted to fly his new kite. Say that he probably wished that he could make the snow melt as the children will do in this activity.

Build with sand and ice. Have the children find places at the sand table (or find containers of sand). Place an ice cube in the sand in front of each child and encourage the child to feel how cold the ice is. Join in and show what you can do with an ice cube in the sand, by burying it, rolling it in the sand, or making designs in the sand around the ice cube. Comment on different ways the children play with the ice in the sand, and encourage them to think of more ideas. As they play, also help them notice that the ice is getting smaller, emphasizing the word *melt.*

MATERIALS

- Sand table or large containers of sand
- Ice cubes, at least five for each child
- Small pitchers containing warm water
- Variety of utensils for building with sand, such as shovels and spoons, assorted containers, cookie cutters, plastic numbers and letters, or other objects for making shapes and forms in the sand

Add warm water to the sand. Before the ice completely melts, let the children pour warm water over the ice cubes, as you remind them that the boy took a bath in hot water. Encourage them to talk about what the warm water does to the ice cubes. Then encourage them to play with the wet sand.

Experiment with ice and warm water in sand. Let the children add more ice and warm water to the sand as they wish. Encourage them to talk about what happens to the materials as they experiment with them.

Add building utensils to sand play. After they have used the ice and water for a while, add other utensils to the sand to encourage the children to dig, build, and create patterns. Join in and show how to use wet sand to make hills that have defined forms, such as a hill with straight sides and a flat top, or a pyramid shape. This will help children see that they can plan and build a definite shape, even if they are not ready to build representational forms. Also show how to use cookie cutters or other utensils to create a pattern in the sand, such as a star shape then a round shape, a star shape then a round shape, and so on.

Theme of the Day: Hot/Cold

Day 2: Make-Believe Center

What to Do:

Relate the activity to the story. Use a bowl and spoon (or chopsticks) and pretend to eat something as you remind the children that the boy's mother made him some hot food to eat. Ask what kinds of hot food they like to eat. Say that they may pretend they are the boy's mother or father preparing food.

Introduce the materials. Look at the materials with the children. Ask them to name some of the things and demonstrate how they are used.

Name some favorite foods. Ask the children to name some foods that they like to eat. After each child names a food, ask if the child eats the food hot or cold. Tell them they may pretend to make some of the foods they named.

MATERIALS

- One set of chopsticks (optional)
- Cooking utensils and appliances, such as pots and pans, mixing spoons, large bowls, old mixers, toasters
- Play stove and refrigerator, or large boxes
- Table and chairs
- Dishware—plates, bowls, cups, eating utensils
- Empty food boxes (optional)

Use the materials. Let the children use the materials freely to pretend to prepare food. As they work, join in and demonstrate using materials in ways that will extend the children's play. For example, if a child is stirring "cookie dough" with a spoon, you might demonstrate putting the pretend batter on a cookie sheet or piece of cardboard and placing it in the hot oven. Encourage the children to work with each other and engage in conversations together: "Tell Tyler where to put the ice cream carton to keep it cold."

Pretend to eat the food. Remind the children to pretend to eat the food that they prepare. As they eat, ask them to describe the food. "How does it taste?" "Is it salty or sweet?" "Is it hot or cold?" "How could you make it taste better?" "How did you make the pizza?"

Clean up the pretend kitchen. Near the end of the activity, tell the children to clean up as they would clean a real kitchen. Emphasize the words *hot* and *cold* as you work with them. They might pretend to wash dishes in hot water, put food away in the cold refrigerator, make sure they turn off the hot oven, wipe off the table, sweep the floor, and put things away.

Theme of the Day:
Open/Close

Day 3 Group Time: Introducing the Theme of the Day

What to Do:

Create the mood by playing Japanese or Asian music.

Review the previous day's activities. Start the review by singing "I'm a little snowman." Discuss the sounds that they made with ice strikers and by walking in ice boots. Were the sounds crunchy? Ask the children what happened when they put their ice strikers in warm water. Did they melt? Ask the children to recall some of the foods they pretended to make in the make-believe center and tell if each one is a hot or a cold food. Discuss the sand activities they did in the art center and how they made the sand feel cold or hot.

Read the story. Read the story, emphasizing the words *open* and *close* as they occur and asking the children to tell what the characters opened and closed (doors and windows).

Introduce the theme of the day: Open/Close. Turn to page 6 and ask the children to tell what the boy is opening in the picture. Then ask one of the children to open a real door in the classroom. Have another child close the door. Then turn to page 16 and ask the children to tell what the boy is opening in that picture. Ask a child to open or pretend to open a real window in the classroom. Have another child close or pretend to close the window. Tell the children that they can open and close things in the centers today.

Sing a song about *open* and *close*. Tell the children you know a song about opening and closing things. Sing the following words to the tune of "Skip to My Lou," modeling the actions and encouraging the children to perform the actions as they occur in the song. For example, tell them to open and close their hands as the song tells them when to do it.

> *Open them and close them, Open them and close them,*
> *Open them and close them, Then put them on the floor.*

Tell the children that now you want them to open and close their mouths.

> *Open it and close it, Open it and close it,*
> *Open it and close it, Then give a great big smile!*

MATERIALS

- Book, *Tree of Cranes*
- One paper bag
- One jingle bell
- Transparent tape
- Plastic sandwich bag
- Uncolored playdough from the art center
- Food coloring
- Small box with a lid
- Object small enough to fit in box
- Gift bow (optional)

continues . . .

If appropriate, sing another verse telling the children to open and close their eyes.

Open them and close them, Open them and close them,
Open them and close them, Then look at a friend and smile.

Introduce the arts activities.

Music and Movement Center

What the children will do: Put jingle bells in paper bags, then tape the bag closed. Show the children the paper bag. Show them that the bag is open. Ask what will happen if you put something in it and don't close it. Wait for an answer. Demonstrate by placing a jingle bell in the bag. Turn it upside down and shake it till the bell falls out. Ask if the bell is still in the bag. What should you do? Put the bell back in the bag and tape it closed. Shake it gently so they can hear the jingle bell inside. Again, turn the bag upside down and shake it. Help the children to understand that now that the bag is closed the bell will stay inside. Tell them that in the music and movement center they will open bags and put a jingle bell inside, then put the closed bags on the parachute and play a game.

Art Center

What the children will do: Put playdough and food coloring in plastic bags and mix them together. Show the children a plastic bag and open it as you describe what you are doing. Then put in some playdough and a few drops of food coloring and close the bag, emphasizing the word *close.* Let each child have a turn to squeeze the playdough in the bag, as you discuss how the playdough is changing to the color that you put with it. Tell them they can change the color of their playdough and then play with it in the art center.

Make-Believe Center

What the children will do: Prepare pretend gifts to give away. Remind the children that the boy in the story received a gift from his parents. Ask them what the gift was and how they think the boy felt when he saw his gift. Then show them the box and discuss the fact that we often put gifts in boxes for the person to open to see what's inside. Open the box as you explain what you are doing. Then put in the small toy and close the box. Put a bow on it and tell the children that they may put gifts in boxes and give them to others in the make-believe center.

Have each child choose an arts activity.

Notes:

Theme of the Day: Open/Close

Day 3: Music and Movement Center

What to Do:

MATERIALS

- Paper bags, enough for each child and adult to have one
- Jingle bells, preferably of different sizes and colors
- Transparent tape
- Parachute or sheet
- Crayons

Relate the activity to the story. Ask the children what the boy in the story opened and closed. Why did he open the window? Why did his mother tell him to close the window? Say that the story is about Christmas and that one of the sounds they may hear at Christmas is the sound made by bells. They will open bags to put bells inside and then tape them closed so the bells stay inside.

Put bells in the paper bags. Place the bags, bells, and tape where they are easily available. Encourage the children to choose the colors and sizes of jingle bells they prefer, put them in the bags, and tape the bags closed. Ask them to mark the bags with crayons so that they can identify their own bags.

Encourage the children to play with the bags as they remain seated. Show how to shake a bag and toss it very gently in the air. Discuss the sound the bells make as they are gently shaken and tossed in the air. Sing to the tune of "Mary Had a Little Lamb":

Shake it and shake it, shake it, shake it,
Shake it and shake it and toss it in the air!

If the children know the song "Jingle Bells," also have them sing it as they shake their bags.

Open and close the parachute with the bags on top. Spread the parachute on the floor. Place your bag on the parachute, and encourage the children to follow your example. Stand around the parachute with the children. Sing the the following words to the tune of "Skip to My Lou," moving together when you say "close it" and moving apart when you say "open it."

Close it and close it, close it, close it,
Close it and close it, then walk and walk around.
Open it and open it, open it, open it,
Open it and open it, then walk and walk around.

(Older children may be able to follow "open" and "close" directions in the same verse: "Open it and close it, close it, close it. Open it and open it then walk and walk around.")

Repeat the song for as long as the children seem interested.

End the activity. End by suggesting that the children lie on the floor and open and close their eyes as you quietly sing, "Open them, close them."

Theme of the Day: Open/Close

Day 3: Art Center

What to Do:

Relate the activity to the story. Remind the children that the boy opened the window to see what his mother was doing and that she told him to close it. Suggest that we can open and close many things. In this activity they will put playdough and coloring in a bag and close the bag so they can mix the color into the playdough.

Choose colors. Show the children the uncolored playdough and remark that it needs color in it. Put out the food coloring and let each child label (or point to) the color she would like to use.

MATERIALS

- Plastic sandwich bags
- Uncolored playdough (see recipe)
- Food coloring
- Tape

Put playdough and coloring in bags. Tell the children to open their bags. Prompt each child to get a piece of playdough to put in the bag. Then let the children put a few drops of food coloring in their bags. Tell them to close their bags, so the playdough and food coloring will stay inside. Help them tape the bags shut, as you explain that this will keep them closed.

Squeeze the bags to mix the playdough. Show how you squeeze the playdough in the bag as you encourage the children to squeeze their own bags. Talk about how this will make the playdough turn into the color of the food coloring.

Introduce a chant. To keep the children interested in mixing the playdough, chant the following rhyme for them as they squeeze their bags:

> *<u>Squeeze</u> the <u>dough</u> and <u>squeeze</u> it <u>hard</u>*
> *<u>Ish</u>ie, <u>squish</u>ie, <u>bipple</u>, <u>bard.</u>*
> *<u>Squeeze</u> the <u>dough</u> and <u>squeeze</u> it <u>hard,</u>*
> *<u>Ish</u>ie, <u>squish</u>ie, <u>bipple</u>, <u>bard.</u>*

Ask the children to think of other silly words to say while they squeeze the bags, such as *mishie.* You might use the words they suggest to extend the chant: "Mishie, mashie, boople, tard."

Some children may want to add different colors to their bags to change the color of the playdough.

Play with the playdough. When the children are satisfied with the colors of their playdough, tell them to open their bags and take out the playdough. Let them play with the playdough freely.

Put the playdough in bags for storage. When they are finished playing, tell them to open their bags again and put the playdough inside. Then have them close their bags and use tape to keep them closed. Explain that they can use the playdough later or take it home.

continues . . .

RECIPES FOR HOMEMADE PLAYDOUGH

(the cooked recipe makes better playdough)

Cooked Playdough

Mix in a saucepan:

- *2 cups water*
- *2 cups flour*
- *1 cup salt*
- *4 teaspoons cream of tartar*
- *4 tablespoons oil*

Stir the mixture and cook over a low heat until it is thick.

Uncooked Playdough

Mix in a bowl:

- *3 cups flour*
- *1 cup salt*

Add:

- *3 tablespoons oil*
- *1 cup water*

Add more water if needed to make the dough softer.

Day 3: Make-Believe Center

What to Do:

Relate the activity to the story. Remind the children that the boy in the story received a gift from his parents and ask the children to tell what it was. Then show them the taped box and tell them that you have put a pretend gift in the box. Ask the children to guess what is in the box, encouraging each child to make at least one guess. Then say, "I'm going to open the box. Let's see what's in it." After you open the box and discuss what is in it, tell the children that they may put things in boxes, like presents, and give them to other people.

Prepare gift boxes. Let each child choose a box and put something in it, emphasizing the words *open* and *close* as you discuss what they are doing. "Open your box, and put something in it." "Find the lid, so you can close the box." Encourage the children to use tape so that their boxes will stay closed, and to decorate them with markers and bows to make them look like real presents.

Deliver presents and open them. As the children finish their gift boxes, encourage them to think of someone to give them to. They might name someone at home or someone in the group. If they want to give them to someone in the group, let them deliver the presents to each other and open the boxes to see what is inside.

Set up gift-giving make-believe. Older children might want to extend the make-believe and pretend that it is someone's birthday or a holiday when people give gifts to each other. Help them collect and set up props to carry out their ideas.

MATERIALS

- A variety of boxes with lids
- A variety of objects small enough to put in the boxes
- Transparent tape
- Markers
- Gift bows (optional)
- Box with an object inside, taped shut

Theme of the Day:
Quiet

Day 4 Group Time: Introducing the Theme of the Day

What to Do:

Create the mood by playing Japanese or Asian music.

Review previous day's activities. Show the children your paper bag. Ask the children to tell what they did with the paper bags in the music center the day before. What did they put in their bags? How did they close them? Show the children the box with the bow on it. Discuss how they put things in boxes and gave them to others in the make-believe center. Show them the plastic bag containing playdough and ask them to tell how they mixed the playdough and food coloring in the art center.

Read the story. After you finish the story, say in a very soft voice that the mother wanted a day that was quiet.

Introduce the theme of the day: Quiet. Ask the children if they can clap quietly, allowing volunteers to demonstrate. Then play the recorded music at a low volume and encourage the children to clap quietly too. When they are finished clapping to the music, explain that they will do things quietly in the centers today.

MATERIALS

- **Box with a bow on it**
- **Plastic bag containing playdough**
- **Paper bag with bell inside from the previous day**
- **Book, *Tree of Cranes***
- **Cassette player**
- **Recording of quiet music**
- **Resonator bells if available (C#, D#, F#, G#, A#) (a keyboard may be substituted)**
- **Cookie tray**
- **Several building blocks**
- **Mixture of ¼ cup flour, ¼ cup pancake mix, and ¼ cup water**
- **Cotton balls**
- **Blankets, cushions, or other soft things from make-believe center**

Introduce the arts activities.

Music and Movement Center

What the children will do: Play a quiet music game. Show the children the bells. Play up and down the bells once. Tell them that this is the kind of music that the boy in the story might play. Ask one child to play the bells or keyboard quietly. (On a keyboard, play the black notes, starting with a group of two.) Say that in the music center they will play the bells quietly to music and then play a music game. Tell them that in the game one child will get to pretend to be a dog and the other children will be rabbits hopping quietly around. Ask someone to show you how a rabbit hops. Ask someone else to show you how a dog would look if it were asleep. Say that they will get to play this game in the music center.

Art Center

What the children will do: Use quiet materials to make sculptures. Stack some blocks on a cookie tray as you tell the children that you are trying to build something quietly. Continue to stack blocks until the tower

continues . . .

falls down and the blocks clatter on the tray. Comment that it's hard to stack blocks quietly. Then dip some cotton balls in the batter mixture and stack them until they fall over. Discuss how easy it is to build quietly with cotton balls. Tell the children that they can build quietly with cotton balls in the art center.

Make-Believe Center

What the children will do: Create a "quiet place" for doing quiet things. Arrange a blanket and some cushions, pillows, or other soft things to make a comfortable place to sit, as you explain that you are making a quiet place to do quiet things. Sit in your "quiet place" with a copy of *Tree of Cranes,* and tell the children that one thing you will do in your quiet place is look at books. Name one or two other quiet activities, such as drawing pictures or listening to quiet music, and tell the children that they can make their own quiet places in the make-believe center.

Have each child choose an arts activity.

Notes:

Day 4: Music and Movement Center

What to Do:

MATERIALS

- Cassette player
- Recorded Japanese music or music that is quiet
- Bells
- Cymbal and striker

Relate the activity to the story. Remind the children that the mother in the story wanted a quiet day. Say that the boy wanted to give his mother what she wished for, so he would have to do quiet things. Say that they will play the bells very quietly to some quiet music. Then they will play a quiet game.

Play the bells to recorded music. Discuss and demonstrate how to play bells quietly. Encourage each child to choose one bell. Hold the cymbal and striker. Tell them that they will play the kind of music the boy in the story might play. Play the recorded music, encouraging the children to play along quietly to the music as you tap the cymbal quietly with the striker. At the end of the song, hit the cymbal hard to make it sound like a gong. Repeat if the children seem interested, encouraging the children to trade bells and take turns playing the gong at the end of the song. Praise the children for quiet playing.

Play a game. Tell the children that in every country there is music that people like and there are games that children like to play. Now they will play a quiet music game. In the game the farmer has told the dog to watch the garden so that the rabbits will not eat all his lettuce. But the dog goes to sleep and little rabbits hop out quietly so they won't wake up the dog. Ask a child to show how rabbits hop. Encourage everyone to practice hopping like rabbits, encouraging creativity in movement as long as the motion is appropriate. Ask for a volunteer to be the dog. Tell the other children that they will be the rabbits. Sing the song and encourage the children to act out the motions as you sing the words.

Sing to the tune of "Mary Had a Little Lamb":

The old brown dog is nodding, nodding, nodding
The old brown dog is nodding, he's falling fast asleep.

The old brown dog is sleeping, sleeping, sleeping
The old brown dog is sleeping. He is fast asleep.

The little rabbits are hopping, hopping, hopping
The little rabbits are hopping because the dog's asleep.

The little rabbits are eating, eating, eating
The little rabbits are eating because the dog's asleep.

The old brown dog starts barking, barking, barking
The old brown dog starts barking, the rabbits hop away.

Sing "If You're Happy." Help the children settle down by sitting with them and very quietly singing, "If You're Happy." Remind them that at first the boy in the story was sad and then he was happy.

Theme of the Day: Quiet

Day 4: Art Center

What to Do:

Relate the activity to the story. Say that the mother in the story wanted a day of quiet. Say that one of the things a child might do on a quiet day is to build with cotton balls, because cotton balls are very quiet. Drop a block, then drop a cotton ball. Ask which one was quieter.

Prepare batter. Have the children help you prepare the batter they will use to stick the cotton balls together. Let them take turns adding 1 cup water, 1 cup flour, and 1 cup pancake mix to a bowl and stirring until the mixture is blended.

Build with the cotton balls. When the batter is ready, dip the cotton balls in the batter and then stick them together to build sculptures. Encourage the children to do the same. As the children build with the cotton balls, comment that the cotton balls are very quiet, and tell the children to be as quiet as they can while they build. Use a very quiet voice, and compliment children who follow your example.

Pretend to build with snow. Show the children page 32 in the book, and remind them that the boy and his father made a snowman. Say that the cotton ball sculptures look like snow, and encourage them to pretend that they are making things out of snow too.

MATERIALS

- Several building blocks
- Cotton balls
- Measuring cup
- Large bowl
- Mixing spoon
- Flour
- Pancake mix
- Small pitcher of water
- Book, *Tree of Cranes*

Theme of the Day: Quiet

Day 4: Make-Believe Center

What to Do:

Relate the activity to the story. Remind the children that the mother in the story wanted a quiet day. Say that sometimes we all need to have a special place where we can be quiet. Say that they will each make their own quiet place and do quiet things in their quiet places.

Choose materials. Put out the materials and help the children divide them among themselves. Help them agree on how to distribute the materials.

Create quiet places. Encourage the children to work as independently as possible as they each create their own quiet place. They might simply arrange blankets and pillows like a bed, or build beds or enclosures with boxes or blocks. Compliment them for their ideas and encourage them to think of additional props to add to make the quiet place even nicer.

Do quiet activities. As each child completes a quiet place, ask him to think of quiet things to do in it. Encourage the child to name at least three quiet activities, then to choose one activity to actually do. Help each child collect materials he needs for the activity and ask him to tell what he will do with the materials. If children have chosen an activity that is not quiet, let them try to do it quietly. If they make noise, ask them to think of something else that is easier to do quietly.

Think of other quiet activities. After individual children have done their quiet activities for a while, ask them to look around at the other children and tell what they are doing. Then ask the children to think of even more activities that are quiet. Write down all the children's observations and suggestions and read them back to them. Then ask them to choose one new activity to do in their quiet places.

MATERIALS

- **Variety of medium-sized and large boxes, or large building blocks**
- **Old sheets, blankets, large pieces of fabric, or carpet squares**
- **Cushions and pillows (optional)**
- **Paper and pencil**

Theme of the Day:
Decorating Trees

Day 5 Group Activity

What to Do:

Teachers have started this activity at the beginning of a week during the holiday season, using a large tree instead of twigs. The children add decorations to the tree every day.

Relate the activity to the story. Show the children page 25 from the book and discuss how the boy and his mother decorated the tree with paper cranes and lights. (Emphasize that it is very dangerous to light candles on a tree, and they should never try it!) Ask the children how they think the boy feels when he looks at the tree. Then say that they can decorate their own little trees.

Prepare twigs. Give each child a twig and a container of sand, and help them stick their twigs in the sand to make them stand up like the tree in the book.

Decorate the twigs. Show the children the scrap materials and ask volunteers to demonstrate how they might use some of them to decorate their twigs.

Let the children use the materials freely. Join in and show how to hang things from the branches, poking branches through materials like paper and Styrofoam to attach them, and gluing on lightweight materials.

The children might also add glitter or paint to their decorated twigs. Encourage them to think of other materials to use.

Display the decorated twigs. When the children have finished decorating the twigs, ask them to think of a special place to put the twigs, or other ways to display them. They might invite other classes to come see their twigs, or display them in a place in the school where many people will see them.

MATERIALS

- **Story, *Tree of Cranes***
- **Large twigs**
- **Containers of sand, such as large margarine containers, one per twig**
- **Scrap materials, such as ribbon, yarn, lace, old jewelry, shiny paper, scraps of fabric, used greeting cards, Styrofoam chips**
- **Glue**
- **Glitter (optional)**
- **Paint (optional)**

SKILLS & GOALS MATRIX

Tree of Cranes

	Skills or Behaviors	Goals and Objectives
Cognitive	• Identify things that are quiet	• Increase ability to group like objects • Increase auditory awareness
	• Discuss change in water from cold to warm	• Increase development of concepts about physical processes • Increase observation skills
	• Manipulate wet and dry sand	• Increase experience with physical processes • Increase understanding of cause and effect
	• Pretend to cook and eat warm and cold food	• Increase representational play • Increase general concept and vocabulary development
Language	• Listen for and label quiet sounds	• Increase auditory awareness and discrimination • Increase receptive and expressive vocabulary
	• Learn, and sing, a song	• Increase receptive and expressive vocabulary • Increase phonological awareness
	• Chant nonsense syllables	• Increase auditory awareness and discrimination • Increase phonological awareness
	• Act out events for others to identify	• Increase sequencing skills • Increase use of language to describe events and actions
	• Open and close plastic bag when directed by an adult	• Increase ability to follow simple directions • Increase concept and vocabulary development

SKILLS & GOALS MATRIX (CONT.)

	Skills or Behaviors	Goals and Objectives
Social	• Participate in games with rotating leadership	• Increase participation as member of a group • Increase ability to follow rules in group activity
	• Identify and discuss expressions of happy and sad feelings in pictures	• Increase understanding of point of view and feelings of others • Increase ability to speak in a group setting
	• Pretend to cook, eat, and clean kitchen with supervision	• Increase appropriate verbal interactions with peers • Increase appropriate social behaviors with adult supervision • Increase ability to represent home routines in play
	• Participate in small-group development of a large mural	• Increase ability to cooperate with peer to increase appropriate interactions in a small group
Fine-Motor	• Paste small pieces of paper onto large mural	• Increase bimanual coordination • Refine pincer grasp and release • Increase visual-motor coordination
	• Identify hot and cold objects by touch	• Increase tactile awareness • Increase finger dexterity
	• Play musical instruments quietly	• Refine grasp, hand use, and manipulation skills • Increase bilateral coordination • Increase visual-motor coordination
	• Squeeze playdough in plastic bags	• Increase bilateral coordination • Increase hand strength • Increase postural support with hand use
Gross-Motor	• Move to happy and sad music	• Increase motor planning and control • Increase dynamic balance • Increase awareness of body in space
	• Follow directions to move parachute	• Increase motor planning • Increase ability to move based on auditory input • Increase awareness of directionality of movement (in and out)
	• Move like rabbits	• Increase gross-motor planning and control • Increase mobility and agility • Increase awareness of body in space
	• Walk with weight and bulk over shoes	• Increase motor planning • Increase leg strength • Increase awareness of movement

STORY OF THE WEEK / EL CUENTO DE ESTA SEMANA

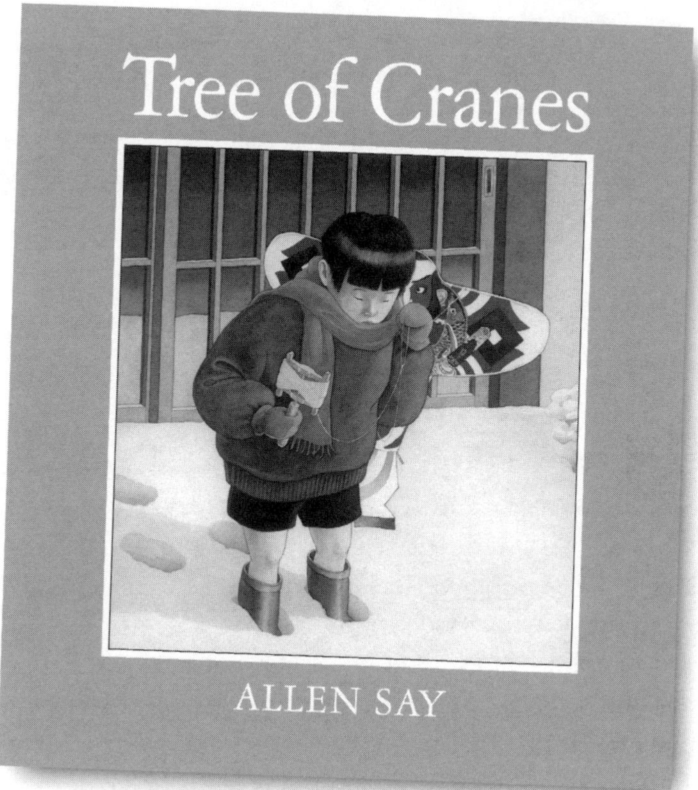

Tree of Cranes

by Allen Say

The Spark story this week is *Tree of Cranes.* It is about a little boy who lives in Japan. You may be able to find this book at the library. In the story the boy's mother tells him about the Christmas holiday and decorates a Christmas tree for him with candles and paper cranes. Ask your child what the little boy did at the beginning of the story that made his mother angry (played in a pond). Ask what present he found under his Christmas tree (a kite). The themes to go with this story are *feelings, hot/cold, open/close,* and *quiet.*

El cuento de Spark de esta semana se llama *Tree of Cranes* (el árbol de los adornos de papel). Usted puede encontrar este libro, en inglés, en cualquier biblioteca. Es sobre un niñito que vive en el Japón. Su mamá le cuenta sobre la fiesta de Navidad y le decora para él un árbol de Navidad con velas y adornos de papel. Pregúntele a su niño o niña que hizo ese niñito, al principio del cuento, que hizo enojar a su mamá (jugando en un estanque). También pregúntele qué regalo él encontró debajo de su árbol de Navidad. (La respuesta es un barrilete). Las ideas temáticas que van con este libro son: *sentimientos, caliente, abierto, cerrado* y *callado.*

© 2001 The Board of Trustees of the University of Illinois. May be reproduced for use by teachers.

The Very Quiet Cricket

by Eric Carle

New York: Philomel Books, 1990

Story Synopsis: *The Very Quiet Cricket* is one of the series of preschool books by Eric Carle. Children enjoy the surprise at the end of the book, the sound of a cricket chirping. *The Very Quiet Cricket* tells the story of a baby cricket that is hatched from an egg at the beginning of the book. As the day progresses he meets many other insects that greet him in various ways. On each page, the words are repeated, "The little cricket wanted to answer, so he rubbed his wings together. But nothing happened. Not a sound." On each page, the little cricket is larger than he was on the previous page. Finally at the end of the story, when night has fallen, he meets a female cricket. This time when he rubs his wings together, the children hear the chirping sound. Children enjoy participating in the story by chanting the repeated lines on each page and rubbing their hands together as the little cricket rubs his wings together.

Classroom Use: This story is most effectively used in the fall of the year when insects are plentiful. Many classroom teachers have used it to introduce an insect unit. It also may be used with stories related to growing up. Such stories as *The Very Hungry Caterpillar* link well with this unit. The themes and concepts for this unit are *rubbing, big/little, together,* and *insects*. Some teachers have brought live insects into the classroom and others have provided insect collections for children to examine with magnifying glasses.

Considerations: If there are children in your classroom who have trouble sitting through story time, this story is a good one to use. Children relate to the story since insects abound all over the world and after hearing the story once, they eagerly anticipate hearing the chirping sound at the end of the story. They understand not being able to do something because they are too young and they can participate both verbally and physically in the story reading.

Special Materials: In addition to the materials typically found in preschool classrooms, Styrofoam balls, plastic insects, liquid starch, and liquid dishwashing detergent are suggested for activities in this unit.

ACTIVITY MATRIX

The Very Quiet Cricket

Day	Concept	Music Activity	Art Activity	Make-Believe Activity
Day 1	Rubbing (Cognitive, Language, Motor)	Different musical instruments to determine which ones can be played by rubbing them.	Make crayon or chalk rubbings.	Rub table with sponge to get it clean for a pretend birthday party.
Day 2	Big/Little (Cognitive, Language, Social)	Discriminate big and little shapes as they play the "Hokey Pokey."	Make big and little items with playdough.	Pretend to be adults taking care of babies.
Day 3	Together (Cognitive, Language, Social)	Move to music together. Do mirror movements.	Mix ingredients for fingerpaint.	Rub fabrics together and pretend to wash doll clothes.
Day 4	Insects (Cognitive, Language, Science)	Use kazoos to sound like insects and streamers to "fly" like insects.	Make insects from boxes, Styrofoam balls, and other materials.	Make pretend insect homes and pretend to be insects.
Day 5	Insect World			

Theme of the Day:
Rubbing

Day 1 Group Time: Introducing the Book

What to Do:

Read the story. Read *The Very Quiet Cricket.* At the end of the book, as the children listen to the chirping sound, talk about how quiet the sound is. Ask if anyone has ever heard the sound before. Is the sound always quiet or can it be loud? Where have they heard the sound?

Rub hands together to demonstrate how to make a sound by rubbing. Show the first few pages of the book and discuss how the little cricket rubbed his wings together, but could not make a sound. Tell the children to pretend they are the little cricket and their hands are wings. Show how to rub your hands together very slowly and softly so that there is no sound. Encourage the children to do this too, emphasizing that there is "not a sound" and it is "quiet." Then rub your hands fast to make a sound encouraging the children to make as loud a sound as they can in this way.

Introduce the theme of the day: Rubbing. Sing the following words to the tune of "The Farmer in the Dell," rubbing your hands together when you sing the word *rubbed.*

The cricket rubbed his wings,
The cricket rubbed his wings,
He rubbed and rubbed and rubbed and rubbed
The cricket rubbed his wings.

Sing the song through several times, encouraging the children to sing with you as they become familiar with the song.

Show the children the sand blocks and say that sand blocks are rubbed together to make a sound. Demonstrate rubbing them together, singing the cricket song again.

Rub sand blocks and sing. Distribute sets of sand blocks. Ask the children with sand blocks to stand beside you, and rub the sand blocks as you slowly sing the cricket song. Ask the other children to rub their hands together as you sing. (Encourage children to sing with you as they feel able.) Distribute the blocks to other children and go through the procedure again if the children are still interested.

MATERIALS

- Book, *The Very Quiet Cricket*
- Sand blocks (as many sets as are available)
- Guiro tone block and striker
- Cymbals
- Peeled crayon and/or colored sidewalk chalk
- Piece of white paper
- Flat object from the art center
- Classroom table
- Sponge
- Bowl of water

continues . . .

Introduce the arts activities.

Music and Movement Center

What the children will do: Experiment with ways to make sound. Show the children the guiro and the striker. Ask a child to rub it with the striker. State that this is an instrument that is played by rubbing it. Strike the cymbals together. Ask if you rubbed the cymbals to make the sound. Let a child rub a cymbal with her hand to see if she can make the same sound. Suggest that some instruments are played by rubbing them and some are not. State that they will decide which instruments can be played by rubbing them in the music and movement center.

Art Center

What the children will do: Make crayon or chalk rubbings. Rub your hand on the floor and invite the children to do it too. Say that they are rubbing hands on the floor, instead of rubbing wings like the cricket. Place a flat object under a piece of paper and rub a peeled crayon or piece of chalk over it. Show the children the impression that is made, and tell them they can make rubbings in art.

Make-Believe Center

What the children will do: Rub a table with sponges to prepare for a pretend birthday party. Have the children stand around a classroom table. Dip a sponge in some water, wring it out, and then wipe the table, with a circular movement and going from left to right across the table. Say that you are rubbing the table with the sponge to get it clean for a pretend birthday party in make-believe.

Have each child choose an arts activity.

Notes:

Theme of the Day: Rubbing

Day 1: Music and Movement Center

What to Do:

Relate the activity to the story. Remind the children that the little cricket in the story made a sound by rubbing his wings together. Say that they will make sounds by rubbing things too.

Review what *rubbing* means. Have everyone rub their hands together as you sing the following words to the tune of "Row, Row, Row Your Boat":

Rub, rub, rub your hands
Back and forth we go
Rub, rub, rub your hands
Rub them nice and slow.
(As you sing this line, get slower and slower.)

Sing the song several times, substituting appropriate body parts such as stomach, head, elbow, wrist. (Include body parts that children need to learn to label.)

MATERIALS

- **Instruments that can be played by rubbing them, such as guiro tone block and striker, sand blocks, tambourine and large paintbrush, rhythm sticks**
- **Instruments that cannot be played by rubbing them, such as bells, jingle bells, drum, cow bell, maracas**
- **Red and green strips of construction paper**
- **Masking tape**
- **Cassette player**
- **Recorded music with a strong rhythmic beat**

Have children take turns rubbing the drum. When you are sure everyone understands the concept, set the drum where all the children can reach it easily and encourage the children to take turns rubbing it. Ask them questions such as, "Are you making a drum sound when you rub the drum?" and "Are you making a musical sound when you rub the drum?" Some of them may think that the sound produced by rubbing is a musical sound. That's all right; however, help them understand that drums are typically played by striking them.

Experiment with instruments. Place all the instruments where they are easily accessible. Encourage the children to choose an instrument and experiment with ways to make sounds with it. Encourage them to try out more than one instrument. Show some different ways to make sounds with the instruments, and make such statements as, "Lamond is rubbing his maracas. I think I will rub this tambourine. Maybe if I rub it with the brush it will make a sound."

Demonstrate instruments. Have each child demonstrate what his instrument sounds like when he rubs it. Ask if the instrument makes a musical sound when it is rubbed. If the children think that it does, tape a green strip of paper on it. If the children think that it needs to be played in some other way, have them demonstrate the other way and then tape a red piece of paper on it.

Play the recorded music while children play their instruments. Tell the children you will play some music and that anyone who wants to be the leader will have a turn. Say you will be the leader first to show them what to do. State that if the leader holds up green, the children with green paper on their instruments should play them. If the leader holds up red, the children with red paper on

continues . . .

their instruments should play them. Start the tape, holding up first one color of paper, then the other. When you think the children understand the process, choose a child to be the leader of the band. Encourage children to take turns leading the band.

End activity. Sing "The cricket rubbed his wings," encouraging the children to sing with you as they become familiar with the song.

Theme of the Day: Rubbing

Day 1: Art Center

What to Do:

Relate the activity to the story. Ask the children what crickets do to make a sound. Do crickets talk like we do? Do crickets bark like dogs, meow like cats? Say that they will rub things to make pictures the way the cricket rubbed his wings together to make a sound.

Show how to use the materials. Place the materials where they are easily accessible. If you are using crayons, explain that it is easier to rub crayons on paper if they are peeled. Show how to peel a crayon; let each child choose a crayon to use and peel it, telling its color. When each child has a peeled crayon or piece of chalk, ask them each to get a piece of paper and choose something flat to put under it from the assortment of objects you have gathered.

Make rubbings. Place an object under your piece of paper and show the children how to make a rubbing. To help anchor the paper as the child rubs, tape the corners of the paper to the table. Show how to rub the crayon or chalk hard over the object so that the impression shows up clearly. Emphasize the word "rub" as the children work. Let them make rubbings of several things, and suggest that they trade crayons or chalk with each other, so that each rubbing has several different colors.

Label objects in the rubbings. When the children have made rubbings of a few objects, ask everyone to stop to look at the papers. Tell them to try to identify the objects in each other's rubbings. They might also match the real objects to the impressions in the rubbings.

Paint over the rubbings. To extend the activity, let the children paint over the crayon rubbings with watery paint. The crayon markings will resist the paint. (Chalk rubbings will not resist the paint.)

MATERIALS

- **Crayons or colored sidewalk chalk**
- **White paper**
- **Flat, textured objects to place under paper, such as doilies, geometric shapes, cutouts of letters of the alphabet, keys, paper clips, combs**
- **Transparent or masking tape**
- **Watery paint and brushes (optional)**

Theme of the Day: Rubbing

Day 1: Make-Believe Center

What to Do:

Relate the activity to the story. Remind the children that the way the cricket made sound was by rubbing his wings together. Say that we rub things for other reasons too. Ask them how they get their hands clean. Do they rub them together when they wash them? Say that they will rub a table to get it clean for a pretend birthday party.

Dip the sponges in water and wring them out. Give each child a sponge, and put out the bowls of water. Remind them to twist the sponges to wring out the water, before they use them.

Wash the tables. As the children wash the table, show how to rub in a circular motion, from left to right across the table. (This is an excellent prewriting exercise.) Sing a variation of the song you sang in the music activity as they work, to the tune of "Row, Row, Row Your Boat":

Rub, rub, tub the table, Back and forth we go,
Rub, rub, rub the table, Rub it nice and slow.

MATERIALS

- Classroom table
- Bowls of water
- One sponge per child
- Paper towels or dry rags
- Pretend birthday cake, such as a playdough cake
- Cups, plates, forks, spoons, napkins
- Small pitchers of water

Dry the table. Collect the sponges and put out the paper towels or rags. Tell the children to dry the table, encouraging them to use the same left-to-right, circular motion.

Set table. Remove the washing materials from the area and put out the tableware. Set one place at the table with a cup, fork, spoon, plate, and napkin. Draw the children's attention to the place setting, asking them to name each item. Then tell each child to set his own place at the table, making his setting look the same as yours. Help children as needed.

Sing a birthday song. When the table is set, put the pretend birthday cake on the table and ask the children to sit down. Name one child to be the pretend birthday person, and have everyone sing a birthday song. Repeat the procedure until each child has a turn to be the birthday person.

Pretend to eat the birthday treat. Cut the pretend cake. Let the children pour themselves water and pretend to eat the cake.

Theme of the Day:
Big/Little

Day 2 Group Time: Introducing the Theme of the Day

What to Do:

Introduce the activity. Introduce the activity by singing "The cricket rubbed his wings" as on the previous day and rubbing your hands together. Invite the children to sing the song and rub their hands with you.

Review the previous day's activities. Discuss the activities from the previous day, showing the art rubbings the children made and discussing which instruments can be played by rubbing them. Ask the children what they rubbed to get ready for the birthday party.

MATERIALS

- Book, *The Very Quiet Cricket*
- Piece of playdough or modeling compound
- Baby doll
- Big and little cricket pictures

Read the story. Read the story, encouraging the children to join you in rubbing their hands together and saying, "The little cricket wanted to answer, so he rubbed his wings together. But nothing happened. Not a sound," whenever the passage occurs in the story.

Introduce the theme of the day: Big/Little. Go back through the story, drawing the children's attention to the pictures of the little cricket. Look at the cricket at the beginning of the story. Is he big or little? Then look at the cricket on several other pages. Does the little cricket look any bigger? Show the children the picture on the last page where the cricket makes a sound. Does he look little or big?

Discuss babies. Ask the children if any of them have a baby brother or sister. Can the baby do everything they can do? Can the baby talk the way they talk? Tell them that the little cricket was a baby cricket in the beginning of the story. (Show the picture at the beginning of the book where he has just come out of the egg.) Suggest that when crickets make a sound, they are talking, and that the little cricket was still a baby and couldn't talk. Have the children squat down; talk about how they look little, like the baby cricket at the beginning of the story. Then show how to stand part way up, like the cricket in the middle of the book. Stand up with the children, reaching high to be big like the cricket at the end of the book.

Introduce the arts activities.

Music and Movement Center

What the children will do: Discriminate between big and little cricket pictures and move to music. Suggest that children who go to school can play games because they are big enough to follow rules. Sing the first verse of "Hokey Pokey" using the following words and demonstrating the actions with the cricket pictures.

continues . . .

You put your big cricket up
You put your big cricket down
You put your big cricket up and you shake it all around
You do the hokey pokey and you turn yourself around
That's what it's all about.

Say that in the music center they will play this game and another game too.

Art Center

What the children will do: Make big and little items with playdough. Break off a small piece of playdough and talk about how it is little, like the little cricket. Roll it into a ball or a snake. Then show the children the remaining piece of playdough and discuss the fact that it is big, like the big cricket. Roll it into a ball or snake as you tell them they can use little and big pieces of playdough in art.

Make-Believe Center

What the children will do: Pretend to be adults taking care of babies. Show the children the doll and say that it is little because it's a baby. Then state that you are big because you are an adult. Tell the children they can pretend to be big adults and take care of little babies in make-believe.

Have each child choose an arts activity.

Notes:

Theme of the Day: Big/Little

Day 2: Music and Movement Center

What to Do:

MATERIALS

- Big and little cricket pictures, enough for each child and adult to have a set

Relate the activity to the story. Ask the children why the little cricket couldn't talk at the beginning of the story. Be sure they understand that he was too little. He was just a baby. What happened to him during the story? State that he got big. Say that they will play a game with big and little crickets.

Explain the game to the children. Put out the pile of big and little crickets and let each child choose a big cricket and a little cricket. Encourage the children to describe the crickets as *big* or *little* and to identify the color. Stand in a circle with the children. Say that you will be the leader first and that they should do what you do and sing with you when they know the song well enough. Put your crickets on the floor in front of you. Pick the big one up and ask if it is big or little. After the size is correctly identified, compliment the children for good thinking and have them pick up their big cricket.

Play a game. Sing to the tune of "Hokey Pokey": "You put the big cricket in, you take the big cricket out . . . " Sing additional verses, varying the size of the cricket, sometimes using *big* and sometimes *little.* After the children seem to understand, encourage a child to be the leader, encouraging her to select the size of cricket that the children have put in. (You might wish to expand the game for older children to include big and little shapes.) Encourage the children to be creative in their movements, especially as they "do the Hokey Pokey and you turn yourself around." Encourage creativity by praising children's movements.

Discuss the next game. Have everyone sit on the floor with you. Say that you know another song game that big children like them sing and play. Sing the following words to the tune of "The Grand Old Duke of York," encouraging the children to sing with you as they begin to learn the song.

> *Oh, good old Mr. Jicket*
> *He had a great big cricket*
> *It jumped right up to the top of the hill* (move your picture as if it is jumping up)
> *And it jumped back down again* (move your picture as if it is jumping down).

Repeat several times, encouraging the children to move their crickets up and down as you move yours.

Model actions. Ask everyone to stand. Sing the second verse and model the actions, encouraging the children to join you. Say that you are going to sing more things about crickets.

> *And when it was big, it was big* (reach high)
> *And when it was little, it was little* (squat down)
> *And when it was only halfway grown* (stand halfway up)
> *It was neither big nor little* (stand up with arms up and then squat down).

Encourage children who are nonambulatory to raise their hands high for *big* and to bend down low for *little.*

continues . . .

Repeat the song. Sing the song through several times as long as the children are interested, praising them for playing the game like big children.

Sing the Cricket Song. End the activity by singing the "The cricket rubbed his wings" together quietly (see day 1 group time instructions).

Theme of the Day: Big/Little

Day 2: Art Center

What to Do:

Relate the activity to the story. Ask the children if the cricket was big or little at the beginning of the story. If necessary, show them illustrations in the book. Say that babies are little and adults are big. They will have little and big pieces of playdough, and they may pretend that the playdough is the little cricket.

MATERIALS

- Book, *The Very Quiet Cricket*
- Playdough or modeling compound

Distribute small pieces of playdough. Give each child a small piece of playdough. Say that it is little, like the little cricket. Pretend that your piece of playdough is the little cricket, by moving it around the table and saying, "I'm little. I can't make a sound." Encourage the children to pretend with their small pieces of playdough.

Build with small pieces of playdough. Make objects out of the playdough with the children, saying such things as, "Look, I made a little ball! What can you make that is little?" or "I made a little tiny worm. Can you make one too?"

Work with big pieces of playdough. Give each child a big piece of playdough and demonstrate adding it on to the little piece. Encourage them to talk about how their playdough is bigger now, like the big cricket. Make chirping sounds, like a big cricket.

Make big things. Join the children in forming shapes with the big pieces of playdough, emphasizing the word big, as you prompt the children to talk about what they are doing.

Encourage children to ask for little and big pieces of playdough. Tell the children to ask you if they want more playdough to use. When each child requests more playdough, ask, "Do you want a little piece or a big piece?"

Theme of the Day: Big/Little

Day 2: Make-Believe Center

What to Do:

Relate the activity to the story. Remind the children that the little cricket was just a baby at the beginning of the story. Say that baby crickets can take care of themselves, but that our babies have to be taken care of. Say they will pretend to take care of babies.

Take care of babies. Show the children a doll and tell them they can pretend they are adults who are taking care of babies. Let the children play with the dolls, caring for them like mommies and daddies. As they play, remind them that the babies are little and the children are pretending to be big adults. Compliment them for doing things as adults would to take care of the babies. Some things they might do include:

- Feed the babies.
- Bathe the babies.
- Dress the babies and wrap them in blankets.
- Put the babies to bed.
- Take the babies for a walk.
- Take care of sick babies.

MATERIALS

- Baby dolls
- Props for baby care and housekeeping

Theme of the Day:
Together

Day 3 Group Time: Introducing the Theme of the Day

What to Do:

Review the previous day's activities. Review what the children did the day before by talking about how things start out little and then get big. Ask them what they did to take care of the babies in the make-believe center. Sing the "Good old Mr. Jicket" song that you sang in the music center the previous day, encouraging the children to perform the actions to the song. Discuss the big and little objects the children made out of playdough.

Read the story. Read the story, encouraging the children to rub their hands together and repeat the following passage whenever it occurs in the story: "The little cricket wanted to answer, so he rubbed his wings together. But nothing happened. Not a sound."

MATERIALS

- Book, *The Very Quiet Cricket*
- Bowl of liquid starch (with a spoon) from the art center
- Sample of powdered paint from the art center
- Piece of paper
- Bowl of soapy water
- Two pieces of doll clothes or pieces of fabric

Introduce the theme of the day: Together. Place the palms of your hands together and tell the children to put their hands together too. Then rub your hands together as you sing the following song to the tune of "Go in and out the Window," encouraging the children to rub their hands together like you.

Let's rub our hands together,
Let's rub our hands together,
Let's rub our hands together,
As we did before.

Repeat the song several times, asking the children to name other body parts to rub together as you sing. Let them discover for themselves that some body parts cannot be rubbed together, such as head, eyes, and back. Say that they will be thinking about putting things together in the centers today.

Introduce the arts activities.

Music and Movement Center

What the children will do: Mirror movement to music. Have your assistant come up to stand with you before the children. While the children watch, place your hands on the palms of the other adult's hands. As you sing the following words to the tune of "Go in and out the Window," move slowly up, down, around, and so on, as you demonstrate mirror movement.

continues . . .

Let's move our hands together
Let's move our hands together
Let's move our hands together
As we did before!

Tell the children that they will move together this way and play other music games in the music center.

Art Center

What the children will do: Mix ingredients for fingerpaint. Show the children the dish of liquid starch and the powdered paint. Spoon some starch onto a piece of paper and then sprinkle some powdered paint on the starch. Use a finger to mix the paint and starch, as you tell the children that you are mixing them together. Put your fingers in the mixture; then rub them together as you say that you are rubbing your fingers together, like the cricket rubbed his wings together. Then make fingerprints on the piece of paper and tell the children that they can fingerpaint in art.

Make-Believe Center

What the children will do: Rub pieces of fabric together as they pretend to wash doll clothes or other pieces of fabric. Show the children the bowl of soapy water and tell them that you want to wash some things. Dip two pieces of fabric in the water and then rub them together as you talk about how you are rubbing them together as the cricket rubbed his wings together. Tell them they can rub things together to get the dirt out in the make-believe center.

Have each child choose an arts activity.

Notes:

Theme of the Day: Together

Day 3: Music and Movement Center

What to Do:

Limit the number of children to an even number so they can form pairs. If a child has difficulty working closely with another child, provide a mirror.

MATERIALS

- Recorded music that is slow, such as "Georgia on My Mind"
- Cassette player
- Full-length mirror (optional)

Relate activity to the story. Ask the children what the little cricket rubbed together. Say that when two things are next to each other, they are together. They will move together in music.

Move to a song together. Ask the children to stand in a circle with you and hold hands. Walk around in a circle with the children as you sing the following song to the tune of, "Go in and out the Window":

Let's walk around together,
Let's walk around together,
Let's walk around together,
As we did before.

Sing more slowly:

Let's jump around together,
Let's jump around together,
Let's jump around together,
As we did before.

Have the children continue to hold hands and move just as you do. Stress that you are moving *together.* Sing additional verses, such as "Move your feet like I do," "Shake your head like I do," and "Move your shoulders like I do," moving in different ways. Ask the children for ideas, encouraging them to lead, and comment that you are all moving together.

Move to the music in pairs. Help the children form pairs (when possible, place an older child with a younger), then show each pair of children how to face each other and place the palms of their hands together as you and your assistant did when you introduced the activity. Designate one child of each pair to be the leader. The other child should follow what the leader does. Then slowly sing the song again with the following words: "Let's move our hands up high, let's move our hands down low, let's move our hands around, as we did before." Encourage the pairs of children to move their hands together as you sing the song. Compliment the children for working well together. Repeat the activity if the children seem interested and time permits.

Move in pairs to recorded slow music. Have the children remain in pairs with their palms touching. Play the slow music and encourage the pairs to move to the music in this position. As they move, talk about how they are moving together.

Theme of the Day: Together

Day 3: Art Center

What to Do:

This activity will need to be adapted for tactilely defensive children.

Relate the activity to the story. Remind the children that the little cricket rubbed his wings together to make a sound. Say that they are going to put things together too.

Mix materials together. Suggest that each child get one piece of paper, a bowl of starch, and a spoon. Encourage the children to choose the color of powdered paint they want to use. Join in and show how to dip a spoon in the bowl of starch and then pour it on the paper. Sprinkle some powdered paint on the starch. After the children have done this, encourage them to use their hands (or craft sticks) to mix the starch and paint, as you prompt them to discuss how they are mixing them together.

Rub your hands together to make handprints. Encourage the children to place one hand and then the other on the paint mixture. Then show how to rub your hands together, while you talk about what you are doing. "I'm rubbing my hands together, as the cricket rubbed his wings together. Now there is paint all over my hands. You rub your hands together too." Show the children how to make handprints on the paper after rubbing paint on their hands.

Rub different parts of your hands together and make prints. Show how to place different parts of your hands in the paint and then rub them together: knuckles, thumbs, fingernails, and fingertips. Talk with the children about what they are doing as they try this, emphasizing the word *together.* Encourage them to think of different ways to rub their hands together. Then encourage them to use these parts of their hands to make prints on the paper.

Fingerpaint freely. Let the children experiment with the materials, making new paint mixtures whenever needed. Show how to make different kinds of shapes, lines, and simple drawings with the paint, and using different parts of your hands to create different effects. For example, you can pat the paint with your fists, slide your palms and knuckles over it, tap it with your fingers, scratch it with your nails.

Wash your hands. End the activity by encouraging the children to wash the paint off their hands. Have them sing the "Rub our hands together" song as they wash the paint off.

MATERIALS

- Small bowls of liquid starch (one per child)
- Spoons
- Powdered paint (unmixed) in small bowls
- Craft sticks
- Smooth paper or clean tabletop

Theme of the Day: Together

Day 3: Make-Believe Center

What to Do:

Relate the activity to the story. Say that the cricket had to rub his wings together to make a sound. Remind them that on another day, they rubbed the table to get it clean. Now they are going to rub clothes together to make them clean.

Mix soap and water. Have the children stand around the water table or give each child a bowl of water. Let them squirt soap in the water, telling them how many times to squeeze the bottle.

Wash the clothes. Give each child at least two pieces of clothing or other fabric items to wash in the water. Prompt them to rub the items together to get the dirt out.

Wring water out of the clothes. After they have washed for a while, demonstrate swishing the clothes around in the water, squeezing them, and twisting them to get the water out.

Hang clothes to dry. Show the children how to hang the clothes on the clothesline and attach the clothespins, encouraging them to use a pincer grasp to squeeze the clothespins. As the children work, discuss how adults wash and dry clothes at their homes, and how it compares to what they are doing.

MATERIALS

- Water table or one bowl of warm water per child
- Bottles of liquid soap
- Doll clothes or other small fabric items
- Clothesline or heavy string suspended between two chairs
- Spring-type clothespins

Theme of the Day:
Insects

Day 4 Group Time: Introducing the Theme of the Day

What to Do:

(Place markers in the pages showing a cricket, praying mantis, spittlebug, cicada, and bumblebee.)

Review the previous day's activities. Show the children the fingerpaintings from the previous day and discuss how they mixed the starch and paint together to make the fingerpaint. Encourage children to identify the colors they used in their work. Review how they moved together in music and rubbed clothes together to wash them in the make-believe center.

Introduce the activity by discussing the story. Ask the children what happened in the story. Why couldn't the little cricket make a sound at the beginning of the story? Review some of the things that they can do that babies can't do.

MATERIALS

- **Fingerpaintings from previous day**
- **Book, *The Very Quiet Cricket***
- **Plastic insects**
- **Kazoo**
- **Styrofoam ball**
- **Eight pipe cleaners (stems)**
- **Box large enough for child to hide under**

Read the story. Read the story and encourage the children to rub their hands together and chant the repeated phrase as it occurs in the story.

Count the legs of insects in a book. Show the children the cover of the book, and comment that the cricket has many legs. Ask the children to count the legs with you. Then have them help you count the legs of the other insects you marked in the book. Tell them that all insects have six legs, just like the insects in the book. Have them count their legs. How many legs does each insect have? Does the cricket have more legs than they have, or fewer legs than they have?

Introduce the theme of the day: Insects. Show the children the plastic insects. Give each child an insect and count the legs together. Help them realize that all insects have six legs. Say that even though some of the insects are called grasshoppers, flies, ants, or crickets (or whatever you have), they are all insects, just as the children are all children. Encourage the children to "walk" their insects around on the floor in front of them. Say that they will think about *insects* in the centers today.

Introduce the arts activities.

Music and Movement Center
What the children will do: Use kazoos to sound like insects and streamers to "fly" like insects. Play a part of a song the children know on the kazoo. Tell the children that the kazoo sounds like some insects and

continues . . .

that they will play kazoos and sound like insects in the music and movement center. Show them the streamers. Say that some insects can fly, some jump, and others crawl. They will move like insects in the music center.

Art Center

What the children will do: Make insects from boxes, Styrofoam balls, and other materials. Show the children the Styrofoam ball. Stick pipe cleaners into the ball for antennae and legs. Ask the children how many legs your insect needs. If necessary, show them the picture of the cricket on the front of the book again and help them count the legs. Say that they can make their own insects any way they want to make them in the art center.

Make-Believe Center

What the children will do: Make pretend insect homes and pretend to be insects. Show the children the box and turn it upside down. Ask a child to pretend to be an insect and crawl under the box. Lift the box and comment to the group that there is an insect under the box. Tell them they can all be insects in the make-believe center.

Have each child choose an arts activity.

Notes:

Theme of the Day: Insects

Day 4: Music and Movement Center

What to Do:

Make the crepe paper streamers out of different colors and at least 2 feet long if possible.

If you have access to a recording of insect sounds, use it during this activity.

Relate the activity to the story. Remind the children that the little cricket was an insect and that there were many insects in the story. Tell them that some insects fly, some hop or jump, and some crawl around. Show the pictures of the flying insects, helping the children name each one and point to the wings. Say that wings are what the insects use to fly. Say that they will use streamers to pretend they are flying insects; then they can play kazoos to make buzzing sounds like insects.

Introduce the music. Have the children sit with you as you play a short section of each of the recorded music selections. Discuss how the music sounds: Is it fast? slow? quiet? loud? Have children demonstrate how they would move to each segment of the music if they were insects. Accept their decisions, praising them for their good thinking and listening.

Encourage the children to choose streamers. Let each child choose a streamer, encouraging the child to name the color.

Move to the music. Play the fast music and join the children as they move to the music. Encourage the children to move like flying insects. Show how to "land" on certain objects, fly around and around, fly high, and fly low. Provide additional streamers and let each child move with several streamers. Encourage creative movement.

Play slow music. Remind the children that not all insects fly. Ask if ants fly. Mention insects that are prevalent in your area and ask how each one moves. Play the slow music and encourage the children to crawl like beetles or move as other insects move.

Introduce the kazoos. Turn off the cassette player and invite the children to lie on the floor. Tell them to pretend that they are lying outside at night. Ask what kind of insects they might see at night. Distribute the kazoos. Suggest that the children play the kazoos as you sing "Twinkle, Twinkle, Little Star."

MATERIALS

- **Book, *The Very Quiet Cricket* (with page of flying insects marked)**
- **Kazoos, one for each child and adult**
- **Crepe paper streamers, enough for each child and adult to have at least two**
- **Cassette player**
- **Recorded music that is fast (such as "Flight of the Bumble Bee") and music that is slow**

Theme of the Day: Insects

Day 4: Art Center

What to Do:

Relate the activity to the story. Remind the children that the little cricket was an insect and that all insects have six legs. Show them the pictures of insects and help them trace the antennae on the insects and count their body parts. Point out the eyes and mouths on the insects. Say that they will make their own insects any way they want to make them.

Show how to make insects. Place the materials out where they are easily accessible. Join the children as they get boxes or Styrofoam balls to make the bodies of their insects. Place pictures of insects around where they can be easily seen. Show how to put the body pieces together (toothpicks in Styrofoam balls, or glue between boxes) and how to stick various materials onto the insect. Glitter can be used for fireflies; pieces of shiny metallic paper make nice-looking beetles. Encourage creativity.

Make more insects. Encourage the children to work together in pairs to make additional insects. Encourage variety, stressing that there are many different kinds of insects in the world.

Make a display. Make a display of the insects and encourage each child to say where her insect lives and how it moves.

MATERIALS

- Styrofoam balls
- Small boxes
- Pipe stems
- Craft sticks
- Collage materials such as glitter, pieces of felt, spangles, ribbons
- Glue
- Toothpicks

Theme of the Day: Insects

Day 4: Make-Believe Center

What to Do:

Relate the activity to the story. Remind the children that the little cricket was an insect. Say that insects often live in special places. Show the children the pictures of insect homes and talk about where insects can be found—under rocks and logs, on plants, in hives, and under the ground. Show the children the materials and tell them they can make pretend insect homes and pretend that they are insects.

Make insect homes. Put out all the materials, and show how to use them to build an insect home, inviting the children to join you. You might color a box with markers to make it look like a rock to hide under. Or you might cover chairs with pieces of fabric or other materials. Encourage the children to think of different ways to use the materials. Encourage them to refer to the pictures of insect homes to get ideas.

Dress up like insects. Invite the children to dress up in costumes to look like insects. Join in and choose simple costumes from the dress-up clothes. Suggest that they look at the book to help them remember what insects look like. The costumes need not be realistic; they might just be clothes that are the same colors as insects in the book. Praise their creativity.

Pretend to be insects. Encourage the children to pretend to be insects in the homes they created. Show how to walk on hands and feet, make insect sounds, and crawl into the insect homes that the children created.

MATERIALS

- Pictures of insect homes, such as logs, rocks, plants, beehives, ant colonies
- Masking tape
- Boxes large enough for children to sit in
- Markers
- Classroom chairs
- Large pieces of fabric
- Dress-up clothes
- Book, *The Very Quiet Cricket*

Theme of the Day:
Insect World

Day 5 Group Activity

What to Do:

Relate the activity to the story. Ask the children where they think the little cricket lived. Say that insects live in many places. Some live in water, some live under the ground, and some only come out at night. Remind them that some insects even live in our houses. Show them the pictures of insect homes.

Take a walk. Go for a discovery walk to find insect homes. Remind the children that they shouldn't touch strange insects, but help them explore under pieces of wood or logs, in corners, in bushes, or whatever is available in your area. Return to the classroom.

Discuss insect homes. Show the children the pictures of insect homes again and help them describe each of them. See if there are pictures of any of the homes they found on their walk. Remind them that they made insect homes in the make-believe center on a previous day. Ask them to tell how they made the insect homes and how they pretended to be insects. Show them the plastic insects. Say that they can make insect homes for plastic insects with sand and rocks and other things today.

Make insect homes in sand. Give each child a container of sand and at least one plastic insect, and put out the other materials. Join in and show how to put some leaves, rocks, or other things in a container and hide a plastic insect under it. Encourage the children to look at the pictures of insect homes for other ideas. Remind them that many types of insects live under the dirt.

MATERIALS

- Pictures of insect homes
- Plastic insects
- Large containers of sand (bowls, boxes, or a large sand table)
- Rocks
- Sticks, pieces of wood, leaves and other materials from nature
- Water in spray bottles
- Cassette player
- Recorded insect sounds if available

Suggestions for Implementing Insect World Play:

After the children have worked with the materials for a while to make insect homes, encourage them to move the plastic insects around like insects in their settings. Join in and move an insect in ways that are typical of real insects—digging holes in the ground to hide in, crawling under leaves, rocks or pieces of wood, eating leaves or other insects.

If you have a recording of insect sounds, play it for the children to listen to as they play with the materials. Comment about the insect sounds: "Big crickets make the same sounds over and over." "I hear the sound

continues . . .

of crickets outside at night. I hear flies in the daytime." Encourage the children to talk about the sounds too. "How does that fly sound make you feel?" "Does a fly make a fast or a slow sound?" "Do you ever hear cricket sounds in your house? Do you hear fly sounds in your house?"

Encourage the children to rearrange their insect settings by moving around the rocks and other props, removing and adding things. They might also spray water on the sand and pretend that it is raining. It will then be easier for them to build hills or dig tunnels.

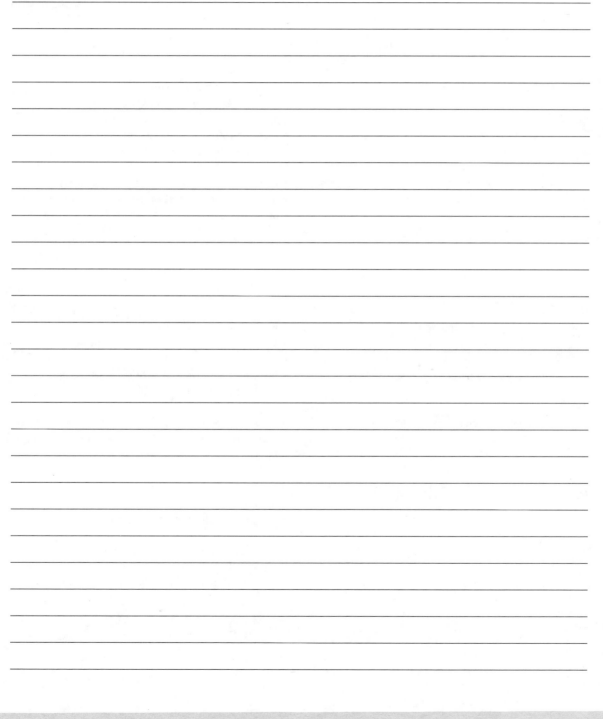

Notes:

SKILLS & GOALS MATRIX

The Very Quiet Cricket

	Skills or Behaviors	Goals and Objectives
Cognitive	• Show understanding of *big* and *little*	• Increase size concept and vocabulary development • Increase understanding of measurement concepts
	• Sing songs and chants from memory	• Increase rote memory skills • Increase phonemic awareness
	• Observe and describe natural objects, such as insects, logs, and plants	• Increase concept development • Increase experience of physical environment
	• Count objects and compare number of objects in sets	• Increase rote and rational counting skills • Increase understanding of one-to-one correspondence
	• Organize objects into groups of similar items	• Increase ability to classify objects by categories • Increase ability to sort objects by one or more attributes
Language	• Follow chanted directions	• Increase receptive vocabulary • Increase ability to respond to a request
	• Identify body parts	• Increase receptive and expressive vocabulary • Increase ability to associate words and objects
	• Imitate characters in a familiar story	• Increase preliteracy skills: link story characters to own experiences, understand story structure, and become familiar with written language
	• Make music by blowing kazoos	• Increase oral-motor coordination • Increase respiratory strength • Increase vocalizations or verbalizations
	• Participate in "Hokey-Pokey"	• Increase vocabulary for body parts • Increase listening skills • Increase ability to follow verbal instructions

SKILLS & GOALS MATRIX (CONT.)

	Skills or Behaviors	Goals and Objectives
Social	• Dress self up in a dress-up costume	• Increase understanding of others' point of view, feelings
	• Sing a song or rap with others	• Increase participation as member of a group
	• Lead others in an activity; follow another's lead	• Increase ability to perform individually in a group setting • Increase ability to perform behavior modeled by peer
	• Take turns and follow the rules while playing a game	• Increase appropriate interactions with peers • Increase appropriate social behaviors with adult supervision
Fine-Motor	• Squeeze soap out of bottles	• Increase hand strength • Increase visual-motor coordination • Refine prewriting grasp and manipulation
	• Rub hands together rhythmically	• Increase bilateral skills • Increase sensory awareness • Increase motor planning skills
	• Play a variety of musical instruments by rubbing and striking	• Increase bilateral coordination • Increase visual-motor coordination • Refine grasp, hand use, and manipulation skills
	• Roll and pinch playdough	• Increase bilateral coordination • Refine pincer grasp • Increase tactile awareness • Increase hand strength
Gross-Motor	• Do mirror movements with a partner	• Increase motor planning and control • Increase dynamic balance • Increase awareness of body in space
	• Wash table with sponges	• Increase tactile awareness • Increase motor planning • Increase bilateral coordination
	• Move to music with streamers	• Increase gross-motor planning and control • Increase dynamic and static balance • Increase body awareness
	• Imitate the movement of insects and animals	• Increase motor planning and control • Increase dynamic and static balance • Increase movement repertoire

STORY OF THE WEEK / EL CUENTO DE ESTA SEMANA

The Very Quiet Cricket

by Eric Carle

This Spark story this week is *The Very Quiet Cricket*. You may be able to find this book at the library. The story is about a tiny cricket who cannot make a sound until he grows up. Each page shows him meeting a different type of insect, but the cricket is unable to talk to the insect because he is still too little. "He rubbed his wings together, but nothing happened, not a sound." If you read this story to your child, encourage him to say these words from the book with you. The Little Cricket is a little bigger on each page. At the end of the book he tries one more time to rub his wings together to make a sound, and he does! Ask your child what happened at the end of the book (the cricket was big and made a chirping sound). The themes to go with this story are *rubbing, big and little, together,* and *insects*.

El cuento de Spark de esta semana se llama *The Very Quiet Cricket* (el grillo muy tranquilo). Usted puede encontrar este libro, en inglés, en cualquier biblioteca. El cuento es sobre un grillito que no podía hacer ningún sonido hasta que creciera. Cada página del libro lo muestra al grillito encontrándose con un insecto diferente, pero el grillo no podía hablar con el insecto porque era todavía muy pequeño. El "frotaba sus alas pero no pasaba nada, no podía hacer ningún sonido". Si usted lee este cuento a su niño o niña, anímelo a que repita con usted las palabras del libro. El grillito es un poco más grande en cada página. Al final del libro trató una vez mas de frotar sus alas juntas para hacer sonido y ¡lo logró! Pregúntele a su niño o niña que pasó al final del libro (el grillo era más grande y produjo un chirrido). Las ideas temáticas que van con este cuento son: *frotar, grande, pequeño, juntos* e *insectos*.

© 2001 The Board of Trustees of the University of Illinois. May be reproduced for use by teachers.

Index

This index covers Volumes 1 and 2 of Activities for the Spark Curriculum for Early Childhood. Pages 1–284 are in Volume 1. Pages 285–558 are in Volume 2.

A

B

C

D

E

F

G

H

I

J

K

L

M

N

O

P

Q

R

S

T

Other Resources from Redleaf Press

Focused Portfolios™: A Complete Assessment for the Young Child
by Gaye Gronlund and Bev Engel
Focused Portfolios™ offers an innovative method to accurately document children's growth and development by observing them in the midst of their everyday activities. Eight chapters include a complete introduction to the Focused Portfolios™ method, many step-by-step examples, and all the necessary forms for portfolio collection.

Help Yourself! Activities to Promote Safety and Self-Esteem
by Kate Ross
Written for use with the CD of the same name by Cathy Fink and Marcy Marxer, *Help Yourself!* is filled with fun and creative ways to use the songs as a springboard into a curriculum for promoting self-esteem and safety skills among young children.

Big as Life: The Everyday Inclusive Curriculum, Volumes 1 and 2
by Stacey York
From the author of *Roots and Wings,* these two curriculum books provide all the information you need to weave culturally relevant and anti-bias activities throughout an early childhood curriculum based on familiar themes such as Families, Friends, Community, and Foods. The perfect curriculum book for beginning teachers—includes curriculum webs, interest areas set-ups, materials lists, and hundreds of activities.

More Than Letters
by Sally Moomaw Sally Moomawand Brenda Hieronymus
Filled with dozens of fun and engaging activities designed to make literacy a meaningful adventure for children. Contains an extensive whole-language curriculum that creates a print-rich classroom environment.

More Than Painting
by Sally Moomaw Sally Moomawand Brenda Hieronymus
Make art a thought-provoking, fun part of your everyday curriculum. *More Than Painting* provides an impressive variety of art activities (over 100) for the classroom. Activities include drawing, collage, painting and printing, sewing and stringing, three-dimensional art, and outdoor art.

Much More Than Counting
by Sally Moomaw Sally Moomawand Brenda Hieronymus
Contains more than 100 activities that will make math more fun for children. This book addresses those questions most asked by teachers, providers, and parents, as well as questions about toddlers, children with disabilities, estimation, and patterning–topics that often are forgotten in an early math curriculum.

Call toll-free 800-423-8309
www.redleafpress.org